LISA CLIFFORD grew up in Sydney. She won a scholarship to the Australian Film, Television and Radio School and went on to work as a radio reporter and newsreader for 3BO, 2GB and 2UW (now HITS FM). After leaving radio, Lisa became a reporter for Channel Ten, before becoming associate producer of the Channel Ten Late News. She is now a freelance journalist, writing for *The Australian*, *The Australian Financial Review* and *Gourmet Traveller,* among many others.

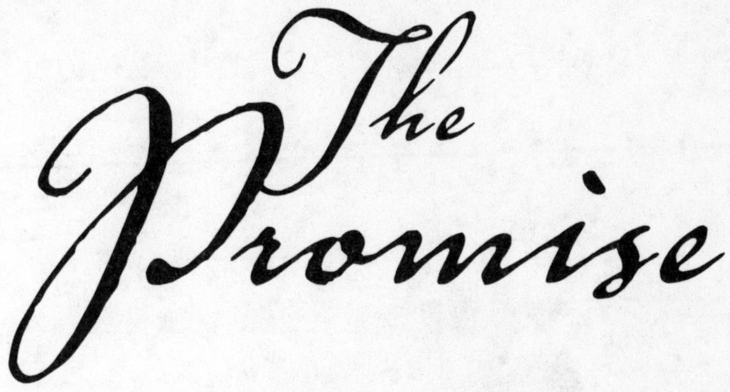

The Promise

AN ITALIAN ROMANCE

LISA CLIFFORD

MACMILLAN
Pan Macmillan Australia

First published 2004 in Macmillan by Pan Macmillan Australia Pty Limited
St Martin's Tower, 31 Market Street, Sydney

National Library of Australia
Cataloguing-in-Publication data:

Clifford, Lisa.
The promise : an Italian romance.

ISBN 1 40503630 3.

1. Love - Italy - Florence. 2. Man-woman relationships - Italy - Florence. 3. Tuscany (Italy) - Social life and customs. I. Title.

945.51

Set in 12/16.5 Stempel Garamond by Midland Typesetters
Printed in Australia by McPherson's Printing Group

Papers used by Pan Macmillan Australia Pty Ltd are natural, recyclable products made from wood grown in sustainable forests. The manufacturing processes conform to the environmental regulations of the country of origin.

For every heart that has left a
love in a faraway land.

And for Paolo, Natalia and Leo.

1

I can recognise most of the faces that appear from underneath the fur-lined hoods, fluffy scarves and woolly hats. Rugged up against the alpine cold, only about fifty locals are in Consuma now. The summer crowds, the holidaymakers who prefer the drier, cooler climate of the mountains to the humidity of the Tuscan seaside, have long gone home. Only the people who were born here are courageous enough to face the winter, and most of them are hardened pensioners with a remarkable resistance to the cold. The Consuma people are tough, rugged, worn – just like their mountains.

The snow hasn't yet arrived at Consuma, though today could be the day. It's almost Christmas and they say that when the clouds across to the other side of the Apennine alps are black and angry, snow is on its way. The official name of the village is Il Passo della Consuma (Consuma Pass). It's at the top of the Tuscan north-central Apennine mountains, and the 'pass' used to be the only way over the alps to the province of Romagna on the other side. Over in the distance, the Romagna clouds look dark and nasty. If the saying is true, snow should fall by this afternoon.

The people I see as I drive through the village gave their children over to the nearby towns of Florence or Arezzo many decades ago so that the new Consuma generation could make a living out of something apart from farming and labouring. But if they don't come back home soon, this tiny slate-grey village will become just another summer vacation destination that is shuttered and deserted during the long winter months. Strangely, I find the thought quite upsetting. I hadn't realised I cared so much.

I drive on further, past the café where Giovanni always goes for coffee. Sure enough, his two best friends are standing outside with their hands stuffed into their pockets, their breath clouds of vapour like two dragons breathing smoke at each other. I'Magnano and Diavolino ('strong man' and 'little devil') are famous for playing tricks on people. They're always ready for a laugh. Even now that they're pushing eighty, they're still the village pranksters. When Giovanni's with them, he laughs so hard his nostrils flare and his eyes get teary. I rarely get the joke, but the sight of Giovanni's nostrils going white with the strain of his glee makes me crack up, too.

I'Magnano and Diavolino aren't their real names; they're nicknames. Everyone up here has one. I don't think I know even one of Giovanni's friends' real names. I have a nickname too – Assuntina, they call me, after a local woman who liked a drink. I like to keep the wine on the table and have another drink after the food has been taken away. Reason enough, according to them, to call me Assuntina.

I spot i'Picchio ('the woodpecker', undoubtedly a reference to his W.C. Fields nose) on his way to the café. He has a crush on my blonde Brisbane girlfriend. They danced together one night after he'd braved the three-kilometre walk down the icy dirt road that runs from the main road through the woods down to Giovanni's isolated farmhouse, known for centuries as Pratiglioni. I'Picchio had squeezed my friend just a little too tightly as he twirled her around the living room to some merry Italian accordion music on the radio. Even though someone had sticky-taped the aerial on to the window, the reception was still appalling. Everyone was red-faced from the laughter, the fire and the heat from our thick sweaters. I'Picchio might be a weather-beaten old farmer from up in the Tuscan mountains, but he's not silly and he is, after all, Italian. If he could give a pretty woman a squeeze, he wasn't going to let the opportunity slip by, even if it meant having to scrabble down the dangerous road to Pratiglioni.

The villagers venture out of their warm homes at around ten in the morning for a coffee at one of the three bars in town. Most people go to Giovanni's favourite, Bar Consumi, because it's bigger and has the best selection of homemade *schiacciatas*, brioches and pastries. It belongs, as does everything up here, to one of Giovanni Consumi's distant cousins. It's a bit like the old TV program *The Waltons*, only everyone up here is a Consumi on Consuma Mountain.

Bar Consumi's counter is eight metres of total food heaven. Three rows of glass shelves curve and straighten around the main meeting area, the espresso machine. On each shelf are silver trays laden with freshly baked Tuscan specialities. To the left of the coffee machine are various pastries stuffed with custard cream, jam or chocolate. Then there are raisin snails, frosted fruit pockets and sugary buns. There are little cakes, like scones, with almonds, sultanas and pine nuts, and sponge cakes filled with freshly whipped cream, then fig or apricot jam tarts, and biscuits dipped in dark chocolate. The shelves to the right of the coffee machine are dedicated to those who prefer *salato* to *dolce* – salt to sugar. The woodfire-baked Florentine *schiacciata* is like a focaccia but a thousand times better. It's rolled flatter (*schiacciata* means 'squashed') and topped with olive oil, rosemary and salt. The *schiacciata* also comes reheated and stuffed with ham, tomato and cheese or *porcini* mushrooms, or with roasted onions, potatoes, herbs and *rucola* (rocket).

Next to the *schiacciata* shelves are the cheeses and salamis. The woodfired oven churns out one-kilogram slabs of Tuscan bread, which is sliced to make thick *panini* – sandwiches, which are lined with the local pecorino (sheep's) cheese and prosciutto. The café walls are a jumble of wooden shelves that display a mountain pantry's essentials – lots of Consuma dried herbs and *porcini* mushrooms, wine, oils, capers, canned tomatoes and, of course, pasta in every shape and size.

The only downside to this Tuscan food mecca are the hairy wild boar legs that hang from the ceiling, soon to be carved up and eaten on a *panino*. During my first visits to Bar Consumi (distracted as I was by the decision of what to have for morning tea), I was constantly being hit on the head by various heavy brown, furry legs. The limbs are rubbed with a peppery seasoning, so invariably I left the café with blotches of pepper on my forehead and a sprinkle of seasoning in my hair. Unnerving, really, and quite macabre, the sight of the dangling limbs sometimes put me off my food, but never for long.

Most of the locals who are now converging on Bar Consumi will have the same breakfast every morning, the classic Italian cappuccino and brioche, which is a plain light pastry and the best for dunking. Normally, I too would stop at Bar Consumi for my favourite breakfast, because after all these years I know everybody. If they don't actually know me, they certainly recognise me. 'It's the Australian girl, Giovanni's son's girlfriend,' they say. But this morning isn't like any other morning and my mood is as churlish as the weather. I don't feel like stopping for a coffee and a chat, because I'd have to force a smile. After almost two decades of heartbreaking travel between Italy and Australia, I've made up my mind and decided to go home.

I drive further down the main road through the village, mentally painting everyone into my memory like pictures or slides that I can look at later when I'm back home in Sydney. I take it slowly and carefully because the road through Consuma is so narrow. Some of the tiny stone houses on either side of the street were built five hundred years ago, when only the odd horse and cart used the road. Now the road can be perilous – drivers must know the width of their vehicles very well so as not to swipe oncoming cars.

The skinny road curves to where Beppino Carletti, the only redhead in Consuma, sells petrol. Beppino's ruddy cheeks are so red his capillaries seem to be bursting before your eyes. I can never see him without thinking of his two little brothers. Up against a wall, they were squashed to death by a reversing German army truck during the war. Terrified, with nowhere to run, they died holding hands.

Zia (Aunty) Piera is outside her house. I've always called her Zia because it's a part of the warm Italian family culture for a nephew's girlfriend to make his family her own and so call people what he calls them. Zia still lives in the original Consumi family house. Her front door opens right on to a fifty-centimetre strip of footpath, barely wide enough to stop a side mirror from taking off her arm. She comes up to my elbow and has pale blue eyes, blonde hair and, even though she's Italian, English rose skin. As I drive past I give her a big friendly wave, a toot of my horn and a wide smile. I make the smile a bright one because she's always been so kind and it feels right that her last impression of me is a happy one. I'm not going to stop and say goodbye, because it would be too hard to answer the endless line of questions. 'Why are you going?' 'Are you coming back?' 'Surely, after all these years, you'll keep in contact?' But Zia Piera would never understand my answers. Maturity has made my love affair with her nephew more complicated, and her attitude to all life matters is simple: 'Eh, you love him? No problem! You marry! Many women leave their families for love.' Hers is a traditional village life, spent mostly sweeping, dusting and weeding the grave where her husband is buried. He died many years ago, but that hasn't diminished her zeal. That's what most of the widows at Consuma do, they tend the cemetery. It's a social thing – they change the linen or polish the chalice on the tiny altar in the minuscule chapel and chat.

I've always envied Zia Piera's simplistic approach to love, because an attitude like hers would make my life so easy. Right now my brain is a muddle of bewildering stumbling blocks to living in Italy. As I imagine Zia Piera serenely dusting down her husband's grave, content in the knowledge that she will one day lie beside him, a new block of resistance is added to my growing pile: 'If I stay, I'd be buried here. What would my headstone read?'

Lisa June Clifford
Nata (born) Sydney, Australia
Morta (died) Consuma
'She loved a good bodysurf.'
May She Rest In Peace

I'Magnano and Diavolino would think that inscription was hilarious, so incongruous would the 'bodysurfing woman's grave' be up here in the snow. It might be worth dying here just to give them one last laugh. But the blocks keep coming and I can't seem to knock them down, so now there's a wall so high in my head I can't see over it.

I'm an Aussie girl, a Bondi bather, a have-a-beer-in-the-beer-garden kind of girl – and even though I love my Italian boyfriend, this isn't my destiny. I won't let it become my fate. I can control my life. The choice is mine, and it's not too late to change everything.

I'm going home to Sydney to find a job as a radio journalist, then I'll work hard to achieve my goals, which include buying a car and a home to call my own. Maybe one day I'll find a job as a television reporter. I am ambitious and so tired of putting my career on the backburner as I pack everything up and leave, only to pack up once more and come back. My life has become a never-ending circle of Florence, Sydney, Florence, and then back again. Most of all, I'm mentally exhausted from the confusion. The endless comparisons between what my life would be like if I stayed on here, in Italy, or went home and made what I could of all the wonderful opportunities in Australia. I can no longer take the pain of that indecision, and neither can my boyfriend. Our relationship has become an emotional seesaw of uncertainty and I want to stop hurting him. I must go and let him get on with his life, even though I still care for him deeply.

I know this is my final leaving because it's so different from my many other leavings. This time, I actually want Paolo to find someone else – perhaps a lovely Florentine girl whom he can marry, someone who will make him happy by giving him children and a family of his own. He deserves it after waiting more than a decade for me to make up my mind. When I met Paolo, I was seventeen years old. How could I have known that our love affair wasn't destined to be a fling, but rather a long, drawn-out relationship that would ultimately prove culturally and geographically impossible?

I think of sarongs and endless, deserted beaches and sunburned, salty shoulders. Mirages above bitumen roads and a relentless, throbbing heat. Eucalyptus and Moreton Bay fig trees. The sound of cicadas and the soft drone of the cricket playing on a distant television. Thoughts of a Sydney summer whirl through my head. Cold eskies and outdoor barbecues shared with my father and mother and brothers and sister. A cup of tea and long talks about anything and everything with the girls that I grew up with. How I love them all, miss them all. They're starting to marry now and have babies, and I'm never there for the weddings or births. Knowing that I'll soon be home sends a thrill of anticipation and excitement down my spine.

I'm out of the village now and on my way down the winding road that clings to the side of the mountains. As the valley of Florence opens out before me, my ears begin to pop from the lower altitude. To my left are the enormous, rustic Tuscan farmhouses built from huge slabs of Vallombrosa indigenous grey stone. These are the farmers' houses and barns, designed around the *aia*, the little courtyard in front of the house, where the workers threshed their wheat and sorted the corn, oats and barley. I've heard all about it, together with the stories about the Consuma people's poverty and backbreaking hard work, all only one generation ago. The stories have been shared lovingly with me, passed on with pride, in the hope that I too will pass the yarns on to the next generation. Now the land is dedicated solely to the production of olive oil and wine. Line upon line of grapevines and olive trees neatly stripe the sloping countryside. And I'm going home. I know that by the time I reach the apartment that I share with Paolo in Florence the mist will have disappeared to be replaced by blue skies and a crisp sunny day. But for now, the farmers have pulled shut their dark-brown shutters and their chimneys are billowing smoke. I can just imagine the huge fireplaces inside, built wide and deep so that they can fit little benches in under the mantle for the old folk to warm their bones alongside the burning grate.

The soft fog of the morning starts to creep into my soul and I think about my departure and wonder if I'll ever truly be free of this place. It has found its way deep into my heart. Every now and then the centre of Florence and its mammoth cathedral, the Duomo, is visible through the trees that line the road. Its huge dome is bigger than any other construction in Florence and its majesty is breathtaking. I can feel the doubt subtly scratching at my resolve. I'm infected with Italy, along with my boyfriend and his family.

I push guilt away and try to ignore the feeling that maybe I owe something to Giovanni and Gemma. Paolo's father and mother have for years loved me as their own daughter. I must go to them now and tell them I am leaving, again.

I sigh, 'Oh for God's *sake*, Lisa. Make a decision. Do you

want to live in Italy or in Australia?' The song, Paolo's song for me, starts ringing in my head again. 'Should I stay or should I go? Should I stay or should I go nowwwah? Should I stay or should I go? Da, da, da, da, da, da, dum'.

2

The Italian passengers showed their appreciation for our safe landing in Rome with a round of hearty applause upon touchdown. A big clap had also accompanied our Singapore landing, so I assumed the cheers were a charming custom to thank the captain for a safe trip. Then it was bedlam. As we taxied towards the Da Vinci terminal, all hell broke loose when the Italians refused to wait for the seatbelt sign to be turned off before getting down their hand luggage. The non-Italians watched in mild amazement as the Italian passengers scrambled out of their seats and stood to undo the overhead luggage compartments. Like dominoes, the compartments started popping open all the way up the plane. Red-faced flight attendants flapped their arms and ran up and down the aisles yelling, 'Sit down'. Warily, the passengers would return to their seats, only to perch on the edge, reluctant to do up their seatbelts and lose the advantage already gained. With one hand on the headrest in front of them, they were ready to race once again for their hand luggage and disembarkation pole position by the plane's door once it had come to a halt.

I had yet to learn it, but queues are a way of life in Italy and ways of beating them have been fine-tuned for centuries. A good line jumper even has a name – *furbo* – and is revered and admired. *Furbo* means smart or cunning, and that's what you have to be in Italy to get ahead in the queues. Instead of forming lines, Italians tend to bunch up in big groups at exits or ticket counters. That way, its easier to jostle your way to the front. Some years ago, in an effort to keep some order, post offices and banks painted red lines on the floor behind which people were required to wait, one by one, for their turn. But the elderly still have difficulty in keeping to that rule and will often wander up to the counter to stand next to the person who is being served. It's not unusual to find a little old man or woman at your elbow peering into your wallet as you count your money, showing no comprehension of personal space, or their infringement of it. The old Italian way of queuing was shoulder to shoulder with some clever manoeuvring of the elbow. Lining up and waiting your turn has improved immeasurably since the days of bottleneck queuing, which secretly, among the Italian men, were the best moments for a good old-fashioned bottom pinch and an 'Oops, *mi scusi Signorina*!' accidental brush against a breast. Italians are probably the worst (or best?) line jumpers in the world, but I didn't know that when I first visited the country. I sat wide-eyed and watched the other passengers, thinking that their desperation to disembark was due to cabin fever after the long flight from Australia.

This wasn't my first international travel experience, though it was my first big trip alone. I was sixteen and thought I knew it all. In truth, I was as green as the grass lawn outside the convent I'd just bombed out from. With the enormous confidence so typical of the young and ignorant, I had set off for Europe to discover life in a faraway place. Italy seemed like a good destination because my sister lived in Milan. It would give me the chance to learn a language, something I'd always wanted to do. But unlike many people who go to Italy because they are intrigued by its art, architecture or food, it wasn't the country's culture that I was searching out. I just wanted to avoid sitting for my Higher School Certificate examination, and setting out on the classic young Australian's overseas adventure trip seemed like the best way to achieve that. Italy, with my sister already there and my brothers close by in London, was the perfect place to start.

In the face of such obstinacy, my father, who is a relatively easy-going man with an aversion to confrontations, eventually gave up trying to dissuade me. His raised objections were met with, 'I know, *I know*, Dad' and 'Yeah, five hundred dollars will be *heaps* of money, don't worry'.

My mother, on the other hand, was all for the trip because her idea of a good education involved lots of travel. Mum and Dad had been divorced since I was a baby and their opposing views on almost every point were, and still are, standard practice. While Dad was worried about my safety and thought that I was too young to go, Mum never tried to dissuade me. She had made it her parental mission to see that her children had plenty of what she called 'The School of Life'. 'Go,' she would say. 'Travel, see the world and enrich your lives. Broaden your views and open your eyes.' Consequently,

I hadn't seen my siblings for more than two years because they were off enriching their lives.

In retrospect, Mum also let me leave home at sixteen because she had big plans for me – her own agenda, so to speak. But that would only be revealed through time. She wanted her youngest daughter to learn the chic, sophisticated ways of the Europeans, to absorb Italian style. As the owner and director of several model agencies and the largest model school in Australia, her plan was to mould me into a cultured woman of the world who could hold her own in any circle. She also wanted to give me the opportunities that she had never had. 'The world is your oyster,' she said. 'And you are its pearl.' Heady words for a girl not yet out of her school uniform.

The plan was to meet my sister, Carel, who is nine years older than me, in Florence where she was preparing for the Pitti Donna Fashion Week with a group of models. Carel worked for one of Milan's most prestigious model agencies, booking and organising the English-speaking models into their jobs. Her week in Florence would involve getting the girls to their fittings, rehearsals and shows on time. My job would be to hang around in the background. Then Carel would head back to work in Milan and I would look for work or start with a language school. It all sounded so incredibly exciting. I was jumping out of my skin with anticipation at the thought of it all.

Much time had been spent ruminating over what clothes to pack so that I could look as good as possible when with the models. However, twelve years at the convent hadn't supplied me with a vast selection of fashion statements. I wasn't exactly a 'surfy chick', but the beach look was popular in Sydney in the late 1970s, so that was what I was after. To achieve a naturally blonde bleached look, I had passed many hours in the midday sun with lemon juice on my hair. My choice of clothing further complemented the surfy image: long, drawstring cotton floral skirts, puka shell necklaces and espadrilles. Black leggings and oversized T-shirts. A few boob tubes with lots of gold thread and some cheesecloth, off-the-shoulder dresses. Vintage clothes were also big in those days, so not to be forgotten was my rather moth-eaten collection of Chinese knitwear, found in several opportunity shops in Sydney's Surry Hills. I thought the embroidered and sequined collars would be particularly groovy for dancing in Florence. I had also packed lots of Pot 'o' Gloss for my lips, eye shadows in frosted blues, greens and browns by Rimmel (sold in gel form and dispensed in a tube), Lady Jayne hair combs and Charlie perfume. It didn't take me long to discover that what's 'in' in Sydney was definitely *not* 'in' in Italy. I soon realised that I had absolutely nothing to wear. What I *did* have made me stand out like a hippie beach babe at a rodeo.

When the plane touched down, I was thrilled that my reunion with my sister was now only a few hours away. But after almost thirty-six hours in transit, I didn't much feel like Mum's pearl. My red eyes stung as I stood at the door of the aircraft and looked out at a brilliant Rome morning. The sky was azure blue and the air already humid with the promise of a hot June day. I filled my lungs with the fresh dawn air and thought of the wet, wintry weather and enormous grey sky that I'd left behind in Australia. Then I hopped to it because those Italians were all pushing in front of me again trying to steal my place in the queue for the bus to take us to the terminal.

In the late 1970s, there were no trains from Da Vinci airport to Rome's central railway station. Air travellers had to find the train station bus and then jostle for a seat (it didn't take long for me to catch on) for the ride into the centre of Rome. Nowadays, new arrivals catch the train connection from the airport to Rome Centrale (called Roma Termini), but before the track was laid, the uninitiated risked their lives and joined in the fabulous chaos that unfolded on the streets above. The bus roared down the highway with no concern for the marked lane it was meant to stay in, while other cars careened around it, with only inches to spare. Once in town, the bus slowed to a crawl, only to accelerate to full speed should a tiny gap offering better progress appear in another lane. Motorbikes and mini motorbikes, called *motorinos*, whizzed in and out of the traffic, buzzing like mosquitoes. The traffic was clogged with loads of Fiats, which my friends and I always called 'Fix It Again, Tony'. They were parked jam-packed on the streets and footpaths, facing any which way. All the time, our bus lurched and zoomed forward and sideways to get us to the train station. I left half-moon indentations under my seat on that bus from the fierce grip of my fingernails.

Rome itself looked like a movie set. There were ancient ruins everywhere, on every corner and in the middle of the road. In fact, everything – even the buildings being used and lived in by the Romans – seemed to be an ancient ruin. Modern-day life carried on normally around beautiful, historic monuments that in my country would have been revered, protected and treasured. Here, everything was hundreds, if not thousands of years old; there was so much that was ancient, the local people probably didn't even notice anymore.

By the time I arrived at Roma Termini, it was almost midday and I still had to grapple with buying my ticket to Florence. I was lighthearted with the adventure of it all and lightheaded from lack of sleep as I dragged my luggage behind me into the cavernous train station that looks like an airplane hangar.

But hang on, where was the train to Florence? I searched the train departure board . . . nothing. No Florence. People swarmed around me. They stopped, looked at the board, found their time of departure and platform, and moved on to the ticket counter. Some chatted to companions while they absent-mindedly took note of the information and floated away. Others looked up only for seconds, hitched their bags further on to their shoulders, then disappeared into the thick crowd. I watched them and tried to gather some clues, as if gaining information from a train departure board was a mystery that they could reveal to me through close observation.

It never occurred to me to go to the ticket counter and ask, as I couldn't speak Italian.

Savona

Venezia

Napoli

Civitavecchia

Milano

Firenze

Ancona

Velletri

But no *Florence*.

The station bustled with people of many nationalities. Filipinos, Africans, Arabs and Japanese, they all seemed to know the trick. As I gazed up and scoured that vast board, with my bags clustered around my feet, I felt my excitement turn to anxiety. I was deflating rapidly in the face of this new obstacle and tears of disappointment were dangerously close to the surface.

An hour passed. I went over my itinerary plans, which required me to 'catch the train to Florence'. No more than that – easy, just get on a train and go to Florence. It had sounded so simple when I was at home, in the kitchen going over my game plan with Mum. Florence was a big town, wasn't it? Maybe it was smaller than I had thought and wasn't a true destination, only a stop on the line. A strike? Line trouble? Why weren't there any trains to Florence today? Fear and loneliness were rising in my stomach and I was limp with travel fatigue. Not yet out of Rome and I was already stuck – no Florence on the departure board. There was no emergency strategy and no way I could drag my gear over to a phone because public phones in Italy only took special coins called *gettoni*; that much I did know. According to Carel, the brass disc with grooves on either side was one of the greatest Italian tourist foils. On her last visit to Sydney she'd showed me a *gettone* and told how tourists didn't know they existed or where to buy them. We'd marvelled at how a country could run a public telephone system with something that looked like it would get you through a turnstyle at Luna Park. Anyway, I didn't have one, or anyone to call. My eyes pooled with tears and my vision blurred.

'*Signorina? Vuole aiuto?*'

I stared down at a short, fat man dressed in a grimy suit and tie that were far too small for him. The way his pudgy neck and round, bald head burst out of his dirty shirt made me think of a turtle dressed up as a man.

'Pardon?'

'Do you need 'elp?'

He stood erect and proud. I had an image of a turtle bowing graciously, sweeping his hands deeply before him, saying, 'May I be of service to you, ma'am?'

'Florence, Florence I can't find a train to Florence'.

'*Ma, li.*' He pointed up to the board, his eyebrows raised high at my ignorance.

'No, no. I'm trying to find Florence. Ffffllllllooorrrrenccc-cce', I said, enunciating the name slowly and clearly.

'*Si, si, si*. There – Florence, *Firenze*, Florence, *Firenze*.'

'*Firenze* is Florence?' I asked incredulously.

'*Si, si, si.*' And with that he picked up my suitcase and tottered off towards the ticket counter. I followed, panicking at the sight of someone, even if he was a turtle, running off with my stuff.

We waited in line for an hour and he stood there next to me like a silent sentinel, his hand glued to the handle of my suitcase. Once I had my ticket, no amount of thanks or protest would send him on his way. He was going to take me to my train and that was that. His body was so sharply inclined to one side from the weight of my luggage that he could manage only a wild wave with his free hand to indicate that we'd arrived at the right platform.

'Oh thank you so much. You really are very kind,' I said, sincerely grateful. 'What a sweetheart, to take so much trouble to help me to my train,' I thought as I moved towards the train door. 'Gee, I hope they're all like this in Italy.'

But the palm of his upturned hand appeared in front of me and stopped me from moving forward.

'Thank you,' I said again loudly, with a dismissive nod of my head. But the hand didn't move, it only barred my way.

Damn it! I realise it's money he wants. The very thing I don't have much of.

I took my purse from my shoulder bag and began to rummage through it. I tried to work out how many lira there were to the Australian dollar, but I had no idea. In my currency, zeroes mean money and lots of it. 'One hundred lira ought to do it. It seems like plenty,' I thought as I laid the coin in his outstretched hand. He snorted with disgust, shuffled his feet in growing irritation but didn't move aside. 'It's obvious he wants more,' I sighed, as I tried to gather all my energy for a display of feisty determination in the face of this money-hungry shyster. With as much indignation as I could muster, I plonked one more 100 lira coin in his palm. At this he virtually spat and then rattled off some rapid, angry Italian and moved away, no doubt in search of another naive traveller.

I later worked out that I had given him, in all, twenty cents for his time and trouble, so his display of fury was probably quite warranted. If it hadn't been for that little man, I would still be standing there, frozen in fear with my bottom lip quivering, waiting for the name 'Florence' to appear on the departure board and too afraid to ask anyone for help.

Unfortunately, with all the confusion, I had missed all the jostling for a seat on the train and had to make do with slumping on my suitcase in the aisle. Not a problem really, except that I am almost six feet tall (two metres) and don't compact easily. My ungainly seat soon became an obstacle course for my fellow aisle travellers who insisted on moving constantly up and down the carriage in search of a better place to smoke their cigarettes. As the Roma/Firenze/Milano express snaked its way out of the hangar and started its three-hour journey north, any notion of some quiet time went out the window with the cigarette butts.

For a while the ruins of an ancient wall ran parallel to the train tracks, as if it were trying to take centre stage from the rows of ugly, identically tall, modern apartment blocks. But, surprisingly, it was only a matter of minutes before we were out of the concrete jungle and into lush green countryside.

I leaned my head against the window and watched the Tiber River wander lazily through flat plains that were neatly ploughed to expose rich, black soil. After pushing through a series of black tunnels, the train broke out into an open valley surrounded by hillocks and mountains, giving me my first glimpse of the thousands of medieval fortress villages for which Italy is famous. Like islands of brown stone upon a sea of green, they were built for inaccessibility – on the very tip of the hills or trickling down their side, their solid perimeter walls making access even harder for invaders. Then the southern province of Lazio gave way to the central province of Tuscany and I was almost 'home'.

Cradled on a plain between softly moulded hills called *colline*, Florence is divided in two by the Arno River. The *colline* are dotted with clusters of houses, churches and their bell towers, and superb villas, most of them complete with beautiful gardens and olive groves. Although the geography of Florence provides beautiful views, it also ensures crazy temperatures in summer and winter. In the hot months, when there is little or no breeze, the city's heat and pollution have nowhere to go because of the mountains on either side. The mercury soars as Florence, built from stone and clay, bakes like a pot in a furnace.

By the time my train eased into Firenze Santa Maria Novella station, Carel was well into rehearsals and fittings for the fashion shows that were due to run the following week. It was late Friday afternoon and all I had to do was find a taxi to our hotel, which wasn't too tricky after the surprises that Rome had thrown at me. Heat blasted me in the face as the train doors slid open and I threw my luggage on to the platform, cursing myself for bringing so much stuff. *Tabacchi*, *San Paolo*, *Sala di Attesa*, *Informazioni Turistiche* – the signs meant nothing to me, so I trundled on through the crowds. A child, filthy and dressed in rags, scampered up to me with his hand out. Pulling at my clothes, he babbled and whined, while his mother, a gypsy woman dressed in a long, brightly patterned skirt, sat with her breast exposed as she fed a baby. A man, with his trousers rolled up to his knees, sat on the flattened cardboard box next to her. He picked at the scabs of a horrible wound to his shins. I tried to shoo the boy away as I floundered with my bags, but his persistence and pestering were new to me. There are no gypsies in Sydney, no beggars that follow you waving their self-inflicted wounds in your face. Shocked and revolted, I was unused to sights like this.

'Leave me alone!' I screamed. It worked and the gypsy beggar dissolved back into the crowd.

Taxi rank discovered and address – 'Hotel Porta Rossa, in Via Porta Rossa' – delivered, the final leg of my journey was underway.

Bumpety-thump, bumpety-thump, bumpety-thump. I loved the sound of the car's wheels on the roads; fast-moving rubber on smooth, uneven cobblestones. There is a rhythm to wheels on cobblestones that you don't get with bitumen. Then great slabs of flagstones led the taxi into Piazza del Duomo and I couldn't believe that I was seeing one of the medieval world's greatest architectural feats up so close, so soon. The cathedral is ninety-one metres high. It takes up the space of several back-to-back football fields and is completely covered in intricate green and white marble. The baptistery, in front of the Duomo's entrance, dates back to the fourth century. Cars, motorbikes, buses, pedestrians and tourists all fight for space on the tiny roads that lead from the Duomo's splendour off into the various areas around the city centre.

My taxi *bumpety-thump*s off to the right where the façades

of all the buildings are in varying shades of brown, cream and beige. They are only ever three or four storeys high and the windows are all the same, with grey stone lintels and chocolate-brown shutters. The uniformity of the Florentine architecture is fortress-like, strong, as though nothing could break through the thick walls of these homes.

We drive through a huge square with a triumphal arch that celebrates Florence's time as Italy's capital, past outdoor cafés with brightly coloured awnings and stalls selling T-shirts and scarves, around elegant street lights with lamps like moons, then out of the square and into another ancient street that is doing its best to accommodate all this modern traffic.

I could have kissed the taxi driver in gratitude when he took it upon himself to heave my bags out of the boot and up the small stairway that led into the hotel. He virtually took my wallet from my hands and found the money for the fare himself; such was my confusion with the zeroes of the currency.

I was *here*. At last.

Something like the remains of a vaulted ceiling jutted out of the hotel over the footpath, which was about thirty centimetres wide. The street itself was narrow enough to cover in just one leap. Ornate lamps with glass panels hung along the hotel's façade. Years ago they would have held burning torches. They were decorated with wrought-iron flowers and leaves that poured out the top. Alongside them were highly arched windows with 'Hotel Porta Rossa' written in old-fashioned curly gold italics. Through the windows I could see couches and coffee tables where, a century ago, Russian princesses and British noblewomen would have met for afternoon tea and to watch the passing parade of the latest fashions.

Once inside, I followed the Corinthian columns to the reception desk, where an old man with a kind face handed me a heavy key and nodded encouragingly for me to wait for the porter. Behind him were odd bits of hotel paraphernalia that time-machined me back to the days when the post was the only means of written communication. Brass plaques engraved with the names *Palermo*, *Napoli*, *Roma* and *Trieste* lined the wall, marking a series of small, dusty shelves waiting for letters that were no longer delivered.

Pretty, full-breasted maidens in flowing gowns, turtles on sails, and smiling Bacchus faces gazed down from the walls where stained-glass windows broke the monotony of continuous walnut panelling. The ceiling, an immense stained-glass dome, was once open to the sky and this foyer a grand inner courtyard. There was a faded glory smell – dry and musty, like a dinosaur display room in a museum.

A young porter, wearing a maroon jacket with brass buttons down the front, appeared before me. He had bright blue eyes and a wide smile with perfectly straight white teeth. He ran his fingers provocatively through thick, brown hair that hung over one eye, all the time smiling at me curiously. I was momentarily startled by his cheek and good looks, so smiled uncertainly when he turned to lead me to the elevator. Once the doors slid shut with a clanking shudder (in what century had this lift been built?), he pointed to his chest.

'I am Fabiano. You friend models?'

'Well, yes. I'm staying with them and my sister, Carel.'

'Your sister? Who your sister? Lauren? Bethany?' He barely seemed able to contain himself.

'No, Carel.'

'Ahh.' Confusion crossed his face as he tried to place Carel, but couldn't. He settled for looking at me irreverently, penetrating me with his eyes.

I flushed, embarrassed by his interest and by my appearance. I felt shockingly dirty. And then I remembered my hair. Somewhere between Singapore and Rome I had lost the elastic for the bane of my life – my eternally untidy, curly hair. After spying the plastic cutlery wrap, with 'Philippine Airlines' emblazoned across it, I'd bunched my hair at the back and wrapped the plastic around it several times to make a ponytail. I'd forgotten it was there until Fabiano's scrutiny reminded me. Every time I moved, the cutlery wrap rustled softly, making my self-assurance, which at sixteen wasn't my strength, plummet even further.

Was he flirting with me? Or was I just imagining it?

He let me into my room and put my luggage down on a rack. 'You call Fabiano any time you have a problem. I will help you. OK?'

'Yes, all right.'

It was the *way* he looked at me, as though he found me attractive and interesting. I found it disconcerting, almost threatening, because I couldn't imagine he would want me for me. My mother, so accustomed to handling models and telling them whether they would make it in the competitive world of beauty, had always told me that one day I would be beautiful. Apparently, all my features were going to miraculously fall into place and bingo! Beauty would be mine. But, unless it had happened on the way over on the plane, I knew that that day hadn't yet come. (And I wasn't holding my breath for that day to come tomorrow, either.) I felt that I was 'all right' looking, but I nursed a keen paranoia about my pimples.

Dubious about Fabiano's interest in me, I realized it was probably the models he was after.

Fabiano held the room key out to me, oozing confidence and Latin style. 'OK. You call me. Bye-bye.' A solicitous grin and he was out the door.

My sister had arrived that morning, and already her clothes and cosmetics were spread throughout the room and over the bed, which looked particularly inviting with its crisp white sheets and ornate gold Renaissance-style bedhead.

I peeled off my clothes, sick of the sight of them, and lay down on the floor next to Carel's bags, the cool tiles refreshing my back. The room was big and deep, with a high ceiling and four curves, rounded and smooth, where the corners should have been. The furniture all matched; the same scrolls cascaded into feathers carved along the top of the wooden cupboard, bedside tables and dresser. I wondered whether we would bother to put our clothes away in them.

Past the suitcases was a set of huge French doors that opened out on to a waist-high balustrade. Beyond it lay an expanse of jumbled rooftops, irregular in size and shape, jutting in and out, over and under and beside each other. The rooftops connected and disconnected in a pattern of textured terracotta crosshatching. Their endless clay colour was broken by patches of green moss and stretches of guttering that offered up tufts of grass, yellow wildflowers and willowy ferns. Smoke-charred chimneys and aerials, along with the turrets and towers, pointed towards the sky. The glass in the doors wasn't perfectly smooth, so everything seen through it looked wiggly and slippery. The glass was old and, like everything else around me, probably handmade; blown complete with flaws, rather than an immaculate modern-day factory finish.

I heaved myself up to pull closed the curtains. Exhaustion was sweeping through my body in waves. After a quick shower, I was unable to stop myself from swaying; delayed motion sickness had finally caught up with me. I slept.

3

A shaft of light cut through the darkness like an axe to my jet-lagged head. My sister peeled back the bedcovers with an excited squeal.

Our reunion was joyous, with giggly looks at each other to check out the changes that two years had brought. Carel looked more glamorous than she had back in Sydney. There was a new elegance and understatement to her style. Her Italian was brilliant as she ordered coffee from room service, and I was in awe of her fluency. She had what I soon learned was a Milanese accent, an Italian punctuated with melodious sing-song inflections.

She talked of her plans for the weekend as we sat cross-legged on the bed. 'The shows start tomorrow. The models are nice girls. One or two of them are a bit whacky, but when you're drop-dead gorgeous you can get away with being eccentric.'

Our door opened and soon our room buzzed with beautiful girls in varying states of nonchalant undress (oddly, there was no sign of Fabiano) as we prepared to go out for dinner. There were three Americans, and one Swedish girl who was rarely seen without a Marlboro in her hand. The fifth model was an Australian brunette whom I recognised immediately from a recent Australian *Vogue* cover. Classical music resonated a calm tranquillity from her room, in contrast to the upbeat disco thump emanating from the Texan girl's room. A violinist studying at the Conservatorium of Music in Sydney, she was supporting her musical studies through modelling. She was quiet and withdrawn and seemed to resent the effervescence of the other girls. Lauren, whose southern drawl was so strong she took forever to finish a sentence, was the chattiest. She wore heavily embroidered cowboy boots with tight jeans, a belt embedded with lapis lazuli, and a cropped leather jacket, and claimed she knew Jerry Hall. This was indeed a true brush with fame. At the time, the model Jerry Hall was dating the singer Brian Ferry and had appeared in his music video 'The Price of Love'.

Leather pants and suede miniskirts teamed with tight little T-shirts appeared to be the models' preferred choice of clothes. Or slim-fitting, straight-legged jeans with high-heeled boots. While they looked fabulously fashionable, my own personal fashion statement for the evening fell way short of the season's must-have wardrobe essentials. An orange vintage Chinese knitted singlet with yellow flowers embroidered around the collar line was teamed with faded flared jeans. To complete the look, I wore side-buckled, flat, natural leather shoes that had cut-out sections on the sides so that you could see my orange socks. After seeing the models and my sister in their funky leather, I felt like the consummate dag. But having been around models all my life, I was used to the physical intimidation. There was no use trying to compete with their brand of extreme gorgeousness. But still . . . perhaps tonight the sparkly boob tube, or even the green knitted singlet with the diamantes, would have been better? Oh, forget it. My suitcase offered nothing better, the orange would just have to do. I had already worked out that I wasn't going to be the centre of any male attention tonight.

We were a startling and statuesque group of seven women – not one of us was less than five feet ten inches (one hundred and seventy-eight centimetres) tall, so it wasn't too much of a surprise when drivers honked their horns and men walked into telegraph poles. Even the women's necks craned to get a better look as we made our way down to the Arno River and the Ponte Vecchio (the old bridge), the most ancient of all the bridges that connect the two sides of Florence. Our hotel was situated on the Duomo side of the river where the streets are lined with grand old *palazzi*, built by wealthy Florentines who wanted to settle near the huge marble cathedral. Most of the city's treasures are found in the *centro* (the main city area) as well as the brand-name shops such as Gucci, Prada and Ferragamo. We were headed towards the Oltrarno, which means, literally, 'the other side of the Arno', home to the workers, artisans and craftsmen of Florence. The atmosphere here is warm, arty and alternative. The beauty of Florence is that the *centro* and Oltrarno are both small enough to cover on foot.

We strolled to the middle of the bridge, where the views up and down the river are magical. Built in 1345, the Ponte Vecchio was originally lined with butcher shops, its stench from the bloody display of carcasses made famous by various medieval poets. Now it is home to dazzling goldsmiths' shops, their sparkling antique and modern jewellery enough to blind window-shoppers.

The weather was perfect, and my stressful arrival in Rome only that morning quite forgotten. The twilight sky promised another lovely day tomorrow. On either side of the Ponte Vecchio, rows of facades in differing hues of yellow stretched along the riverbanks until a tree-lined bend took the Arno out of sight. It was *aperitivo* time, the sunset hour when work is finished and the locals head out to their favourite cafés for a pre-dinner drink and a canapé. The sound of their heels clipped the cobblestones and echoed across the bridge while shop owners pulled down their shutters with a roar and a clang.

Lauren's voice broke my reverie. 'Hey, guys, I'm starting to feel like the Pied Piper.'

Men, clustered in groups near us, guffawed and rough-housed, trying to catch our attention. One guy, clearly the clown and a little gutsier than the rest, called out to Lauren: 'You are milk, I am coffee . . . together we make cappuccino?'

Everybody laughed as the guy clutched at his heart and staggered about under the weight of his undying love.

As we moved on across the bridge, the men followed, waving and calling out, 'Where are you going?' 'What is your name?' They whistled or signalled, as though they had something important to say.

The models appeared to be accustomed to the commotion, all this Italian masculine fuss. Lauren and her co-Texan, Bethany, cracked flippant jokes and teased, while gliding easily through the attention. It was an open display of adoration for beautiful women that, for me, was a surprise.

But that's mainly because of the way the models handled it. They played it like a game. They were the cats and the men were the mice.

Over dinner at Borgo San Jacopo's Il Cammillo restaurant, the conversation turned to the differences between modelling in America, Australia, Japan and Italy. The models chatted about the money they could earn here or there, how the different photographers worked, and international requirements for fashion shows. The Australian violinist remained aloof, still cool to everyone around her. Her unfriendly attitude was intriguing.

'Do you like modelling?' I asked.

Finally she became animated. 'I hate it! I'm only here because the money is so good. I really should be back home working on more important things, like my music.'

'I'm sure that can be arranged,' Bethany drawled.

Someone quickly changed the subject and the Australian girl again retreated into herself, where she was obviously most happy to be.

When our meals arrived, no one else seemed to notice that Lauren cut her veal scaloppine into tiny pieces and produced from her handbag a set of chopsticks.

'Ah, Lauren, do you yearn to be in China, rather than Italy?' I ventured.

'I eat slower, I eat less and I feel fuller faster when I eat with chopsticks,' she said. 'So, I keep my weight down.'

Six pairs of eyes rolled towards the ceiling and the conversation prattled on.

Secretly, while making out that I was listening, I was actually coveting their skin – they all had clear, healthy, radiant, spotless, poreless, perfect bloody skin – even Marika, the Swedish smoker who could single-handedly take the blame for the hole in the ozone layer. I wasn't envious of their overall good looks, only of their skin. In Sydney I'd heard it all: Pizza Face, Volcano Girl, Princess Pimple – not that these insults were said behind my face and its pimples; they were harmless nicknames bandied about and invented in fun.

Just as these thoughts were going through my head, Lauren casually asked: 'When are you going to start modelling?'

'You've got to be joking,' I spluttered, shocked.

'No, I'm not. You're tall enough, you've got a fantastic body, and makeup can always cover a pimple or two.'

'Lauren, my mother has model agencies all over Australia. I think she would've mentioned my potential by now.'

'That's just it,' she insisted. 'Sometimes when you're so close to someone, you can't see their potential, sort of like doctors being unable to diagnose their own children. I think you should try.'

My cheeks throbbed into a blush and I mumbled, 'My mum says I'm a late bloomer. Maybe when I'm older. Best I work on my inner beauty for now.'

The girls laughed and the conversation changed direction. I searched Carel's face for a sign of encouragement, but she stayed silent, only offering a 'we'll see' kind of expression and a small shrug. Perhaps it was a compliment paid in sympathy for a young, impressionable girl who needed a bit of a boost. But still, Lauren, the mighty friend of Jerry Hall's, had suggested that I model and I was deeply flattered.

The models did the Pitti Donna fashion shows, leaving hordes of passionate suitors in their wake, and I went along every day to help and watch. On the night before we all checked out of Hotel Porta Rossa, Fabiano, who now knew that I was looking for work, knocked on my door to tell me that the British Consulate kept a book with a list of jobs available for English speakers. I shook his hand gratefully and thanked him profusely.

'You, me, we do the bedroom thing,' he said, pulling me towards him.

'What?' I replied, like a stunned mullet.

'I have one hour. This is the way we say goodbye in Italy,' he said softly, puckering up.

'Well, this is the way we say goodbye in Australia: SEE YA!' Slam! As hard as I could, I shoved the door closed on his floppy Hugh Grant haircut, while behind me, Carel laughed until the tears ran down her cheeks.

Once she'd regained her composure and I'd stopped punching the air in anger at being so boldly propositioned, Carel shed some light on what had just happened.

'Your problem, Lisa, is that you look older than you are. People here will be shocked to find out that you're so young and so far away from home. Sixteen-year-old Italian girls are still at home with their mammas. You must also remember that the average Italian man, given half the chance, will flirt with you.'

'Yeah, but I didn't give him any encouragement, so why on earth did he feel he had the right to try and kiss me like that?' I replied indignantly.

'Because you are a *straniera* – a foreigner – and Italian men think that all foreign girls are easy. You've left your family, you are independent, so you're therefore more adventurous. Most men here will tend to think that all that adds up to a girl who is more likely to go to bed with them.'

'Oh, great! So all the boys are going to want to park their

boots under my bed just because I'm *here* and not at home learning how to make spaghetti bolognese with my mummy?'

She smiled her warm big-sister smile and said, 'You'll be fine. On the whole, Italian men are really lovely. They'll never force you into anything. Just be careful who you find yourself alone with.'

How right she was.

4

Without the benefit of Carel's agency's expense account, modest lodgings were needed while I looked for work. There could be no courses in Italian until the constant pocket digging had been replaced by some serious pocket padding. The morning Carel left, I found a small, family-run, one-star *pensione* in the quiet residential backstreets behind Via Porta Rossa. The bathroom was shared, but at least I had my own tiny room under the roof's heavy wooden beams, complete with an olive branch sticking out from behind a framed picture of the *Madonna and Child*.

The temperatures in Florence soared higher every day. The European summer season (July–August) brought with it a growing number of tourist groups that clogged the tiny streets like walls of immovable human flesh. The tourists' huge buses and flag-waving guides were everywhere, while the number of local Florentines dwindled. When the tourist forces invaded, the Italians retreated. In massive highway traffic jams and forty-degree heat, they deserted their schools, universities, businesses and shops, leaving only the hospitals on skeleton staff.

It didn't take long for the mighty Lauren to give me a chance to honour her prediction that I could model. When I contacted my sister to tell her of my new address, she gave me the phone numbers of two Florentines whom Lauren had insisted may be able to help me. The first number was for Lorenzo Susini. Apparently, he was a clothes manufacturer with an enormous business that required lots of girls to model his clothes. Carel had never heard of him, but said that Lauren's word was pretty good.

'Why not?' I thought as I eagerly dialled his number. I told the receptionist I was a friend of Lauren's. She put the call through immediately. Rather abruptly, Mr Susini agreed to see me that afternoon, when his showrooms would reopen after the lunch break. To say I was thrilled was an understatement. In my elated state, I saw this immediate appointment as an admission of probable employment; as an indication that he needed models to show his range right now and that he was keen to give an inexperienced Australian a chance.

My only good dress – a pink, red and yellow gold-threaded Fiorucci gingham – was perhaps a tad too garish and girlie for presentation before such an esteemed European fashion manufacturer, but I clung to the knowledge that a fresh model's potential can shine through anything. With a borrowed blow-drier, I gelled and curled my hair into shape and cursed the tiny mirror of my powder compact. The makeup of the day was heavy, so cat's eyes, a lot of foundation, rouge and eye shadow were applied to achieve the desired effect.

On my way down Lungarno Vespucci, I couldn't help thinking that the future was an exciting place. Even though I had a low opinion of my physical attributes (like most post-pubescent creatures), it didn't take long for me to imagine that everyone in Australia had overlooked my unique appeal and that maybe Mr Susini would see my potential. Convinced that my look was more suited to the Italian audience, I thought I was on my way to being 'discovered'. In fact, I already felt beautiful and walked tall so that people would know I was actually a model on my way to an important appointment with a fashion designer. Surely people were looking at me in a new way? A motorbike with two boys on board whizzed past and one of them yelled out *Bella*. I laughed out loud and grew even taller with confidence. The shop windows showed the reflection of a proud sixteen-year-old with a secret smile. The sun was shining and I clutched hope tightly against my chest. If Mr Susini liked me, I would have to have some test shots done, to see how I looked and moved in front of the camera. I would need a model portfolio and composite cards, too. Maybe Mum or Dad would send some money to help. The rest of my life now hinged on Mr Susini and all that I could think of were the positive changes that his nod would bring.

The *palazzi* on either side of the Arno River house some of the most prestigious office space in Italy. It's prime real estate and only the truly successful can afford to rent offices behind those exclusive walls. Many of the *palazzi* towards the Ponte Vecchio belong to consuls general, embassies and internationally renowned fashion labels such as Salvatore Ferragamo. Susini Fashions was located further down the river towards the green fields of the Cascine Park.

A large bronze plaque indicated the showrooms were on the second floor. The entrance was an enormous archway with ancient wooden doors that folded back to reveal a dark enclosed area with an elegant staircase off to one side. Wealthy families constructed these *palazzi* centuries ago. Carriages would drop them off inside the entrance to their stately inner courtyards. They would then make their way upstairs into their homes in private and under cover. I thought of the many women who had passed this way long before me, their long dresses swooshing over the wide flagstones towards the staircase. They must have bent slightly to gracefully lift their voluminous skirts, so as not to trip up the stairs. Then I thought of the modern models who had gone before me wearing stiletto heels, only to be tripped up by the same flagstones. Ah, the pitfalls of modern living in a historic town. The sound of my own beaten leather sandals hit the steps with a lonely *slap-slap*.

Once upstairs and through a glass door, I felt like Alice in Wonderland. Gone was the medieval architecture of a world gone by. Here were the bright lights of the fashion world. Everything gleamed white and beige or wood. A girl behind a milk-coloured wooden curved reception desk told me that Mr Susini would be with me shortly. To the receptionist's left and right were corridors dotted with tiny bright lights that tracked both sides of the polished wooden floors. The corridors looked like catwalks, all lit up and ready for a fashion show. Behind the receptionist were two doors, one of which was flung open so that a silver-haired man with papers in his hand was framed by the natural light that streamed in behind him. It was all very theatrical and I was duly impressed. Mr Susini stood in the doorway like it was his stage and this was the opening act. He stood frozen, frowning down at the papers and puffing occasionally on a cigarette. Eventually he looked up, found my gaze, and after what seemed like an age but was only seconds said, 'Leeza! Come back at 8.30 tonight. I cannot see you now. I'm busy.' He took a step forward, dropped the papers on the desk in front of the receptionist, turned sharply on his heel and slammed the door.

Was this a good sign? I took it as being extremely positive. At least he didn't take one look at me and say, 'Thanks, but no thanks. Yours is not the look I'm looking for.' He'd asked me back! This was a terrific reaction. I walked back to the *pensione* and never felt my feet touch the ground.

Upon my return to Lungarno Vespucci that evening, Mr Susini greeted me personally, flicking lights on up and down the hallway because his staff had gone home and locked up on their way out. He was well dressed in office casualwear; an open-neck shirt, tailored trousers and expensive leather loafers. Close up I could see that he was a good two inches (five centimetres) shorter than me and probably older than I'd first guessed, more like fifty-five than forty-five. I noticed his grey hair had been freshly brushed back and he smelt of a recent splash of aftershave. Another positive sign – one of respect. He'd taken the trouble to freshen up for me.

He led the way down a hallway and into a dressing room. In a brusque, business-like manner he asked how much experience I'd had.

'Not much,' I replied. 'Though I've been around models all my life because my mother has model agencies in Australia. I've also done several model courses.'

'No, no. Courses dey make you stiff. Dey are no good, no good at all. You will now forget all dat dey teach you,' he scoffed with a voice that dripped thick with Italian accent. He glanced around the dressing room and went to a rack full of hanging garments. He seemed to know exactly which dress he wanted because he rummaged with quick, determined purpose.

'I need to see you in an evening gown. 'ere, put dis on.'

It was a long silky number in shiny slate-grey, sleeveless with a deep neckline, plunging back and slits up to the waist. After he left the room, I examined the dress. It felt shimmery and slippery in my hands. I held it up by what I hoped were the shoulders in an effort to work out whether the front was the back, or maybe the back was the front. It didn't seem to be a dress, but rather the top half of a cocktail outfit. Had he forgotten to give me the pants, as surely my underpants will show? The slits were so high they reached the top of my hip-bones, so what was a girl to do about the sides of her panties showing?

I slipped off my Fiorucci gingham and my Berlei trainer bra and pulled the sheath (for want of a better word) over my head. I'd never worn anything like it in my life and puffed with pleasure when I saw that the fall of the garment was superb; it draped well on my long, thin body. I felt elegant and mature. But it also made me feel exposed and uncomfortable with so much flesh showing. The grey shimmered and shone in an uninterrupted flow until it reached my waist, where the sides parted to reveal my underpants. Like white lightning, they flashed every time I moved.

Any good aspiring model knows that a panty line wrecks the look of a garment, so I had been sure to wear my full brief cottontails. It just wouldn't have done to have a pair of bikini briefs create the rubberband effect by pinching the fat at my hips. My trusty Bonds cottontails had half an inch (a centimetre) of thick banding around the leg, a solid cotton gusset and a waist that almost reached my ribs. But there was no way I could hitch those cottontails higher than the slits in that dress. I wrestled and writhed and wiggled and tried to get those underpants a little further up my bottom so they wouldn't show. No success. Those cottontails were like cast-iron around my hips.

As I tried to find a way out of this unprofessional predicament, Mr Susini strode unannounced back into the dressing room. 'Now model it for me,' he said with a commanding wave of his hand.

No problem. I'd seen this done a thousand times and knew just what to do: stride down here, a little half turn there, make sure the feet always look pretty, the head doesn't bob, a perfectly executed full turn with hands on hips to show how the dress moves in motion.

'You aren't wearing a dong.'

'A what?'

'A dong. A DONG!' he shouted, as if I didn't understand English. He pointed his finger at the region of my cottontails. I stopped mid-glide and felt my brains scramble in confusion until I remembered that Italians often can't pronounce 'th' so say 'd' instead. If so, he meant 'thong'. If so, he meant, in Australian, g-string. If so, my cottontails had blown it.

I was disappointed and he sensed it. In a softer tone he said, 'All the good models wear dongs. But let's work on anoder technique.' Mr Susini walked over to a full-length mirror and, like a patient schoolteacher with a slow but potentially good student, explained to me that he wanted to unveil my hidden sexuality. He had developed his very own personal model-training process aimed at revealing the sensual side of my nature. His series of exercises would help me to become one of those sexy models that strutted the catwalks of Milan. He settled his serious brown eyes on mine and told me to stand in front of the mirror. I did what I was told.

'Do you know what an orgasm is?'

Now here was my shot at modelling with the big boys and already I'd botched badly. Something as simple as a bad choice of underwear had almost wrecked my burgeoning career. Not wanting to confirm his suspicions that I was a provincial girl with convent modesty, I said that of course I knew what an orgasm was.

'OK, den touch yourself in the mirror like you're going to have an orgasm.' There is a moment in one-on-one conversations when people connect and know that an understanding has been reached. It can be a moment of recognition, agreement or perception of the other's intentions. This wasn't that moment. I had no idea what he was talking about, so I stood there blankly and rubbed my arms.

'Come on, you must be sexy, *feel* sexy. Touch your breasts.'

I ran my hands numbly across my chest, touched my neck with my fingertips, then opened my palms and ran my hands down my hips. Though I did what he asked, I felt disconnected from my body, like someone else was at the controls and I was just a robot. I could hear a phone ringing in an office somewhere down the corridor, but no one was there to answer it. The neon light above us buzzed monotonously as we stood silently in its hard white light. My senses were alert, but my movements were mechanical.

'But you don't look like you're about to have an orgasm.'

Something was wrong and I couldn't figure out what. I was far too well mannered and in awe of this man's power to reject his teaching methods. I barely understood the concept of 'exploiting an innocent young girl' and just didn't think of myself as green. I thought I had enough worldly experience behind me to identify a tricky situation. I respected Mr Susini because he was a successful fashion manufacturer. He'd taken time out at the end of a busy day to try and teach me how to model like the supermodels in Milan, and initially I was grateful. But a sick feeling of discomfort was growing in my stomach. I had trusted him implicitly, because he was Lauren's friend, but I now felt invaded, compromised. I was also acutely embarrassed because he was persuasive in a matter-of-fact, professional way that made me feel like I was the one acting improperly. The force of his authority seemed unquestionable, so the strength of spirit to rebuff this man was slow to emerge.

I looked in the mirror and saw the reflection of his face peering over my shoulder, the look of barely disguised lust in his eyes, and everything fell into place. My stranger-danger alarm bells rang and I stepped away from the mirror. We looked at each other – this was the moment of understanding. After hours, no staff, no interruptions. He had wanted to get me alone. Carel's advice echoed in my ears.

'I'd like to model the dress again properly,' I said. Not knowing what else to say or how to escape the mirror, parading seemed the only way to get away from his hands. But his eyebrows narrowed and his expression showed determination. He knew that he wasn't yet finished with me.

'Come here, let me guide your hands. You must feel sexy to be a model. I will show you.' He took my shoulders, stood behind me and angled me towards the mirror. With his hands covering mine he rubbed my palms over my body. Fear robbed me of strength. I couldn't resist; I felt powerless and utterly unable physically to fight back. He had the power and I had to be submissive. But I wasn't a willing puppet and he could feel that. My hands were limp and my body motionless. Mr Susini could see that this little modelling technique wasn't working. I was far from turned on.

'Bah, we try somding else,' he said impatiently. 'Put your clodes back on. Come into my office drew dis door,' he said, pointing to a door I hadn't noticed on one side of the dressing room.

When he strode from the room, I almost fell to the floor with relief. Snatching up my dress, I ripped off Mr Susini's silver sheath and threw it over the back of a chair. Like a snake, it slithered to the floor and I didn't bother to pick it up. As I pulled my gingham on over my head and buckled up my shoes, my mind raced. 'Bloody hell, I bet he's moving on to Plan B.'

'Maybe I should go now,' I said timidly, opening the door, feeling afraid of what I'd find. But he was fully clothed, in front of his big mahogany desk, jauntily leaning back with his arms folded. He flicked his wrist and motioned for me to stand in front of him.

'We dry anoder ding. I am master of meditation. I will go into a trance. I do not know where I am when in dis trance, I do not even know who I am wid. And I *cannot* remember what 'appens. You can touch me; feel me all over, anywhere you like. When you finish, clap your hands dree times and I will come out of de trance. Dis exercise will make you feel like a beautiful model. Den, when you are finished, we will talk about your modelling career.' He then proceeded to close his eyes, lean back further against his desk and hum.

'He has *got* to be kidding,' I thought as he ohm-ed his way into a self-induced state of make-believe oblivion. 'He really expects me to believe this crap?' The ridiculousness of the scene and his farcical behaviour were making me angry, but I was too scared to turn on my heels and run. He still had the authority and power and I was still his junior, in his office. So, I stood in front of him and sent him powerful thought messages: 'You are such a thoroughly demented, desperate old man. You make me sick, you kinky old scumbag.' I sent him all the thoughts that I would never have had the courage to actually say out loud. I wanted the messages to smash into his pretend transcendental plane, so that he would know of the disappointment and humiliation I felt.

We stood there face to face, his aftershave nauseatingly strong, for about sixty seconds and I never lifted a finger to touch him. When I clapped my hands three times, he shook his head as though he was clearing cobwebs, looked at me and said: 'I don't dink you 'ave a future in modelling.'

I flew down the steps and out on to the pavement beside the Arno River. He was right, I would never have a future in modelling.

Like a rape victim who feels guilty, as though she brought the attack on herself, I never told anyone about Lorenzo Susini. I was too embarrassed to talk about what had happened. I spent my time wandering the streets of Florence, exploring the piazzas and markets, mostly checking out the picnic food that I could eat sitting on my bed. I found much comfort in the cafés, or bars as they are called in Italy, and couldn't resist the ever-present temptation to snack. I had developed an insatiable appetite for pizza, pastries and rolls – soft 'milk' buns that are filled with ham or tuna and mayonnaise with spicy *rucola* salad. I discovered the bars that served fresh *bombolone*, hot doughnuts full of warm, runny raspberry jam or custard. I stopped at little *latterias* (milk bars), where open fridges had shelves lined with yoghurts, seasoned cheese chunks and cream cheeses such as ricotta and *stracchino*. There were always little tastettes of food to take home, like the 'Mukki' (similar to Dairy Farmers) cheeses that are wrapped in grease paper with a picture of a jersey cow wearing a red-and-white-chequered hanky at its throat. I bought huge mozzarellas made from buffalo milk, fist-fulls of salad, fresh bread, pizza slices, a bottle of oil, and pastries and spent the afternoons eating. My figure also showed that I was enjoying my food. My once-lithe body had new curves, and for the first time, my boobs looked more like cupcakes than pancakes.

During the daily three-hour siesta I lay on my bed, listened to the Porta Rossa families having their lunch and thought of my friends back home. I wished that Janet, Mary, Stephanie or Fiona were here to share this adventure with me. It was strange living my life alone after years of sharing such tight companionship with my girlfriends. Their Higher School Certificate exams would almost be upon them, their studying and last-minute cramming in full swing. I could just see their heads bowed over their books in the little cubicles in the library. They would be deskbound until at least October.

I'd bombed out in the final year, only weeks before the trial exams. To go through with it would have been a farce. Study was like a dirty puddle in the middle of the footpath.

When I saw it coming, I walked around it and past it and never looked back. I adored reading and always had. But no latchkey kid would choose study over play or television. While my friends' mothers were watching over their children's shoulders, pushing them to do their homework, I was watching *Bewitched*, then *The Young Doctors* and *Countdown*. Mum came home to cook dinner some time after *Hogan's Heroes*.

The year I started kindergarten at Kincoppal in Elizabeth Bay in Sydney's eastern suburbs, the convent closed down and all the students moved to Rose Bay Convent nearby, which subsequently changed its name to Kincoppal Rose Bay Convent. But somehow I was two years too young for first class and never caught up. At age sixteen I found myself looking down the barrel of the Higher School Certificate and couldn't cope. I thought it prudent to just slip away. The gang, about six of them in their blue school uniforms, skipped school to come out and see me off at the airport. They'd pooled their money and bought me a gold ring and a gold chain with a single dangling freshwater pearl. A teary group of gangly schoolgirls, we'd cried and hugged and waved until the very last moment of my departure. Afterwards they were called into Sister Ann McGrath's office and threatened with expulsion for leaving the school grounds.

I felt lonely listening to the woman in the apartment across the way. The sounds that came from her home made me homesick for Sydney, my family, my friends. All that separated my little *pensione* room from the woman's home was a small back lane about a metre wide. The acoustics bounced her voice from her kitchen, across the laneway, through my window and into my room. She sounded so close, I felt as though I could reach out and touch her. Her two university-aged children would come home for lunch every day. Their chairs scraped the tiled floor and their dishes clanged, while the strong aromas of their *pasta al pomodoro*, basil and *parmigiano* would waft into my room. Once they'd finished their meal, they would have their lie-downs and other voices would filter up from the street below. In the second hour of siesta there was no more noise, save the sound of the swallows' songs as they swooped and dived into their nests. The Italians have a saying that if the swallows choose to make their nests under your windowsill or rafter, you'll have good fortune all year. (Your house will also have streaks of concrete-hard black and white poo down the walls, but they don't dwell on that.) I hoped that the swallows would bring me luck in my job hunt, because it was time to investigate Fabiano's tip and head back down to the beautiful *palazzi* on the Arno to check out the British Consulate.

The huge Union Jack, attached to the wall by a wrought-iron flag holder, was hard to miss. Inside and up the spacious stairwell into the office itself, a woman indicated a red plastic folder that was shackled by a chain to the front desk. Obviously a popular read, its loose-leaf pages were dog-eared and stained. There was plenty of work on offer for au pairs, nannies, part-time afternoon babysitters, English teachers and promotions officers (a nice way of saying you'll be handing out leaflets at the Piazza del Duomo). I took note of all the offers, but I felt that even though I was underage and had no experience, a barmaid's position that was advertised for a pub near the centre of Florence was more for me. Red, yellow and black, the bar's logo adhesive had been stuck to the page with information on the job. It had a cartoon of a frothy beer mug and a jolly fat man with a handlebar moustache playing a banjo.

Barmaid wanted
Start immediately
8 pm to 1 am five nights a week, more if wanted.
Call in after 7 pm and ask for Franco Cappelli.

My only concern was the pub's name, The Red Garter. After my crushing experience at Susini Fashions, I was taking no chances. Would I have to wear one?

5

All the beautiful people who shopped and worked in the glamorous, upmarket area of Lungarno/Via Tournabouni were on their way home when I set out for the Red Garter. The Italian women were tanned to perfection, wearing their fashions of the moment – pencil-thin miniskirts with high-heeled shoes or tailored light cotton trousers with superbly crafted leather sandals. Their crisply ironed white shirts revealed thick, coordinating gold jewellery that gleamed at their throats and wrists. Their shoes matched their handbags, and their hair was brushed into the latest style. The look was simple elegance, an image that would ultimately earn them the descriptive fashion term 'Euro chic'. I felt pretty confident in my flared, faded jeans, because all the young people were wearing V-neck Fruit of the Loom T-shirts and I'd bought a pack of three at the markets.

Dinner was takeaway pizza on the steps of the Palazzo Vecchio (the town hall) in Piazza Signoria, on the fringes of a grunge backbackers' circle. There were thousands of them travelling around Europe in those days and they were always out in force in the evening. Mostly from Germany, Britain or Sweden, they hitched from country to country with their dogs and dreadlocks. Some of them were spiky, orange- and pink-haired punks from England. Anarchy and 'God Save the Queen, the Fascist Regime' was big back then. The traffic police – *vigili urbani* – turned a blind eye to the backpackers' takeover of the major architectural landmarks, so they sat undisturbed in large groups. They sang, played the guitar and bongos, chatted in different languages, passed joints and took swigs from bottles of red chianti wine on the steps of the Uffizi Gallery or the Palazzo Vecchio. It was a friendly, happy hippie scene that went on late into the night until they'd snuggle down into their sleeping bags and pass out where they lay. It wasn't really my scene, though, even without the blast of ice-cold bore water from the high-powered water hose that they would receive tomorrow at dawn. Just after the street-sweepers, a council cleaning truck with a little water tank on top would pass by and hose the motionless sleeping bags down if they didn't respond to an early morning wake-up yell.

The grungies' dogs snapped voraciously at my leftover pizza margherita. My appetite had lost out to a feeling of apprehension about the barmaid job interview, probably because I'd never been behind a bar (though I had spent some time in *front* of one or two). Being underage didn't concern me too much because by putting on a show of haughty bravado, I had managed back in Sydney to bluster my way past burly bouncers and had never been asked for proof of age.

The worry was more connected to an image evoked by the bar's name. The picture dancing through my mind was of a blonde, leggy barmaid wearing nothing but a red garter. She held her drinks tray artfully high, while she dodged and weaved through the lecherous hands of leering Italians.

Via de' Benci didn't inspire confidence. In total contrast to the Lungarno area, the street where the Red Garter was located, down towards the river from Piazza Santa Croce, was dark and brooding. A narrow stretch of sky above the four-storey buildings didn't allow much light to filter down on to the footpath, and after years of incessant traffic, the walls were stained with a black sooty substance. The façades, with their dingy, grime-encrusted roll-a-door shutters and gloomy doorways, appeared threatening. There was no one else on the street. With every dank doorway and dog-piss damp corner I passed, my heart picked up a beat.

Light from an open archway up ahead made me slow my pace. There was no sign, but from the thumping music, I knew this was the bar. My intention had been to walk straight in, ask for the boss and go for the job, but my legs chickened out. I walked straight past the archway, throwing a casual glance inside as I did so.

There were three men inside a well-lit alcove. One sat on a very high stool, like an umpire's seat. Another man lounged against the wall, while the third man, whose voice could be heard over the music, stood in front of them both and gesticulated something that was clearly obvious to him but that eluded the others. In an agitated staccato Italian, he gave the word 'no' three passionate and melodious syllables. He was a short, nuggety man and, to an English speaker, his feisty voice and air-punching finger would have him labelled as a fight-picker immediately. But not so in Italy. Here, what appears to be an argument may be only a passionate explanation. The other men's body language showed they were bored with what he was saying. All three men wore black trousers, white short-sleeved shirts, and red-and-white-striped vests.

The waiters (bouncers?) hadn't noticed me, so there was no risk of embarrassment when I turned around and walked past a second time. The scene had changed slightly: the guy on the umpire's seat was now on his feet poking Shorty's shoulder and apparently telling him he was nuts. All three men then went inside. I followed.

Once inside the alcove, through the door and into the bar area, one of the men turned and noticed me standing hesitantly in the doorway. He threw one last quip over his shoulder and started to move towards me. He had the body of a weightlifter, not too big, just muscled in a broad, sculptured kind of way. Long, dark wavy hair curled softly down to his collar, short behind the ears, with length at the back. His jaw was very strong too, in keeping with the strength of his body, and he had a remarkably deep cleft in his chin. I'd always had a thing for strong, square jaws, ever since I spied Larry Hagman on *I Dream of Jeannie* (not on *Dallas*) as a little girl. But it was his eyes that were different. They were a strange mix of blue and yellow, in stark contrast to his dark hair and very tanned skin.

'Is Franco Cappelli in?' I asked him in English, too shy to try out my phrase-book Italian.

'Yes, just wait a minute while I find him.' He responded with a good accent and a kind smile. As he walked off, I automatically put the blue-and-yellow-eyed waiter into my 'Too Gorgeous For Me' category, a classification I used for men that were so good-looking they would never be interested in me.

So far, everything appeared to be regular. There were no girls carousing about in bikinis and red garters. However, there was a crunching sensation under my feet and my suspicions were aroused when I saw that the tiled floors were covered in sawdust. This was a concern, because sawdust is often used in wild bars to camouflage and absorb spilt drinks, cigarette butts and, in the worst-case scenario, vomit.

A very serious cocktail barman concentrated on preparing potions behind a glossy black bartop. Rows of heavy glass beer mugs sat on shelves lined with bright red towels and backed with mirrors. The bar area was clean and shiny, with no sign of the standard Italian espresso machine with its piles of demitasse coffee cups, only brass beer taps that glistened with British beer logos.

It dawned on me then that the Red Garter was a form of Ye Olde English Pub. The little straw baskets of peanuts for drinkers to shell and throw on the floor (this eased my 'wild bar' worries), the waiters' red-and-white-striped vests, the beer kegs, the beer pitchers, and the photographs of men with handlebar moustaches were all 'English' gimmicks. Relief. Not a skimpy barmaid in sight. At this early hour only the waiters were about, busying themselves with their preparations for another busy night.

'*Buona sera*. I'm Franco. Are you looking for a job? What is your name?' With one hand plunged deep into his trouser pocket, the other waving a cigarette, Franco Cappelli squinted up at me as though he were shortsighted.

'Yes, there was a barmaid position advertised at the British Consulate. I'm Lisa.'

I drew breath and nervously prepared to launch into a litany of lies . . . false age, loads of previous bar work, the possibility of a work visa. But all Franco did was turn and say,

'Stan, show Lisa around and get her a drink.' Then he sidled off to the bar and the job interview was over.

'What would you like to drink?' asked Stan, whose American accent came as a surprise. 'Australian? Which city? We get a lot of Australians in here.'

'Vodka and orange, and Sydney.'

Tall, lean, sporty and tanned, Stan further raised the standards of quality service at the Red. By now, I was considering paying Franco to let me work there.

Stan led the way back to the bar, ordered my drink, and then left, as people had begun to arrive. The far side of the bar, where the benchtop doglegged around to the wall, looked like a good, discreet place to settle. Better there than perched up in front like a siren on a barstool.

The waiters were pulling benches off trestle tables and teasing each other loudly enough for me to hear. The short one boisterously cracked jokes and then took sidelong glances to see if I was watching him. I couldn't help but smile, because his silliness made me feel welcome and not so alone. Perhaps he was just kind, or perhaps he fancied taller women? In time I realised that it was a mixture of both, and months later I didn't know whether to thank or berate him for my nickname, Lunghina – Little-long-girl. In any case, Geppa was an outrageous flirt, and trying it on became the way he operated his friendship with me. He'd sigh, look towards heaven and ask God why He hadn't made him taller so that we could marry and have lots of tall children. Then he'd swear loudly, shake his fist at me and yell, 'What's wrong with a man who is shorter than you? Who made the rules that a man has to be taller than a woman, eh? Oh, *Lunghina mia*, one day you'll be mine.' I doubted it.

Before long, tour groups of Australians and New Zealanders arrived by the busload. They were instantly recognisable as Aussies because of their accents and clothes: jeans with T-shirts and thongs, leggings with floppy T-shirts, sloppy-joes tied around waists, and white canvas Dunlop tennis shoes with the green and gold at the back. Some of the men wore grey King Gee shorts and thongs, and a few of the women wore incredibly short shorts that showed the bottom of their bottoms. They walked in single file through the bar area down to a second room, so I followed them and found a cavernous hall full of more long wooden tables and benches. A gallery level above the hall looked down upon a small stage with instruments but no musicians. Within an hour the hall was packed with people smoking, drinking and laughing. There was a holiday atmosphere, as though everyone was really letting themselves go because there were no cars to drive home tonight and no work tomorrow.

The waiters took the tourists' orders, with varying degrees of English proficiency. The more English they didn't understand the angrier they became and the more they'd yell, as if shouting would increase their chances of being understood. Their Italian accents were '*oi*-ish', different to my sister's Milanese, as though they were pronouncing their words with lots of airy *oi*, *oi*, *oi*'s. They also dropped their *c*'s and replaced them with a heavy *hhh* sound. It was Fiorentino, the Florentine dialect and accent.

The waiters' striped vests stood out like beacons as they marched down to the bar and yelled 'cinque zombie, tre pitcher, due White Russian e un Harvey Wallbanger!' The cocktail barman mixed all the cocktails, while the barmaid only pulled the beers and mixed drinks for the people at the bar. No nip measures were used, which explained why the crowd was so rapidly getting trashed. The barmaid generously splashed out the gin, then poured in a bit of tonic. She was from Newcastle in England and her name was Loraine. This small bit of information took many minutes to understand, because Loraine's accent was like the drinks she poured – laced with such a heavy dash of Geordie accent I could barely understand her. But she was friendly and funny, and we giggled at how we needed a translator.

By now I was buying my own drinks and the barman was no longer serious, but smiling and Franco, too, occasionally inclined his head. Their glances encouraged me to just hang around and relax. I chatted with Loraine and wandered backwards and forwards from the bar to the back hall.

A man had started playing old-fashioned ditties on the piano, songs like 'It's a Long Way to Tipperary', 'Oh My Darlin' Clementine' and 'Pack Up Your Troubles'. The Yanks and Brits enjoyed it, but didn't seem to think it particularly strange that an out-of-the-way theme pub in Florence was practically playing their national anthems. But when the piano player started on 'Waltzing Matilda', the Aussies went berserk. So unused to having their remote country's music played in a distant land, they showed their appreciation with roars of 'Encore!' Pucci, the piano player, went on to play 'Shuddupayaface' (a song that took the mickey out of Italian migrants with accents). Well-lubricated, the tour groups rolled along to the jolly sing-a-long, as everyone thought about their homes and smiled. I got the warm and fuzzies, too.

Once Pucci left the stage, three men with a lead guitar, bass guitar and drums took his place. Huge loudspeakers on either side of the tiny stage made talking impossible, and a small dance floor to the side of the stage began to swell with jiggling bodies. For a trio, they did a good job. They would always finish their sets with a slow song – 'Hotel California' by The Eagles, Rod Stewart's 'Sailing' or 'Jealous Guy' by John Lennon – which would see the Aussie men flee the dance floor in droves. This opened the way for the Italian men, who now moved through the crowd asking girls to dance or leaned nonchalantly up against the walls, chainsmoking while raking the tables with intense gazes, to try and catch a girl's eye. Then, if eyes did meet, the man's glare was so intense that the girl would turn away quickly. Some of the girls were confused, some were flattered, but all were ultimately courted. The Italian men had no shame and the Australian girls clearly found their behaviour extreme.

That night, and for many nights to come, I was protected from the dance-floor sharks because I was working. I was there 'officially' and so I was free to observe everyone communicating with each other. I could roam the bar and watch the Italian boys picking up the *straniere*. In fact, it became a favourite pastime during my breaks. From the shadows under the stairs, or from the dogleg at the bar, or from beside the door to the women's toilet, none of the guys knew that I was keeping tabs on their movements.

When the band closed their last set with a slow Lionel Ritchie song, I took it upon myself to tell them that they had the words all wrong. As they came off the stage, I confidently approached the lead singer.

'Excuse me, but I speak English fluently and I just wanted to let you know that the Lionel Ritchie song is called "I'm Leaving", not "Easy". The words go, "I'm leaving like Sunday morning", not "Easy like Sunday morning". I think you've misunderstood the words.'

'*Cosa?* Eh, no, eh. We have the real words. It's *easy*, not leaving.' But he was worried enough to consult with the other band members, who then proceeded to look me up and down over his shoulder. Then they all approached.

'No, *you* are wrong. *You* must check your English words.'

Feeling like an idiot, I retreated to the shadows under the stairs. Well, how about that? I always thought that Lionel was *leaving* on a Sunday morning. It was an inauspicious start with the band. I was humbled and stood corrected. I would never again assume that, because English was my mother tongue, I knew everything.

As the evening wore on, I felt very much at home and knew that I would enjoy working at the Red Garter. It was fun, though the sawdust and peanut shells got on my nerves when they jammed up between my toes in my summer sandals. Had someone turned the airconditioning off, or didn't it work? The heat on the gallery level had become unbearable as the humidity rose to the ceiling. The cigarette smoke was so thick it was like standing downwind from a bonfire. The waiters' hair stuck to their skulls, and under their jolly vests their crisp white shirts looked like wet, crumpled rags. As the party raged, Franco, holding a cigarette between his thumb and his forefinger, hollered in my ear: 'You want to come back and work tomorrow night?'

'Sure!' I yelled down to the top of his head.

'Then come back at eight.'

Once my name appeared regularly on the roster, there was only one strongly enforced rule for the barmaids: under no circumstances were we allowed to date the waiters. In the past, a barmaid and her boyfriend waiter had ripped off the owners and they didn't want that to happen again. So, with that in mind, I set about understanding the machinations of the bar and its clients.

The Red Garter was an established part of the itinerary for the big Australian and British tour groups. On the European tour it was their partying pitstop, a place where the bottom-sore bus travellers could let their hair down, have a decent drink and boogey to live music. Over the years, it had developed a reputation for being the place where people got drunk and did silly things. Then all the couriers (tour leaders) would come back, stand around the bar and reminisce, saying things like, 'Remember the time such-and-such drank six pitchers of beer, then fell down the stairs and landed on the guitar player? Ha ha ha.' Or, 'That group had such a good time here, they can't remember a thing about Florence.' Or, 'Now, *this* is the famous zombie – you should drink three.'

It was all very Australian. And often very British and American, too.

The Florentine regulars would come almost every night for the company, rather than the alcohol. All very Italian. Italians don't drink much, and rarely to excess. They tend to drink only when they eat, not while socialising. That's too expensive and makes you lose control – which isn't cool, in their eyes.

Attracted by the bar's easy-going, foreign atmosphere, the regular Red-goer wasn't your average Mario. Most Italian nightclubs for the young are hip, with the latest minimalist interior design and modern spotlights that illuminate glossy tables. They are places where the fashionable can showcase their fabulous outfits. The Red, as the regulars called it, was the watering hole for the kind of man who didn't like the competitive, fashionable scene of the Italian bars. Perhaps he felt he couldn't compete with the trendy clothes and in-vogue hairstyles, or maybe he just didn't want to. To find an Italian girlfriend among the trendsetters wouldn't be easy, for they are hard to pick up, difficult nuts to crack, especially the beautiful ones, who have learned from an early age that their looks bring them many unwanted compliments and advances. A beautiful Florentine girl will rarely act warm and friendly in a bar. It's more effective for her to appear to be aloof and therefore to keep her admirers at a distance. Because of the social stigma attached to socialising without men as chaperones, or more adequately, as buffers against a pick-up onslaught, you would never see groups of single Italian girls out and about. The Red Garter was home to the kind of Italian boy who preferred the easy-going warmth of the Anglo-Saxon girl, or simply found her easier to approach than an Italian girl.

Many of the Italian men also came with a purpose: sex. The foreign women who crowded the Red had no strings attached because they were leaving Florence soon. Many of them had a casual attitude towards sex (certainly more casual than a Florentine girl's) and that made for the perfect combination. The girls imbibed freely, which loosened them up. The AIDS epidemic hadn't yet arrived, so the atmosphere was free, fun. The plainer or less sophisticated Aussie girls were the easiest prey. They had had little or no experience in brushing off persistent men, and when an Italian playboy makes a play, he sticks like glue. A typical conversation would go something like this:

'*Ciao*, I am Bruno.'

'Hello.'

'You are name?'

'My name is Sharon.'

'You American?'

'No, I am Australian.'

'Oh, very beautiful country. Very big. Long time in aeroplano.'

'Yes.'

'You very beautiful, Sharon.'

'Oh, thank you.'

Then much mime would follow as they discussed where in Australia the girl came from and where she was going next. At the very least, the guys then went after a kiss and a cuddle in the dark, medieval doorways outside or on the steps of the church next door. If 'Bruno' was in luck, he might persuade 'Sharon' to go for a drive so that he could show her the spectacular view from Piazzale Michelangelo. There they could join all the other parked cars with steamed-up windows. But he always had to have her back down to the Red Garter in time for her tour-bus departure at 1 am.

For a handful of these guys, this flirt, chase, kiss routine was their evening pastime. Even though the men rarely spoke to each other, I discovered that they did indeed know each other. It's just that they preferred to operate alone. There were curt nods of acknowledgment when they arrived and a weary *ciao* when they left for home, as if they'd knocked off from work. Bundy on. Bundy off.

One unpredictable drawback did on occasion creep up and surprise the Florentines. Sometimes the Florentines fell deeply in love with their Anglo-Saxon one- or three-night stand and wanted to follow her back to Australia, Britain or the United States. Usually, the girl wasn't interested in carrying the romance on to home turf, so then the boy would spend months, sometimes years, yearning for a girl who was never coming back.

Some of the girls regarded the men as Latin lovers with

whom they could have trophy sex. They had their Romeo to create a souvenir memory to take home, and used the men just as much as the men used them.

In defence of the flirting Florentine, not all were in search of sexual gratification. Many just wanted easy-going company without feeling the age-old Italian pressure to walk down the aisle. These were the guys that the girls found most endearing. The women were flattered by the flirting but then felt they could say 'no' without hurting the guy's feelings. After a rebuff, they often hung around offering up further flattery. The women found the attention refreshing, because at home they were treated like a mate, when what they really wanted was to be treated like a princess. The Italian men offered their own special brand of romance, telling the girls why they liked them, why they were special. Most of these relationships only lasted a day or so, but for the whole duration the man was charmed, entranced by the woman, and she was thrilled to be getting such incredible attention.

Every night that summer, the mirror ball turned above the dance floor at the Red Garter and my little world was filled with flirting and laughter. But there were no dates and few signs of romance on the horizon. Sixteen-year-olds often measure their success as a person by their success rate with boys. So far, I was flunking out. But I didn't really feel like a failure and I certainly wasn't feeling dejected. I was OK by myself and didn't let the lack of male interest get me down. I saw myself through all those men's eyes and realised that I was very inexperienced.

Soon life in Florence took on a routine, a comfortable

rhythm. The little alleyways were all familiar now, and Via de Benci had lost its menace. Late at night after work I would wander back to my *pensione* and feel safe on the streets, much safer than at home in Sydney where the after-pub drunkards lurched. A friendship with Loraine was being cemented with meetings for coffee or pizza before and after work. Thrillingly, I could carry on a conversation in Italian. I was studying on my own during the day and it had resulted in a stunted, halting kind of Italian, but still it was Italian and incredibly, I was speaking it.

6

'Hey, Lunghina, voi venire al Calcio Storico?' It was Geppa, waving at me with a bunch of tickets. 'Hey, Little-long-girl, do you want to come to a football game with me?'

'Si, si,' I couldn't agree quickly enough. This football game, or whatever it was, had been the only topic of conversation at work for the past few weeks. The bar had been buzzing with excitement, hands flying as Mediterranean miming gestures wound into full-force description mode. Groups of the regulars stood around *hhh*-ing their macho-sounding Florentine, talking about who was playing, how strong the player was and, most importantly, who had some payback to deliver after a pounding received during last year's match. The word was that this was no ordinary game. It was Florence's own no-regulations, no-holds-barred, traditional footy match –

famous for being the roughest, toughest, meanest football game in the world. Many of our regulars were on the team for the Red Garter's *quartiere* (area/zone), Santa Croce.

Florence, as it has been since the sixteenth century, is divided into four quarters, each named after its local church, *Santa Croce, Santo Spirito, Santa Maria Novella* and *San Giovanni.* Every summer for the last five hundred years, these four areas have competed to establish which quarter has the strongest men. The tradition of the game is like the *palio* in Siena, only this game isn't about which *contrada* (Siena's areas) has the fastest horse; it's about which *quartiere* can more effectively and legally beat the crap out of the other *quartiere.*

I was to go to the game with Too Gorgeous For Me, whose real name was Paolo. I hadn't seen too much of him outside work hours because he was immersed in study for his final year of medicine at the University of Florence. Geppa was marching in the parade (I had an idea that he had invited me so that I could admire him in his special outfit), so he would meet us afterwards. We were to get together late in the afternoon of *La Festa di San Giovanni*, a public holiday to honour the patron saint of Florence, Saint John. The holiday culminates with a grand parade that winds its way through town to finish up at Piazza Santa Croce for the Calcio Storico finals.

Via de' Benci was packed with cheering Florentines when I spotted Paolo standing at the appointed corner. Tanned, dressed in khaki shorts, a white T-shirt and leather sandals, he looked easy-going and relaxed in his civvies. Without the black pants and striped work vest, Paolo had lost the look of an authoritative iron-pumping waiter and gained the appearance of a fit, confident man. He was also wearing a serious frown, as though everything around him was worthy of careful examination. Cutting through the crowd towards him, as yet unnoticed, I was nervous that such a handsome man was waiting for me. When he saw me, the frown disappeared and he welcomed me with a warm smile, a kiss on each cheek and a 'Leeza!' instead of 'Lisa'. Even with his good accent, he still couldn't conquer the soft 's' of the English language. After a lifetime of telling people that I'm Lisa with an 's', not Leeza or Liza with a 'z', it looked like I'd have to settle for Leeza when in Italy.

We stood side by side and watched the colourful pageant that passed before us. There were hundreds of men in sixteenth-century style bloomers and tights, their mutton-sleeved velvet doublets slashed to reveal colourful garments underneath. Every costume, trumpet and flag had been copied from centuries-old original designs. In the forty-degree heat, the men, some in the perfect statistical target age group for a heart attack, grunted and sweated while they dragged medieval cannons and archaic crossbows. I kept waiting for one of the old-timers in full metal armour to keel over backwards, a river of sweat running out of his breast-plate on to the scorching cobblestones. Slayed by the sun.

At the tail end of the parade were the football players. Huge, muscly men, also dressed in medieval-style below-the-knee bloomers, only they wore their costumes with either white or blue T-shirts, the colour and namesake of their teams. The finals were between the Blues, *Gli Azzuri*, representing Santa Croce (our team), and the Whites, *I Bianchi* playing for Santo Spirito. A hushed awe descended upon the crowd as the group of players, who looked more like thugs and mugs, passed. They were physically powerful, ruthless men in the prime of their lives.

'Look at their scars,' whispered Paolo. 'Every face has been in many fights, I think.'

He was right. Broken noses, thick, heavy brows, scarred cheeks.

'They look dangerous,' I said, feeling their menacing aura.

'You must know some of them. Look, there is Gabriele Zena, Gianni and Giuseppe. Have you seen them at the Red Garter?'

'Yes, but, wow, they look different today.'

The men looked straight ahead, not at the crowd of gawkers. On the surface, they seemed arrogantly confident and proud, but it soon was clear that they were anxious. Their gaits were grave, and they had edgy mannerisms such as clenching and unclenching their fists or jamming their mouths shut so tight that tension ticked their jaw muscles. I didn't know it then, but these guys were warriors about to go into a violent conflict. It's no wonder they were feeling disturbed. They knew they were unlikely to finish the game in one piece. A posse of protectors, more hunks and punks – big blokes that jostled the crowd out of the way – surrounded both *Gli Azzuri* and *I Bianchi*.

Bringing up the rear was Geppa, smiling and high-stepping, looking more than ever like a little boy. But this time it was as though he was in the school play, making sure that Mummy was looking at him. In a navy doublet, blue tights and shoes that looked like tap shoes, he marched proudly to the pounding beat of the drums. BOOM ... BOOM ... BOOM. The sound reverberated off the close stone walls and made the ground grumble.

Once the parade had passed, Paolo grabbed my arm and whispered that we had better get to our seats because there was a heavy police presence in case of rioting. 'It's better we get settled,' he said. I raised my eyebrows but said nothing as he hustled me past the barriers and SWAT teams that had batons at the ready.

Piazza Santa Croce had been transformed into a grand football arena, with four big stands surrounding what looked like an enormous sandpit. Enclosing the sand was a thick wooden fence that was padded with foam and swathes of red cloth. Each grandstand was packed with excited spectators, many of them shirtless young men. They gave off a vibe that felt intimidatingly masculine. I was struck not so much by the excitement in the air, but by the palpable feeling of pride in the tradition of this spectacle. You could feel the crowd's passion swelling as though they were all thinking in unison, 'This is Florence and this is our game.' In our second-row seats, I found myself gravitating towards Paolo. Intuitively, I knew that he was an honourable man who would protect me if the spectators did get out of hand. I trusted him to do the right thing by me.

During a spectacular bit of flag throwing, Paolo explained that the match had evolved from a ball game that had been played by the ancient Greeks and legionnaires of Rome. 'It's a mixture of rugby, wrestling and football, with no rules,' he said. 'Basically, the idea is to get the ball down to your team's end of the field and throw it into a long net that hangs about two feet above the wall. That will earn the team one point. Missing the net and landing it just above results in an extra half a point.'

The players, a couple of referees and first-aid men jogged into the sandpit. Then, BANG! The game was under way after what looked like an Aussie Rules start. The men leapt high into the air for the ball, but from that point forward any similarities to any kind of football game ended.

The men lunged, swiped punches at passing heads and boofed elbows into temples. Other men sat on their opponents' chests, or held them down in complicated wrestling grips so that they couldn't run. They were allowed to do anything to shield or get the ball. Some started brawling to stop the other team from getting near the ball. The pitch became a bloody battlefield, or better still, it became the Colosseum. These mugs were modern-day gladiators.

Someone threw Gianni the ball, but he didn't seem to know what to do with it. Players are meant to throw the ball on (they're not allowed to kick it), but instead he tucked it safely under his arm and jogged slowly, warily, towards the goal net, slugging anyone who came within punching distance. That wasn't against the rules, either. He got three good whacks in (I could hear the shlapping sound of fist on skin from my seat) before three men surrounded him. They circled him, jumped on him together and forced him to the ground. When Gianni was down, they viciously kicked him in the head.

'*Eiyyah, non si puo!* No! No!' yelled Paolo, standing up, while my eyes stood out on storks. This was grievous bodily harm in fancy dress.

'Can they do that?' I screamed at Paolo over the noise of the fans who had gone wild around us.

'No, no. He's been marked. They want him out of the game, so clearly they have decided to hurt him badly at the start.'

'But why? This is savage!' I cried.

'Gianni has been a bad boy in the matches leading up to the finals. He is the Italian boxing and kickboxing champion and he has injured too many players. He is dangerous, so they want him out.'

Gianni lay motionless, so the players on the *Azzuri* team, having achieved their goal, climbed off him and stalked off in search of the ball. The crowd had disintegrated into a screaming mass of hysteria. The boys in the stands were baying for blood to avenge the attack against their key player. His name was the buzzword up and down the aisles. Incredibly, he wobbled to his feet, then walked towards the game. But he was a shadow of his former self. The *Gli Azzuri* thugs had done a good job on him, and he would cause no trouble for the rest of the game.

Pretty soon the umpires were fighting with each other. A player was stretchered off, while another's face was shoved into the sand so that he couldn't breathe. The only point-scoring plan that really seemed to work was the distraction technique: start a big fight down the end of the field, involve eight to ten players, and then when everyone's attention was fixed on the brawl, snatch the ball and run like a fox with the hounds behind you down to your end of the field to score a goal. The brilliant passes and fancy footwork present in a good game of rugby were sadly lacking on this pitch. The essential qualities a player needed were aggression and the courage to take a hammering.

While I was disgusted and appalled by the violence, the macabre scene also wholly consumed me. For an hour my adrenaline pumped and I couldn't take my eyes off the field.

Paolo, at some point, stood to wave at a group of people sitting at the end of our row.

'That is Gianni's mother, grandmother and father,' he said.

'They're *here*, to see their son get *thrashed*?' I ask incredulously.

'*Certamente*. They are proud of their son. He is very famous in Florence, even if he has a violent reputation. Wouldn't you come to see your son play?'

I didn't think so. 'No, I wouldn't want to see him get beaten up. It would make me sick to see my child get hurt and hurt others.'

Paolo seemed to consider this an interesting response. Just as he asked me if the violence really bothered me, two men smashed into the wooden fence in front of us, the force of their landing ripping off the protective padding. Like raging bulls in a ring, one man kept pounding the other into the fence, until the palings splintered and fell. Paolo leaned forward slightly, as if to protect me from the flailing limbs.

'*Si*, you are right. A mother would be very sad to see her son like this.' He nodded gravely.

When the horn blew, *Gli Azzuri* had won a decisive victory against *I Bianchi* – eight-and-a-half points to six. The players were exhausted. They sank into the sand, every one of them emotionally and physically shattered. The *Gli Azzuri* players could barely muster a triumphant stance. They were blood-splattered and limping, their T-shirts ripped from their bodies; their shredded shorts stayed up only because they had been taped to their waists.

Once the players had caught their breath, much of the macho bravado disappeared and they all started hugging and backslapping each other. When one man broke down and cried, a teammate consoled him with a hug, his thoughtful affection so at odds with the violence only moments ago. Some of the winners even went over to hug the losers.

'I don't get it,' I said to Paolo. 'Moments ago they all hated each other, and now they all seem to be best friends.'

'Even though they play on opposing teams, many of them

went to school together,' he explained. 'Some are even married to each other's sisters.'

As we walked back to the corner to meet Geppa, Paolo told me that many of the men worked together as removalists, forklift drivers and market stallholders. 'Tomorrow they will all wave *ciao* to each other on the streets,' he said.

'But don't you think that's a little weird, that after all this violence and hate they can so easily go back to being friendly neighbours? It seems very strange to me.'

Paolo waved my concerns away with the Italian gesture of holding up his palms, shrugging his shoulders and pouting out his bottom lip. '*I Fiorentini sono cosi*,' he said. 'That's the way the Florentines are.' I got the impression that Florentine men liked a bit of a dust-up and were well known for it.

The heat was still suffocating. Our heels sank into the melted, sticky bitumen, leaving semicircular heel dents in our wake. Paolo asked me about football in Australia and marvelled that soccer wasn't a popular game. I told him about Rugby Union, League and Aussie Rules. He had seen international rugby on TV, but had never heard of Australia's Union, League or Aussie Rules games. He barely understood the word 'cricket'.

I asked him why he spoke English so well and he explained that he loved music. Not being able to understand the lyrics in his favourite songs drove him crazy, he said. He would buy records and then study the words to the songs using dictionaries.

'What, like "YMCA, it's fun to stay at the YMCA"?' I sang, doing my best to imitate The Village People.

'Yes. Or "Le Freak, c'est chic",' he sang, and paused to look at me with an encouraging expression, as if to invite me to sing with him.

Together we yelled, 'Ohh, freak out!'

Paolo felt no inhibitions when singing. He moved straight on to that year's hit song: 'First I was afraid, I was petrified, thinking I could never live without you by my side.'

It was hysterical and I couldn't resist joining in. 'But then I spent so many nights thinking how you did me wrong and I grew strong and I learnt how to get along.'

'Wow, you sound just like Gloria Gaynor.' I teased. 'Your accent's good too. Your English has an American twang.'

'English has become the language of the world. If you don't speak it, you don't understand what's going on in the world. Most of the English we hear in Italy is American. It's in the movies, songs, the news on TV.'

'Hmm,' I thought. 'And I bet every night you practise your English lyrics on all those American girls at the Red Garter.' The thought irked me. He didn't seem to be the playboy type, but all the waiters were on the make. I began to hope that he was different. 'Do you play a musical instrument?' I asked.

'I play the guitar. Not very well, but I can play. And you?'

'I play the piano. I really miss it, actually. Hey, we could start a band if you like.'

'*Certo, certo!* Sure, sure!' he said, but his tone sounded more like 'As *if*.'

The conversation flowed easily. Paolo wanted to know why a young girl would leave her home to come and work in a bar in Florence. I told him about the goals I'd set for myself before leaving Sydney. I wanted to learn to speak the language fluently. But also I wanted to be a part of Florentine life, to feel as though I belonged on the inside, and wasn't just looking in from the outside. Paolo's expression told me that he understood and was curious to know more. I told him that I felt ready to leave the *pensione*, and wanted to find an apartment to share and that my dream was to buy a small motorbike.

'Te lo trovo io un motorino usato,' he said, reverting back to Italian in his enthusiasm. 'I will help you find a used *motorino*. Tonight, I will bring you the address and name of a friend who sells them. You tell him you are a friend of mine.'

I was disappointed that Paolo didn't join Geppa and me for pizza. He went home to eat with his parents and to change into his work gear. While I feigned great interest in what Geppa had to say about the parade and the game, my mind kept wandering back to Paolo. He had seemed so interested in what I'd had to say, and in turn I had found his insights into the Florentines fascinating. But there was little time for further talk with Paolo that night, as the Red Garter was especially busy with the Santa Croce players lumbering in for a drink and a slap on the back. As the evening wore on, I sometimes caught his eye and smiled. During my break he gave me the address of the *motorino* shop.

It was now time to venture outside the safe world that I had created for myself at the Red Garter and improve my living standards. I had another phone number that Lauren had passed on to me through my sister. It was time to make the call.

This time, Lauren's contact didn't turn out to be a disaster. Suzy, a British girl who ran her own modest model agency called Vanity, helped my goals fall together remarkably quickly. Suzy had many years' experience in Florence and was most willing to part with advice on how to get on in the city. She knew of two girls looking for a third to share a house at Poggio Imperiale (Imperial Hill), just ten minutes outside the historical centre's city walls. The girls weren't models, which was reassuring. I didn't feel bold enough to try and keep up with those in the whirlwind world of fashion. Grania was a British secretary doing translation work for an Italian import/export business, while Terry was an American nurse.

The house itself was lovely. Attached on both sides to other houses, it looked a little like a Paddington terrace in Sydney. Only it had Italian touches, like a big fireplace, worn terracotta-tiled floors, and an old kitchen with a sagging roof that was held up by thick wooden beams. My room was long and narrow, with one cupboard, a single bed, a bedside table, and a pretty bay window that looked out on to trees and a tiny bit of garden.

Grania and Terry were both keen for me to move in that afternoon. They would supply sheets and towels until I could afford to buy some of my own. The best part of the deal was the rent; twenty dollars a week! The Italians have a strict rental law that favours the occupants rather than the owners. No putting up the rent until the occupants have moved out. Grania had been living in that pretty little house for more than a decade, so the rent had never been increased. I packed up my suitcases, piled everything into a taxi and waved goodbye to Via Porta Rossa.

It had only been five days since the *Calcio Storico* game, a fact that Paolo pointed out when I told him about my new shared accommodation.

'*Brava*,' he said, smiling. 'You are living your dreams.'

In the weeks prior to the game, Paolo and I had shared little conversation. We'd smiled at each other during friendly moments at work, but we knew nothing about each other. In many ways, his good looks had overwhelmed me. He was popular, always joking with the locals, the other waiters and other girls. Paolo was also the only one of the waiters who appeared to be moving towards a career beyond the bar. It all made me assume that he wouldn't be interested in someone as young as me. However, of one thing I was certain. Since the game, we had formed a friendship. Now, of all the people at work, I couldn't wait to share my good news with Paolo.

Creeping into my new room after work that night, I found that the girls had left a vase full of fresh flowers on my bedside table. Florence was beginning to feel like home.

The idea of buying a *motorino* and riding it around Florence conjured up a range of emotions: excitement because of the freedom and independence it would give me, pleasure at not having to depend on the unreliable bus system and pride at having made it so far in my new life in Florence. What I really should have been feeling was fear and acute panic.

Paolo's friend did have a *motorino* that was just right for an awkward, uninitiated driver on the precarious streets of Italy. It was a red Boxer, quite a bulky, heavy bike when compared with the zippy little Ciao's that were the flavour of the month among the *motorino* set. The mechanic who sold it to me explained that there was no need to wear a helmet, or to register or insure the Boxer, because it only had a 50cc engine and wasn't very fast.

'No worries,' I said, thinking that speed wasn't my thing anyway. It wasn't until I got it out on to the streets that I realised speed, the ability to power out of a prickly situation, was an essential part of Florentine road safety. If you can't quickly zoom in front of, or away from, some idiot performing an unbelievable U-turn right in front of you, you are dead meat. A *motorino* has to be able to get away from any danger, not be stuck with it. And on Italy's roads, danger comes in a thousand and one disguises. The innocuous-looking tour bus that tries to kill you by slowly forcing you into a row of parked cars. Or the pack of motorinos that won't make space as you try to merge because a break in the traffic never comes. There is no mercy shown on the streets of Florence; it's a war out there, and for every inch of space gained there is a battle fought. At the end of the day, if the idiots behind the wheels of tour buses, other *motorinos* or garbage trucks didn't get you, the carbon monoxide belching from a dilapidated truck that you didn't have power enough to overtake, would. I quickly learned why the awkward and rather cumbersome Boxer wasn't as popular as the speedy little Ciao.

Nevertheless, I humbly took my place among all the *motorinos* and Vespas lined up at the traffic lights and revved my engine too. Once the green light flashed, we were off in a bellow of engines, each driver jostling the other out of the lead position. It's no secret that the Italians love their speed and their motorbikes (let's not even start on their passion for cars), but combine speed with a bunch of fourteen-year-old boys who have just come of age to ride their 50ccs and you've got a pack of testosterone-propelled missiles. Dangerous.

The majority of Vespa and *motorino* riders assume the standard *motorino* driving position: hunched shoulders, torsos screwed up tight into little balls and with their faces just inches from the handlebars. It's as though hunkering down will make you go faster. The position certainly gives you a more wily agility, as you dodge and weave through the traffic, but it took me a long time to become that proficient. I would sit up straight, feet perched neatly on the bar that runs between the handlebars and the seat, ignoring my more aerodynamically correct comrades. I didn't care if my Jurassic-era Boxer coughed along, because it was all exhilarating for me. The feeling of freedom was indescribable. Talk about the wind in your hair! My Boxer may have only reached sixty kilometres an hour, but it felt like one hundred and fifty to me. I guess there's a little bit of hoon in everyone.

These were experiences that I chose to leave out of the telephone conversations I was having with my mother. It was hard to explain what my life was like in Florence. Though I did my best.

'The Red Garter? What do you have to wear?'

'Just jeans, nothing special.'

'Why do they call it the Red Garter if the barmaids don't have to wear one?'

'Oh, it's just a gimmick, really. There's nothing like that going on there.'

Or . . . 'Hey, I've bought a *motorino*!'

'Oh, my God! You're driving a motorbike? You're a moving target! You'll be killed!'

'No, no. It's not that dangerous, really.'

Or . . . 'How did that appointment go with that Texan model's contact?'

'Oh, fine. He just said I wasn't right for modelling.'

After a few weeks in my new home, my sister called to say she was moving back to Australia. She felt that the timing was right to go home and open her own model agency, as well as oversee Mum's existing agencies. I'd been up to Milan to see her on the odd weekend off and had taken great comfort in having her only a phone call away. I would miss having her so close, and the thought of staying on in Italy alone did spark some feelings of insecurity. But life was full of daily distractions, and the nights at the Red Garter were fun.

Also I was developing a deep love of Florence. It was so beautiful, so ancient and different from Sydney, that it was spellbinding. I had friends here now, a home, a motorbike, a reliable job and a basic understanding of the language. It was way too soon for me to return home. Carel was going, but I felt more grown-up than when I'd arrived and therefore able to cope with any surprises that Italy might throw my way.

7

Carel left for home as the weather changed from searingly hot to refreshingly cool, seemingly overnight. The seasons in Tuscany change dramatically, with short to non-existent *mezza stagione* – mid-seasons. The unbearably hot summer finished so quickly that within just a week the Florentines went from wearing singlets to T-shirts to cardigans. A month later, thick pants, warm socks and a padded windbreaker were needed for riding the *motorino*. Within days, that wasn't enough, resulting in the purchase of my first-ever woollen hat, sheepskin gloves, thick scarf and a *really* warm, waterproof coat. It took less than six weeks for summer to become winter.

For my seventeenth birthday, Grania and Terry took me out for a Chinese dinner. In many ways, they replaced Carel.

They were both ten to thirteen years older than me and motherly, protective types. They shared their cultures, telling me how they had grown up in England and America, their favourite old records (Grania, the Rolling Stones, and Terry, Phoebe Snow) and their most-loved books.

Then, one night, a surprising event altered everything as I knew it from that moment onward. The Italians call it *un colpo di fulmine* – a lightning strike. Australians would call it a bolt from the blue. I call it Cupid. And because of that one split second, I truly do believe in Cupid. I've seen him draw his bow, take aim and POW . . . make someone fall in love from one minute to the next.

During Italy's short autumn, my relationship with Paolo had stalled. Our friendship hadn't developed into anything more than catching up with each other at work. It was difficult to see whether the smile he smiled for me was any different from the smile he gave to the other barmaids. Until Geppa changed the pace.

Paolo was leaning up against the doorway gazing towards me. Geppa nudged him. '*E Lunghina la piu simpatica di tutte.*' He yelled. 'Little-long-girl is the nicest of them all. If only I wasn't so short, you'd go out with me, wouldn't you, Lunghina?'

I ignored him, embarrassed, and made myself busy wiping down the bar. But when I looked up again, it was as though a little fairy had come along and sprinkled Paolo with stardust. He looked at me as though a feeling had dawned on him, a realisation had broken through into his consciousness. Paolo's eyes were alight. Cupid had struck him with a bull's-eye through the heart. He kept on looking at me, then walked straight up to the bar and asked me if I'd like to go somewhere for coffee after work. I was flustered because the change in his attitude was obvious and he wasn't trying to hide it. Like Italy's mid-seasons, there was no middle ground. He'd gone from being a friend to a suitor in ten minutes.

'Look, it's really cold,' I said. 'Why don't we go back to my place for coffee, instead of riding around town on our *motorinos* looking for a bar?'

'*Benissimo*,' he responded. 'A very good idea.' His grin was wide.

It was a clear, frosty night. The moon was high in a black sky as we sped over the bridge of Ponte Santa Trinita. It never failed to give me a profound moment of pleasure, that late-night view on the way home after work: the Arno glistening like mercury, the sky a black liquid and the graceful *palazzi* that kept watch over the now-quiet streets. Paolo's navy-blue Ciao had been *truccato* – souped up – so it was much faster than my old Boxer. He kept the accelerator on half throttle and rode beside me so that we could chat, almost as though we were in a car, side by side through the enormous ancient gateway called the Roman Door, Porta Romana, that has led people out of Florence and towards Rome for centuries. The door itself is at least six metres high and is studded with massive nails. It provides a thousand-year-old exit on to the Poggio Imperiale hill and home.

When we were inside, I did what many Australians do when they arrive home. I kicked off my shoes and socks, and then sighed with relief at the wonderful sensation of having my feet bare. Paolo's eyes lit up at the sight of my toes.

'Isn't he sweet?' I thought. 'He must have a thing for feet.'

'Would you like a Nescafé?' I asked him.

'No, no, no,' he said, screwing up his nose and vigorously shaking his head. Strange, I ask him back for coffee, he agrees and then refuses to drink any. I boiled the water, then added lots of milk to my coffee, while he watched with interest. It was madness to offer an Italian freeze-dried coffee, a totally unacceptable drink.

'What about a fresh espresso?' But he declined and would accept only a glass of water.

As we settled on to the couch, which was actually a single bed with a throw over it and a couple of cushions. Paolo's eyes grew shy. It was as though he had a secret and he wasn't going to let me in on it. As he answered my questions about his family, his voice became low and deep. It rumbled through the wall and up my back.

'My parents take care of the oldest theatre in Florence, Teatro della Pergola. My father was a bricklayer, but now he just looks after the theatre and my mum brings the actors their snacks and coffees before and during their performances.'

'Do you want to specialise in any particular kind of medicine?' I asked, clutching my coffee cup protectively to my chest. He was so *gorgeous*! He had a straight nose that reminded me of the profiles on old Roman coins.

'Probably surgery, though I'm not sure if I want to do the extra years. I'm twenty-four years old and all I've ever done is study. I'm starting to get very tired of it. How old are you?'

'Nineteen,' I lied. It was a risky business, this age thing. Everyone at the Red Garter believed I was almost twenty. It also wouldn't do to have Paolo think I was too young for him. 'Have you done much travelling?'

'America and England, and some parts of Eastern Europe, but right now I am almost at my finals, so I must study.'

As I leaned down to put my mug on the floor, Paolo came closer and whispered something.

'Pardon?'

'*Lo facciamo qui?*'

'Sorry, what did you say?'

'*Lo facciamo qui?*' He repeated the phrase again, but I still had no idea what he was talking about.

'*Qui.*' He pointed at the couch/bed, but the colour in his cheeks had risen and he was squirming uncomfortably. Why had he reverted to Italian? We understood each other so well in English. This spelled trouble.

'What do you mean, "*Qui*" – here? Tell me in English.'

'Nothing, nothing. I just thought, no, well, nothing. I had better go now.'

A sinking feeling began to grow in my stomach as I realised that something had been botched, misunderstood. Everything had been going fine.

'What's the matter, Paolo? Tell me.' Bewildered, I insisted.

'I just thought that you wanted to go to bed,' he said bashfully.

'Whatever gave you that idea?'

'We are on a bed, no? You have your shoes off, no?'

'But this is the couch, and I always take my shoes off at home.'

'Italian girls don't do any of this. If she invites you home, she wants to be with you. And if she takes her shoes off, it's a sign that, well . . .' His voice tapered off uncertainly and his eyes showed confusion.

I realised then that an Italian man would think my behaviour was very odd. I had sent him all the wrong (right?) signals. When Italians come home, especially with company, they either leave their shoes on or put on their slippers. Paolo was telling me that when a woman invites a man home and then walks around the house barefoot, it means she's about to strip.

'I'm sorry I gave you the wrong impression. I hardly even know you. Maybe we could see each other again, though.'

He smiled, closed his eyes and rubbed his forehead with his fingers and thumb, as though he was thinking, deciding. Then he brought his hand down to his nose, inhaled and stared at me. His silence churned my stomach. I hoped so much that he wanted to see me again. But maybe he was like the other men at the Red Garter, after all. Maybe this sudden interest in me was because he thought I was just as easy as the other girls that flit through Florence.

He stood to go. My heart sank with disappointment.

'Do you have a very warm jacket?'

'No.' It was my turn to be confused.

'Then I'll bring one for you if you'd like to come for a ride on my motorbike tomorrow?'

As I waved goodbye from the door (another unusual Australian habit, according to him), I knew that we would be good friends. What I didn't know was that our first coffee date together was going to be symbolic of our whole relationship. We were about to embark on a journey that would challenge our entrenched beliefs, the foundations established through our upbringings. The demystifying and deciphering of our mixed cultural habits had only just begun.

8

My footsteps faltered at the sight of his super-duper deluxe Suzuki 1100 GSX, parked in front of the house the following afternoon.

'Um, I've never actually been on a proper motorbike,' I laughed shakily.

'*Niente problema.* No problem. Just hold on tight and lean into the corners with me,' Paolo said, passing me a helmet. There goes the hairdo, I thought as I squished it on over the curls that I'd spent all morning artfully scrunching in all the right places. The strap was difficult to do up and I felt terribly self-conscious as Paolo stood close to do it for me. I struggled into his thermal ski parka then zipped it up to my jaw. Paolo then passed over a pair of huge, battered men's ski gloves.

'Sorry about the gloves. They're all I have.'

'No, no, don't worry about it. Thanks for bringing everything,' I said, genuinely grateful for his thoughtfulness.

Like the Michelin man, I lumbered over to the motorbike and tried to lithely lift my leg over and settle in behind him. I rested my hands lightly on his waist and kept a modest distance between my chest and his back. He revved up and we were off.

Seven hundred metres down the road to the traffic lights and a huge smile had spread across my face. This had to be paradise. The power of the machine was awesome. It was like being on a fabulous roller-coaster ride, only you were free to go wherever you wanted – a sensation of unconfined space, freedom and speed.

Paolo raised his visor. 'You'll have to move closer. And put your arms tightly around my waist. We have to move as one body around the corners, and when I go fast there cannot be any air moving between us. Don't resist me; move with me and the bike.'

Well, just die and go to heaven, please. You won't get any argument from me, matey.

'OK,' I said cheerfully.

There we were at the traffic lights, looking down on all those plebeian *motorinos* when he catapulted away from the pack. I felt like a helpless koala clinging on to the back of a panther in full flight. It quickly became apparent that Paolo had no regard for road rules. He flouted the law in a dozen ways. We sailed smoothly around corners at eighty kilometres an hour (in the city). He overtook on the double lines as cars headed towards us, so that we were sandwiched in-between two moving vehicles. Round and round the curves we leaned, so that we were almost horizontal to the bitumen. We were headed north, up the winding road to Fiesole. The view of Florence below me was breathtaking.

Even a novice could tell that Paolo handled the bike exceedingly well. Though frightened, I tried to relax and trust in his judgment and experience. (It was that or give him severe internal bruising from vice-like squeezes to his waist.) His trick seemed to be speed. The faster you go, the faster people get out of your way. By the time we went through Fiesole (about eight kilometres from Florence) and the next village, Olmo, Paolo was topping one hundred and sixty kilometres an hour in third gear. It was unlikely that anyone could read his surname, 'CONSUMI', which was printed in big black letters across the back of his helmet.

Eventually he turned off the road and on to an overgrown gravel path and parked. Invisible from the road further up the path were the dilapidated ruins of an Etruscan church, a treasure that only a local would know about. We climbed over broken pillars to examine where the altar must have been and jumped over the stone foundations to try and work out the church's proportions. After a while, we sat down to watch the sun sinking over Pian del Mugnone.

Paolo's eyes took on the reflection of the sunset, the yellow inside the blue of his irises more pronounced than ever. His face had an intensity, the same serious expression he'd had when I'd met him at the football game. When he suddenly smiled, everything changed; he appeared innocent, boyish and alarmingly cute. A low beam of late-afternoon sunlight skittered across his face. Impulsively, we kissed.

On the way home, hanging on to his waist felt different from the way it had felt earlier. It was as though I now had a right to hold on to him so tightly. I felt peaceful and very, very happy.

We made plans to meet for pizza before work the following night, then the next night he came over to my place for dinner . . . and so it went on. We spent every possible moment together. Then he said that his parents wanted to meet me. In fact, they insisted we have a meal together, because they never saw their son anymore. Paolo was their only child, and at twenty-four he'd never before introduced them to a girlfriend. I was the first girl that Paolo had ever taken home to meet his mum and dad.

Paolo's front door was between the Theatre Pergola's entrance and the ticket office, with a bell that read 'Custode' (custodian). His home was in the heart of the city's historical centre, a stone's throw from the Duomo, and his street was probably one of the quietest in Florence. The theatre and backstage garage took up most of Via della Pergola, while across the road was the mostly unused rear entrance to the Santa Maria Nuova hospital. There was an unusual atmosphere of calm in the street. It was a pedestrian-only area with no other apartment blocks or businesses around, in contrast to the rest of medieval Florence where peak hour lasts all day.

Every night without fail, the Consumis ate dinner at 7.30 pm on the dot. Gemma had to get to work preparing the actors' or singers' coffees and chamomile teas and Giovanni had to stand by to deal with any last-minute problems before the performances started at 9 pm. The TV news had to be watched, and dinner eaten and cleaned up, beforehand.

On the way up the stairs to their first-floor apartment I took a few deep breaths to contain my nerves. I wanted to make a good impression, but I had no notion of what to expect. Just in case Signora Consumi held store by presentation-type details, I'd applied light makeup, my nails were done and my hair was freshly washed.

Paolo didn't seem at all anxious.

'Relax, relax. My parents are very easy-going people,' he said, pausing on the landing before we approached the door of the apartment.

'Do they speak any English?'

'No way. They are *semplice* – simple people, unpretentious, from the country. They were both born in tiny villages up in the Apennine alps near Florence.'

'Have they travelled?'

'I think my mother's been to Paris, but no, they haven't travelled. They don't like to leave their farm. They are frightened something would happen to their chickens, so they go back to their village every weekend. And who would feed the rabbits, the pigeons and the ducks if *they* didn't?' He laughed, as if he was imitating an oft-repeated line of his father's.

When Paolo opened his front door I knew that something wonderful was going on in the kitchen. A delicious aroma wafted down the hall! I felt like a cartoon character dreamily being lured by the nostrils to a steaming plate of food. Paolo's mother came out when she heard us and at first glance she smashed all my stereotypical expectations of what an Italian mamma should look like. Far from being dark, Gemma was blonde with beautiful skin the colour of golden honey. While we were being introduced she wrung her hands as though she were the nervous one, then sheepishly stood on tippy-toes to give me a kiss on both cheeks.

Though short, Gemma wasn't little. As if accustomed to much physical work, her body was broad, very fit and strong.

She had dressed in a simple, colourful dress, and her hair was natural, short with a light curl, not a hair-salon tease and spray. What stuck out more than anything was that my boyfriend bore absolutely no resemblance to his mother. This was undoubtedly because of Gemma's extraordinary nose. Somehow, without being ugly, it dominated her face. It rose from a knobby ridge between her two happy light-blue eyes, then flowed down into two distinct cartilages, so that the tip of her nose had a couple of substantial mountains and a valley. I was to discover that Gemma was one of six girls and that this nose was the Rossi family's trademark. The Rossis lived at the bottom of an alpine valley, and people would joke about the sisters, saying, 'We're going down to visit the Rossis' while they crooked their fingers into a downward pointing, nose-like hook. Only one of the six daughters had escaped the Rossi nose, some had even bigger ones than Gemma's, but they all wore them with pride (and, thankfully, a sense of humour).

Gemma was very chatty, smiley and warm. She may have talked a lot because she was excited at the prospect of meeting a potential daughter-in-law. Or perhaps she was just like that. Excluding Paolo, she took my arm and led me over to the stove to show me what was for dinner. She described the contents of each pot and pan with enthusiasm, as if there was no question that cooking was a love that we would share. Gemma took it for granted that because I was a girl, I would be interested. Cooking was a woman-to-woman thing, just for us.

'A Tuscan speciality', she was saying, 'called *nudi*.' She giggled like a naughty little girl and went on to explain. '*Nudi* means nude. They're the stuffing for tortellini but without their clothes on, without the pasta around them.'

I laughed, too, and she took her cue to list the ingredients.

'Spinach, ricotta, flour, eggs and salt all rolled into teaspoon-sized balls and rolled again in flour. Then you boil them like gnocchi . . . oh, *guarda*! They're floating to the top right now, so they must be ready. Giampaolo, call your father!'

'*Giam*paolo?' I mouthed at him.

He shrugged and nodded. 'That's my full name.'

'*Babbo*!' yelled Paolo through a door off the kitchen that opened on to a corridor that looked more like a tunnel.

'*Babbo*?'

'That's Florentine for "Daddy".'

Giovanni was a bear of a man who managed a grunt and a timid glance when we were introduced. His voice sounded like a sixty-cigarettes-a-day induced growl. It rumbled from deep within him and made him seem gruff, even scary. He had thick, wiry snow-white hair that at one time must have been very curly because it was now tamed into ripples like corrugated iron. I could see exactly where Paolo got his nose, square jaw, and determined blue and yellow eyes. Giovanni had spent his lifetime outdoors laying bricks, so his skin was thick and craggy, like his voice. In a rough yet refined way, he was handsome. He sat down at his place at the table, not the head of the table, but the seat with the best view of the TV. I was relieved when he didn't turn it on.

Gemma had set the table beautifully. A crisp dark-blue and white checked tablecloth, dinner plates with matching pasta bowls on top, and tumblers for our water and wine. There was also an *oliera*, which held matching bottles and containers for the olive oil, vinegar, and salt and pepper. An enormous loaf of bread, half the size of a pillow, was placed near Giovanni's plate. A one-litre flask of chianti wine was also placed near his tumbler. This is the classic way of setting an Italian table.

Gemma dished up everyone's *nudi* at the stove and then came around to serve us individually with either a butter sage sauce or a gorgonzola cream sauce. Then she sat down to eat with us. Hunched over his meal, his face only inches from his plate, Giovanni said little, apart from barking the odd command at Gemma. If he wanted more cheese, Gemma would jump up and fetch it for him. If more wine was required, she was the one who would race into the larder to get it. Neither Paolo nor Giovanni ever rose from the table to lend her a hand. I had never seen a woman serve men the way Gemma did with Giovanni and Paolo. She did, however, place the main meal on the table for everyone to help themselves. Steak had been cooked on a griddle iron with rosemary, salt and olive oil, and potatoes and carrots had been stewed in garlic and broth in a heavy-based pan. It was delicious, and I told Gemma so.

In stumbling Italian, I tried to answer Gemma's questions about Australia. She was intrigued about life in a land so far away and constantly confused Australia with America.

'So, what's the weather like in America? Is it mostly hot or cold?'

'I'm not sure, but I can tell you what the weather is like in Australia.'

She laughed good-naturedly at her confusion and went on to ask what language we spoke. Once we'd established that English was the spoken language in Australia, she asked me about the religion, if there were Catholics who followed the Pope. Then about the food – were there little food shops, or supermarkets?

Paolo teased her and accused her of not knowing where

Australia was, which I thought was a bit rough until I realised that she really didn't know where it was. Happy to oblige, I mimed a globe of the world and pointed to the bottom. It did strike me as peculiar that in this day and age Gemma didn't know where Australia was. But I could see that she was a simple, good woman who had probably been farming since she was old enough to walk, with no time for school. Goodness knows, there were enough old bushies back home in the same situation. But Gemma had an incredible thirst to know and would often, while Paolo was speaking, ask another question. She was never fussed that Paolo was already talking and in the middle of a sentence. It was as though she couldn't hear him; she would go right ahead and talk over the top of him.

Her interruptions made for disconcerting dinner conversation because I never knew who to answer or listen to. I was torn between nodding at Paolo and acknowledging Gemma. I wanted (and, due to my shocking Italian, needed) to give my full attention to my boyfriend, but out of respect for his mum, I felt I should have been smiling encouragingly at her. The struggle of trying to translate one train of thought while another came over the top was too much. I ended up swivelling my head from Paolo to Gemma as if I were watching a tennis match but couldn't see the balls land. Paolo, on the other hand, coped well with simultaneous interjections from his mother and conversation with me. He would respond to his mother when he felt like it or else just ignore her. In time I would understand that this is how most Italians, especially the older generation, converse. Interruption is a characteristic of their conversational technique; butting in is normal.

Giovanni didn't look at me much, though I could tell that he was listening to the conversation. I thought he was a man of few words until Paolo explained that he suffered from terrible migraines and never said much if he could feel one coming on. Like a grumpy old bear disturbed out of hibernation, he kept his head down and ate, mainly with his bread and hands. He used his huge bricklayer's fingers to rub his bread until his slice was crumbed down to the crust. Then, with his fork in his left hand and the crust in his right, he would soak the sauce, prod the meat and scoop the vegetables, all with his crust. His bread was pawed so much there were big piles of crumbs all around his plate.

No one in this Tuscan family appeared to like the middle of their bread. They all passed the loaf around so that everyone could slice off their piece then remove the soft, stodgy, inner part – the part that I love. Their way of slicing bread is an art, obviously something learned young. They tried to teach me how to hold the one-kilogram loaf in the crook of my elbow, then to cleanly slice the bread in one swift upward motion. There was no way I could manage it; the crust was as hard as a rock and my wrist wasn't strong enough. Everyone laughed when Giovanni repeated an old Tuscan saying: 'If you can't cut your bread, you can't earn your bread.' I mentally pegged a breadboard to their names on my Christmas-present list.

In the meantime, sidelong glances at my boyfriend had revealed some monumental behavioural changes. When we had gone out to dinner together alone, Paolo had minded his Ps and Qs. At home with his mum and dad, it was clearly a different story. He appeared to have slipped into a childish world where anything goes at the dinner table. When he had something to say he said it, no matter how big his mouthful of *nudi*. I looked at him aghast. Paolo, in his natural habitat, was a slob. I had an uneasy feeling that this could become an issue between us. If his mother and father ate badly, it wasn't my concern. (As if to punctuate my point, Giovanni spat out his steak gristle without covering his mouth.) But it was important to me that *Paolo* didn't eat too badly.

In contrast, I was on my best behavior. If you want to make a good impression on your boyfriend's parents, you smile brightly, look them in the eye and watch your manners. I knew the code. The rules of table etiquette had been drummed into me before I was out of a highchair. No scooping your peas on to your fork sideways, you had to smush them on to the upside-down tongs. When we were older we used bread plates that were placed on our left. We had to break off small pieces of our bread, then butter them with a separate bread knife. Definitely no elbows on the table, or Dad would lean over and whack you with the back side of his knife. We had to sit up straight and behave. My family wasn't unusual. All of my friends were subjected to the same kind of rigorous training, so that good eating habits were second nature. My mother had gone to great pains to teach my brothers how to twist a wine bottle after pouring so that there were no drips. At this Italian family table the habit was to shove the glass upwards towards the neck of the flask to indicate that enough had been poured.

After he'd ashed over his finished meal, Giovanni stabbed his cigarette out on his leftover steak while I daintily wiped my mouth with my napkin. No one else said anything about the food, so once again I complimented Gemma on a wonderful dinner. She seemed thrilled by my compliments, so I kept them coming.

It was soon time for everyone to go to work. Giovanni pushed his chair back and said the Italian equivalent of 'Well, I'll be off, then. Bye now', and disappeared down the mysterious tunnel. Gemma, however, walked us to the front door where she produced a present for me. Beautifully wrapped in glossy paper and spangly string, it was a pure-wool, navy-blue, crewneck jumper.

'Paolo says you don't have enough warm winter clothes.'

I was touched by her gesture.

She then presented me with a plastic bag filled with homemade tomato pasta sauces in glass preservative jars and fresh vegetables from her farm. Gemma sure knew how to make a girl feel welcome. A great meal, a new jumper and take-home food. Her hospitality and warmth made me feel warmly accepted.

Then I realised that during the whole evening I had never felt judged. Not once did Gemma make me feel that *my* rigid manners were strange. Nor was she checking me out to see whether I was good enough for her son. If anything, it was my thoroughly disciplined upbringing that had unwittingly made me judge the Consumis.

It wasn't that I found Paolo's manners vulgar, it was more that I felt disheartened, disappointed. I hadn't expected his family's customs to be so different from mine. It meant that Paolo had ways of thinking and behaving that we differed greatly on and that, perhaps, was a worry.

Still, I walked down the stairs just as in love as when I'd walked up them. The dinner, in my mind, had been a success. I understood now that Gemma's sole objective in meeting me wasn't to inspect her son's new girlfriend, but to make her feel part of her family.

When Mum rang the next morning, I couldn't wait to make Paolo a part of my own family.

'You've been hard to catch lately. Are you all right?'

'I'm great! I've got a boyfriend. I really like him.'

'Lisa, that's wonderful. Is he from Florence?'

'Yes. He's studying to become a doctor. I've already met his parents and they're really nice people.'

'Oh? What do they do?'

'They're the custodians of the oldest theatre in Florence, Teatro Pergola.'

'Are you seeing a lot of him?'

'We go out together every night.'

'I think I'll come and visit you in a couple of months. How would you like that?'

She didn't wait for me to answer. Dubbed Australia's doyenne of etiquette, icon of style or legendary model maker, it was time for my mother, June Dally-Watkins, to come over and see for herself what her youngest daughter was up to in Florence.

9

After pulling beers all night at the Red Garter, *motorino* trips home to Poggio Imperiale had started to resemble the icy endurance tests on Japanese game shows. Florence was freezing! During the day the temperature would struggle to a maximum of about five degrees, then sink to about five below zero at night. The cold forced me to finally assume the standard *motorino* driving position. By drawing my torso into a tight ball, the amount of body exposed to the sleet and snow was minimised, but the wind still cut into my eyes. I invariably arrived home with semi-frozen tears on my cheeks.

Accustomed to Sydney's mild winters, Italy's extreme cold and damp was a shock. There was nothing warm in my suitcase; in any case, warm clothes from Sydney would do nothing to keep out the Italian cold. Freezing weather requires a complete sub-zero wardrobe and an education to match, neither of which I possessed. It was as though I couldn't grasp the insidious nature of cold weather.

'Oh, a singlet will do fine underneath this warm jumper,' I'd think, as I leapt about on the numbingly cold marble floor under the illusion that everything would miraculously warm up. It never did, so I'd spend the night quivering with a bone-deep chill that I could never shake.

Enter Paolo and his lectures on how to ward off the shivers. He introduced me to the wonders of a high-powered blow-drier to warm up your sheets when they were frigorifically stiff with cold. He saved my red, chaffed cheeks from the icy wind by buying a windscreen for the Boxer. It was a small, plastic windshield that he screwed on to the handlebars one freezing evening before we went to work. He berated me about my slack attitude to proper spencers and woollen tights, then surprised me with thermal goodies that were better than flowers any winter's day. His presents included a thermex jacket, specially designed for use on motorbikes in the cold, while his mother gave me a thickly padded brown suede jacket that she'd picked up at the markets.

As our relationship gathered speed, it was difficult for me to accept Paolo's gifts because of my defiant independence. But Paolo's character was strong and he would overrule my protestations until I came to enjoy being looked after. He showed his love in practical ways that were as foreign to me as his father's manners. He cared for and protected me. No one had ever loved me that way. He enveloped me in a blanket of security that made me feel precious, safe.

Paolo also delighted in making sure that I understood everything. Sometimes Italy's ways stumped me. He never tired of explaining or translating, so that patience and trust became the cornerstones of our romance. In those first months together, Paolo gave himself over to me and I came to believe in him. Neither of us had ever been in love before and we were smitten.

One night he found my passport on the bedside table and started flicking through it. He was lying on his side on my bed with his arm stuck out trying to read the print in a shaft of moonlight that was coming through the window. He stopped still, then thoughtfully closed the passport and put it down. He turned to me with a deadly serious look on his face.

'Any other surprises?'

It took me a while to realise what he was talking about.

'No, I promise.'

He never brought up my age, or my lie, again.

Just as Paolo had never taken anyone home to meet his parents, the same applied to his best friends. He may have been seeing someone regularly on the quiet, but he had never invited her along to dinners or parties, preferring always to be seen and perceived as single. Many Italian men feel the same way. If the girl they are dating is unimportant to their future, they won't include her in any get-togethers of family or friends. They maintain that they would rather not waste anyone's time.

Paolo's best friends, Francesco and Anna, were already married, while Stefano and Piero were engaged to their long-time girlfriends. The group had been hanging out together for years so knew each other well. When we buzzed on Francesco and Anna's doorbell, I had already resigned myself to the fact that I wasn't going to have them rolling in the aisles with my wit and parry. These people were your everyday Florentines with no English, and I was still trying to grasp Italian, shakily translating in my head before speaking and struggling with the complicated grammar. This was a shame, because I had a great repertoire of jokes and could quite easily go on for hours telling funny stories. In Sydney we would often play a dinner-party game – say a word, any word, and then you had to tell a joke using that word. I could always out-joke anyone with that game. Accustomed as I was to using my sense of humour as my social entrée card, I knew that tonight I wouldn't be able to cut it with humour. Perhaps I should have translated a few jokes in my head before arriving. Too late for that now, because the door was already opening to reveal a big bear of a man who was already laughing (oh, dear).

Francesco, a baker who rose daily at three in morning and was consequently as pallid as an uncooked pastry, welcomed me with a kiss on both cheeks. I gave him the casserole dish full of zucchini ratatouille that I'd slaved over, wanting it to be just right for this meal. When he led us into the kitchen, Anna was standing over the sink in a cloud of steam as she strained the pasta. After she had delivered more friendly cheek kisses, I was ushered towards the table. Tuscans don't go in for much drinking before dinner. They want to eat, and when the guests arrive, everyone goes straight to the table.

Lucia and Stefano were already seated. While I was being introduced, I got the impression that this was a celebration. Paolo had brought a date! The vibe made me feel special. When Lucia stood to shake my hand, everyone laughed at the enormous difference in our heights. She was on the petite side of petite, while I looked like a giant next to her even though she had on her trademark heels. Stefano, Lucia's fiancé and

Paolo's best friend since junior school, gave me a hug and a meaningful look.

The same friendliness couldn't be said to emanate from Gina, who arrived shortly afterwards with a superior flourish and a menacing glare while hanging on to Piero's arm. Laden with thick gold jewellery and a gorgeous outfit that was clearly new, Gina tilted her head back and looked down her nose, snubbing me with a glance. The mannerism made her nose all the more noticeable. Now, I may have been a convent teenager from the Sydney 'burbs, but because of my mother's business I could pick a nose job with the best of them, especially a bad nose job. And Gina's was so badly done I wanted to ask her if she'd sued. The cartilage on either side of her ridge and nostrils had been shaved so concave the tip of her nose was the size of a cotton bud. It looked like she'd given her surgeon a photo of Michael Jackson and said, 'I want that nose'. Whenever her attitude towards me became too intimidating, I consoled myself with the knowledge that her nose job was a *really* bad one.

The kitchen was now full of kissing, hugging and *ciao*ing people all manoeuvring into their places around the table. Wonderful smells were coming from the oven where various dishes bubbled away. When a huge porcelain bowl full of *tagliatelle al ragu* (basically a spag bol) was placed in the centre of the table everybody cheered. Using tongs, the guests heaped great loads of it into their pasta bowls and tucked straight in. No one waited for anyone else. Still so conscious of my manners, I ate slowly, putting my fork down between mouthfuls. I knew there was much more to come. The others were chewing, talking and swallowing – all at the same time. Waving their knives and forks in the air and hanging their heads right over their plates, they ate with great 'gusto', saying 'mmm', '*buonissimo*', '*si, si, ancora*'. I was starting to feel pompously restrained.

Once everyone was eating, a woman wearing an apron and slippers quietly took her place at the table, almost unnoticed until I introduced myself.

'*La mia mamma*,' Anna explained. 'My mother. She lives next door and often comes in for meals.'

It was becoming apparent that either Italian children didn't leave home, or they lived next door to their parents. It's as though the Italians always buy one or two extra apartments so that their children can live nearby. Later, Paolo told me that Signora Baldini did all of Anna and Roberto's washing, ironing and cleaning. Even though Anna's brother was over thirty and unmarried, he also lived in a unit on the same floor. According to Paolo, Signora Baldini did everything for him. He came to her flat for breakfast, lunch and dinner. Basically, he lived in a serviced apartment with a restaurant next door. No wonder her son hadn't yet found a wife. In most Italian families, this is the rule, not the exception. Signora Baldini seemed so quiet and nice. I marvelled that someone could be so dedicated to their adult children.

The food was delicious. Lucia had floured thinly sliced chicken breasts, then pan-fried them with fresh rosemary, garlic, olive oil and, finally, a splash of stock to keep them moist. Anna had made peas boiled in stock with bacon and garlic. Gina had thrown an enormous salad together with lots of *rucola* and cherry tomatoes. It all went rather well with my zucchini ratatouille, until Signora Baldini spoke for the first time that evening.

'Who made these zucchinis?' As I put my hand up, I had the feeling that she already knew it was me.

'What kind of tomatoes did you use for this?' she asked, holding up an impaled zucchini. Her face was stern.

'Canned tomatoes, but I can't remember the brand.'

'You mean you didn't use fresh tomatoes?'

'No.'

'You must always use fresh tomatoes with this dish. It just doesn't taste any good with the canned ones.'

'Right.'

Then she pushed my offering to the side of her plate and sat quietly munching the rest of her meal. No one seemed to notice my surprise, then humiliation and finally embarrassment. On they chatted. Then I felt a growing sense of rage. How *dare* she criticise my dish? The woman has no manners! No one in Australia would ever make a negative comment about someone else's cooking. We might *think* it, but we'd never say it out loud. We would lie and say it all tasted great.

Italians not only have a different set of table manners, but different tasting rules. For them, any dish is fair game for a comment or suggestion. Italians like to have their cooking critiqued by tasters at the table. In the reverse situation, Mrs Baldini would probably be mortified if I didn't tell her that there wasn't enough cheese, sauce or salt on my food. Italians want you to enjoy your meal, and if they think they can help you make it taste better, they won't hold back.

After dinner (when Signora Baldini stood up to clear the table and wash up), Francesco suggested a word game. Enthusiastically, they all agreed. Apparently, it was a game they played all the time. Each person had a piece of paper and a pen. First everyone would write down the name of a man and pass the paper on. Then they'd write down the name of a woman and pass it on, then write what they were doing, what they were saying. The pieces of paper went around the table until everyone at the table had made up a story. A lot of it involved slang and complicated double entendres.

It felt peculiar to be so left out, so isolated from the game. The awkward beats of silence in the rhythm of the game while they waited for me to read or respond were painful. Lucia, Stefano and Francesco acted as though I understood everything that was going on. They were kind and tried to include me in the group. Anna squeezed my arm and nodded vigorously, her expression saying 'isn't that funny?', as tears rolled down her face. I'd 'heh, heh' back, trying to juggle looking like I understood (a bit) and not looking like a goose that giggled at jokes she didn't understand. I felt like a failure, as though I'd let the team down. So I stopped listening and tuned out. My easy relationships and conversations in Australia seemed long ago and far away. I felt dislocated and disoriented, with an overwhelming sense of bewilderment at this group's energy and cohesion. My new friends' gaiety only made me feel sad at not being home among people I knew and understood.

When my face muscles could take no more fixed smiling, Paolo rose and said it was time to go. I couldn't leave quickly enough. I was exhausted from concentrating so hard on the language. Translating results in a unique kind of brain fatigue.

Once out the door, my Florentine boyfriend pulled me towards him for a big, supportive hug. It seemed he did know how I felt.

'I know it's hard meeting all these new people, but once your Italian improves you'll have much more fun.'

'Yeah, yeah,' I said despondently.

'Tell me where you are from again?' he said, holding me close.

'Australia,' I murmured.

'No, that's *Austria*. Everyone thinks you're from Austria because you say *Orst-raay-lya*. In Italian, you must pronounce Australia like this: *OUW-OOh-strah-leea.* Every time you do it right, I'll give you a kiss.'

Walking down the street towards the car, I called out, '*OUW-OOh-strah-leea*' – just to test him out. Then *shmack* on the lips! On the way home, I said it again several times, and each time he pulled over and rewarded me with a kiss. The loneliness and foolishness I had felt at Francesco and Anna's table faded away as the harmony and happiness in our relationship, when alone, returned.

By Christmas I was warmly tucked under the Consumi family's wing. At their insistence, Paolo and I ate dinner every night at their house. Often I would stop in for lunch, too, and Gemma would hold court over her sizzling pots and pans, giving instructions on how to prepare all her family's favourite dishes.

'With Florentine liver, it's important to use purple onions. In fact, don't ever bother with white onions for anything; they're not tender or sweet enough.'

'Did you batter the liver or only flour it?'

'Just a light dusting. Oh, my father used to love this dish.'

Gemma and Giovanni never referred to my home back in Sydney or asked if there were any plans to return there. It was as though Florence was my new home; for them, my old home had faded away. Paolo, too, ignored the eventuality of a return to Sydney. It was something we never discussed.

Now that the Higher School Certificate exams were over, many friends were planning to come over and visit in the new year. My brothers had also promised to visit while Mum was in town, so we were all trying to find a time that suited everyone. The get-togethers were pushed back until the European spring because of Paolo's exams, the last one scheduled for March. Once he had them out of the way, we could all spend some quality time together.

A steer from the New South Wales country town of Taree had also made life financially easier. An old family friend had given me the beast during the school holidays when he let me ride his horses. (They used to shoot the Marlboro television commercials that featured herds of stampeding horses on his property.) Darling Ivan Livermoore had bought the steer and sent me the princely sum of three hundred and seventy-five dollars. (It must have been when cattle prices were good.) That steer paid for my first Italian course.

On weekends off, Paolo would load up his little Fiat with all his ski clothes and drive us up to Cervinia or Abetone for a couple of days' skiing. During the week, when we weren't studying or working at the Red Garter, we'd pop in to the Red for a drink.

Paolo, who in a past life must have been a singer, would approach the band and request his favourite song, John Lennon's 'Imagine'. The lead singer and a friend, Marco Doni, would then make a big deal about introducing their guest singer who was 'here especially to do a one-off solo appearance'. Paolo would spring on to the stage, grab the microphone and start singing 'Imagine' like he was some famous Italian artist that the audience had been incredibly lucky to catch. A hush crept through the crowd as the tourists tried to work out if this guy was really someone well known to the European audience but unknown to them. They'd whisper back and forth, 'Who *is* this guy?'

I'd stand in my favourite spot in the shadows under the stairs and try to avoid Paolo's eyes searching me out. 'Imagine all the people living life in peace,' he'd sing in his softly accented English. I'd shuffle and look at my feet, embarrassed that he was directing the song so obviously to me. Then the band would play *un lento,* a slow dance, and we'd wander onto the dance floor and just hold on to each other as we turned around in slow circles. The bliss of being in each other's arms made everyone else a blur.

Then I was fired for going out with a waiter.

10

Florence at Christmas is festooned with bright neon lights in the shapes of praying angels, stars, Santas, candles and carrot-nosed snowmen. In town, golden lights are stretched elegantly up and down the roads, rather than across them, giving the historical streets and piazzas golden ceilings that glow like halos. The major ring roads around the centre are decorated with thousands of twinkling fairy lights, laced through the branches of the trees.

On a damp night the lights are softened, muted by the misty air. Sometimes there are light snowfalls, providing a white, swirling backdrop to the colourful angels. For an Australian accustomed to heatwaves and fake spray-on snow, this cold, white, European Christmas looked exactly like all the Santa pictures in my childhood storybooks.

Little children who rarely came into town from the small outlying Tuscan villages flocked into Florence to experience the glowing magic. Special merry-go-rounds were erected for them in the main piazza – Piazza della Republica. Dressed up in their winter's best, they looked like mini fashion models on a *Vogue Bambini* shoot. Fake leopard-skin jackets with matching leopard-skin stockings on five-year-olds, pink faux-fur full-length coats on three-year-olds. Also popular was a white lambskin jacket, something an Australian mother would think many times about before buying for her energetic child. The Italian parents would stand around the carousel and take Christmas photos of their kids before moving over to the roasted chestnut cart. There they would buy paper bags full of hot chestnuts to put into their child's pocket to help keep them snug and warm.

Grania, Terry, Loraine and I sipped cappuccinos and thick hot chocolates in warm cafés in-between my doorknocking attempts to try and find a job as a sales assistant. But the tourist season was over, with no employment in sight until at least May. Paolo thought my relaxed attitude to finding a job, coupled with the Australian saying 'It'll be right', very strange. He couldn't understand why I didn't ring home and ask my mother or father to send me money. Italian parents are incredibly generous with their children, making sure their kids have money in their pockets at all times. If they can afford to, they buy their children cars and motorbikes. They'll find them jobs, and do their banking and shopping, if asked.

While falling back on Mum or Dad for money was my final option, to be used only if I was desperate, Paolo often used his parents' financial security blanket. In the classic Italian clan system, the family's wealth was shared. All three used the same bank account. In most Australian families, there is no 'ours' with family money. Paolo couldn't understand this and, while I was unemployed, it was a constant issue between us. But I refused to ask my parents to send money when I wasn't really desperate.

Worried about his jobless foreign girlfriend, Paolo suggested I join his extended family for Christmas lunch. Zio (uncle) Franco was coming and he owned a restaurant at Consuma, the family's village in the mountains. Zio Franco needed a waitress to help out with his New Year's Eve dinner dance, which was fully booked with more than two hundred people. Paolo had helped out every year since he was old enough to hold a tray and said the hours were long and gruelling, but at the end the pay packet was very fat.

On Christmas Day, there were phone calls from home and a sumptuous English breakfast prepared by Grania. A big mistake. Paolo should have warned that to do justice to the traditional Italian Christmas lunch, fasting for at least twenty-four hours beforehand is essential.

The Consumi family had a highly organised tradition of sharing the responsibility for preparing the meal. Their custom was to eat eight courses that had been prepared by Gemma and two of her five sisters. The tiny dining room in Via della Pergola, which throughout the year was kept closed and as cool as a larder, was warmed up and the kitchen table connected to the dining-room table.

Gemma's father, Nonno Armando, had passed away many years ago, but sitting quietly in the kitchen watching the preparations with faded blue eyes was Nonna Angiolina, Gemma's mother. Her eighty-seven-year-old face was devoid of expression. It was as though there was a layer of cellophane over her eyes to protect her thoughts from intrusion while she travelled about the cosmos. Brought back to earth with loudly repeated calls of 'Nonna!' Nonna!', the cling wrap came off and she scrambled to her spindly little feet with an alert smile to meet me. 'Paolo's girlfriend!' the women yelled, as they pointed and nodded their heads up and down at me. I almost had to kneel to reach her cheeks for a kiss. She looked like Gemma a hundred years from now, the same forehead, nose and mouth. I commented on the colourful crocheted shawl that she had wrapped around her shoulders.

'Eh?' she said, cupping her hand to her ear. With added volume and the use of mime, she got it the third time around and told me proudly that she had made it herself. Then Paolo stepped in behind her and grabbed her under the arms and swung her feeble frame into the air like she was a toddler.

'Oh, my God! Paolo, don't *do* that!' I spluttered, shocked. But everyone else laughed, including Nonna Angiolina. Paolo had been greeting her with a hearty toss in the air since he was sixteen. It's a wonder she didn't tell her wizened old legs to make a break for it whenever she saw him coming.

Zia Maria, the sister who didn't inherit the nose, set to work arranging the antipasto trays that she brought to every Christmas lunch. She thinly sliced several loaves of bagette-type bread, dipped one end into hot broth, then spread the other with chicken liver pate or minced steamed chicken with mayonnaise and capers. Another tray was laden with stewed onion and capsicum, and several types of Tuscan salamis and prosciutto.

Gemma always made the second course: chicken broth, in which she boiled delicate little prosciutto-stuffed tortellini. Gemma also made the lasagne that followed. Zia Dina, who, unfortunately, had inherited the biggest nose of them all, had arrived early to roast different cuts of turkey, chicken and lamb with potatoes and sausages. I don't know who made the salad and peas, but Zia Dina's daughter Carla was the undisputed queen of the desserts. Her contribution was a tiramisu. Paolo brought the spumante and the panettone – a traditional Italian Christmas cake. Then, the finale: hot chestnuts that had been collected from the chestnut trees up at the farm and roasted while we ate lunch.

The atmosphere was made merry with a 'new' and mischievous Giovanni. Several months before, the grumbly bear had been replaced by a chuckling joker with a penchant for one-liners. Over Christmas lunch, Giovanni cheekily told his family how his migraines had been miraculously cured by his own son, the almost doctor. Paolo had suggested that Giovanni visit a dentist for an X-ray and it was discovered that Giovanni had a small tooth below his canine that had never emerged. For years it had lain painfully lodged against a major nerve in his lower jaw. With the removal of the baby tooth, Giovanni the clown returned. No other medic had diagnosed a dental problem, so the father teased his son about his diagnostic brilliance, while the son teased his father about Giovanni being back to his old, naughty self.

The Florentines are famous in Italy for their style of humour, largely based on *a prendere in giro* – teasing. No other province in Italy can lay claim to the laughs that these guys get at the expense of others. With an uncanny sixth sense about your sensitivities, they'll jibe until you are either really annoyed or no longer susceptible to offence. The only person to attend Christmas lunch from Giovanni's side of the family was Zio Franco, a burly man with a lopsided potbelly and a glass eye. Apparently, a stomach operation performed years before had left him with badly knitted scar tissue so that the fatter he became, the more crooked his tummy became. He lost his left eye when, at six years old, someone threw a glass that hit him in the face. Of Giovanni's five brothers and sisters, Zio Franco and Zia Beppina were the only ones still alive. Guiseppe (nicknamed Beppino), Graziella and Silvio had all passed away from various forms of cancer.

Together, Zio Franco and Giovanni were incorrigible. Clearly best mates, they also shared similar traits. They chainsmoked, drank lots of red wine, preferred to use their crusts rather than their forks, and incessantly took the mickey out of everyone. My nickname for the day was Kangurina ('little kangaroo'). As yet, I couldn't roll my Rs so their requests for wine or food were made with an Anglo-Saxon accent, like the *kangurina*. Franco's teasing was made all the more baffling by his tricky way of not really focusing on you with his good eye. With one eye gazing glassily at nothing and the other staring over my shoulder, I was never sure whether he was talking to me or the person next to me.

After the feast, the men collapsed in the armchairs or settled on to the couch for some afternoon TV or a nap, while the women gathered in the kitchen to clean up. Even though they did all the shopping, cooking and washing up, the women didn't complain that their husbands never lifted themselves from their chairs, unless it was to move to a more comfortable one. Not for a moment did it cross anybody's mind that perhaps the men should help. When this was guilelessly mentioned by the *kangurina*, the women thought I was hilarious. For them, it was the best joke cracked all day.

'As *if*!' Gemma howled. 'Giovanni doesn't even know where the plates are kept.'

Of the six Consumi children, only Zio Franco had stayed on where he was born, the others preferring to live and work in Florence. Zio Franco owned The Baita (The Refuge),

Consuma's biggest trattoria and unofficial information centre. It was to Franco that the villagers turned for gossip on anything from houses for sale to who had been taken to hospital last night. Almost everyone on Consuma Mountain came to Franco Consumi's New Year's Eve party, the year's largest indoor event.

Zio Franco said he would be delighted to have Kangurina wait on the tables this year. Gemma said, *'Venite qualche giorno prima*. Come a few days earlier.'

So it was during my first freezing days up at the old farm that parts of the Rossi and Consumi family histories were revealed to me. And with those revelations came a far deeper understanding of my boyfriend.

To know Paolo, you had to know his people and his village.

11

As we climbed the thirty-three kilometres to the Apennines and Consuma, the frozen rain on the side of the road gradually changed to icy banks of snow, dirtied brown by the flow of traffic. Where the cypresses gave way to the more hardy pine trees, the roadside snow banks were clean and thick from fresh overnight snowfalls. Twisted and buffeted, the guard-rails gave a far more eloquent testimony to the dangers of speeding than Australia's 'Slippery when wet' signs. Here, that was obvious.

Driving with easy familiarity, Paolo had a story to accompany almost every bend. He'd been coming up here all his life, in many different cars and on all sorts of motorbikes. As a ten-year-old he sat in the back of his parents' Prinz NSU, with all the windows up while Giovanni chainsmoked. At fourteen, he'd come on his own, lost control of his little Vespa and skidded the bottom off his pants. Later, on his first high-powered motorbike, he'd hit the road's shoulder, swerved on the corner's gravel and flown over the barrier. He was never seriously hurt, unlike his grandfather, Armando Rossi. The story goes that Nonno Armando was walking down the hill at Ponticelli, about five kilometres past Consuma, when a girl on a bicycle came racing towards him screaming for help. Her brakes had failed, so Nonno Armando put his hands out to try and stop her. He succeeded in stopping the bike, but in the process he fell, smashing his head on the ground. He slipped into a coma and was put into a bed at the girl's house. Due to the area's isolation there was no medical help and no one was game to take him in a horse and cart down to Florence. He remained comatose in the girl's house for two months. When Nonno Armando finally opened his eyes, he was left with a stutter until the day he died.

We drove through the still-sleeping Consuma village, past the house where Giovanni was born, on higher still and over the mountain pass. Then down along the seven winding kilometres that separate Consuma from Pratiglioni – the little farm where Gemma Rossi was born.

We turned off the main road on to a neatly gravelled laneway that was lined on both sides with well-tended box-shaped hedges. Paolo explained that Arezzo council took care of this part of the road to Pratiglioni because it led first to a derelict little church called the Badiola. He stopped the car beside the church to put chains on the tyres before he attempted the hair-raisingly steep descent to his family's isolated farmhouse. I climbed out of the car to better inspect the Badiola while Paolo yelled out its history.

'The church's full name is Santa Maria di Pietrafitta

because it was built on the site of a large rock that had been cleverly embedded into the ground. *Pietrafitta* means a tight rock,' he called.

'Where is the rock?' I asked, searching around the structure.

'Underneath the church, I think. It could have been a big gravestone. But it was definitely worshipped by pagans. This place is ancient. The Catholic Church built the Badiola over the top of the rock to Christianise the site.'

Abandoned, partly roofless and deconsecrated, the Badiola still had two rotten rows of ten pews inside. In its heyday, it would have housed a congregation of about eighty. Its altar at one time must have been beautiful. Now it was only an empty stone stair with a yawning vacant archway behind it. Even so, I spoke in a whisper out of respect when Paolo followed me inside.

'Why do you call it the Badiola?'

'Everyone does. It's a derivative of the word *badia* – which means abbey. It's name has always been The Little Abbey – Badiola – because of its size.'

'It's the sweetest church I've ever seen.'

'Mamma and all my aunties were married here, the first one in 1949. Only the people born around here know of it. You'll never find Pratiglioni on a map of Tuscany.'

'Do you think they'll ever restore it? It's so sad that it's become a ruin.'

'Maybe. Someone has petitioned the Vatican for money to rebuild it. They may give the money in time. Who knows? My family used to do Saint Mary processions to this church with all the village people from around here. It was the focus of their religious life.'

Arms draped around each other's waists, we sauntered back to the car. Paolo swung an iron gate back into the bushes beside the Badiola and fixed it on to a branch with a wire coat hanger. Once through the gate we were on to his family's part of the mountain. For three kilometres the rutted, dirt road dipped and wound its way turbulently through rugged woodland.

Cemented into a rock beside the road was a wooden cross, the size of a tall man. Through the clank and thunk of the chains, Paolo said that no one really knew how long the cross had been there, but that the tale passed down tells of a hunter who had been shot down in a fit of anger by his best friend. Apparently, the two friends had been out together looking for wild pigs – *cinghiale.* Catching sight of a big one, they fired at the same time and killed it. Then they got into a fierce argument about who had shot the pig until one man shot the other. The cross marks the spot where the man was murdered.

'No, they weren't relations,' laughed Paolo.

The final curve in the road opened up on to a small area of flat land, nestled into the sway and fall of the mountains around it. *Prato* means 'meadow', and the name Pratiglioni gives the idea of a small field. There were four houses spaced at discreet distances from each other on the little plateau. Two of the farmhouses were five hundred-year-old grey-stone originals. The others were of the same stone, but more recent in style and connected.

'They are my father's houses,' explained Paolo. 'Babbo built them with his own hands on the old barn site during the early seventies.'

We drove the car around to the back of Giovanni's houses on to a private little green meadow where wood stacks hid the sheer drop of the mountain below.

There was a flurry of activity inside the house when we walked through the back door. Everyone moved towards us at once, hugging us as though we were long-lost children coming in from the cold. Their acceptance of me almost bowled me over. It was as though Paolo and I had been together for years. They made me feel treasured.

The house itself was full of early-morning sunshine and as warm as toast. A fire that seemed to take up most of the living room roared in a corner fireplace. It stretched from mid-wall to mid-wall with a thick wooden beam for a mantlepiece and a stone hood that protruded from the corner. Over the flames, suspended by a chain and hook, was a sooty black pot that reminded me of a witch's cauldron. The kitchen, to where Gemma had flown to put on some coffee, was off to the side of the living room, along with a big pantry and a bathroom. Paolo jerked his head up to indicate 'follow me' as he trundled up a steep (everything around here was steep) flight of stairs with our bags. Upstairs were two master bedrooms and one small bedroom. I trailed after Paolo into one of the big bedrooms, relieved to know that Gemma and Giovanni had no problems about us sharing a bed together under their roof. It appeared they had a modern attitude towards sex before marriage.

Our room was beautiful, with a long, wide window and old family pieces of furniture. Our bed, with the compulsory *Madonna and Child* print above it, had a massive wooden bedhead with matching bedside tables. Gemma had taken the trouble to add thoughtful, cosy touches to the room, such as dried lavender in a bowl on the chest of drawers under the mirror. She'd spread a patchwork quilt over the bed and draped an extra hand-crocheted rug across a chair.

'What's that?' I said, pointing to a long, semicircular wooden frame that had a terracotta pot hanging from its centre. It looked like a medieval instrument of torture.

'A bed warmer,' said Paolo. 'You put hot coals in the pot, then put the frame in your bed.'

The smell of freshly brewed coffee wafted up the stairs, so we followed it back down to the living room. Around the table, waiting for us, were Gemma, Giovanni and Gemma's sister Dina, or Zia (Aunty) Dina, as I was instructed to call her. She was the eldest Rossi girl and a widow. She'd been invited up to Pratiglioni with Gemma and Giovanni to spend time enjoying her old home. Shaking her head with a wistful smile, she said she wasn't interested in Zio Franco's big dinner dance. Zia Dina's hands were busy while she spoke. She nursed an obsessive habit that was left over from the old days when 'idle hands' were viewed poorly. She was always folding, dusting or polishing something. To everything she said, there was a shaking uncertainty. I realised that she was probably minutes away from full-blown Alzheimer's disease.

Chirpy and clearly happy with the way things had worked out, Gemma said that four of her five sisters would be joining us for dinner tonight.

'Where is your fifth sister?' I asked, not expecting the pall of sadness the question would evoke.

'Gina is in a mental institution, my dear. It is unlikely that she will ever be well enough to join us.'

We were quiet except for the rustling sound of Zia Dina folding plastic supermarket bags. She liked to fold them into small triangular shapes and secrete them away in drawers around the house.

On the walls around the living room were enlarged photos of the Consumis standing in various proud poses before piles of huge mushrooms. Eyeing them, I asked if they'd picked the mushrooms in their own woods.

'*Ohh, non sono una meraviglia?* Aren't they a marvel?'

sighed Gemma. 'That was a record day. The most *porcini* we ever found. And the biggest. They're all from our forests. You'll be having some of them for lunch.' She sounded positively in love with her mushrooms.

At that point, Zia Maria swirled in through the front door. Famous for her fabulous dancing, Zia Maria twirled rather than walked. At sixty she had a small waist, which she liked to show off with cinch belts and full skirts. I wondered whose womb she had come from. All her sisters were small with large, hooked noses. She had long legs, blue eyes and a small, straight nose. Zia Maria had bought the original Rossi house, where most of the six girls were born, next door. It had come on to the market in 1972 when the previous owners – the Catholic Church – put a large proportion of its mountain land up for sale. She paid one thousand eight hundred dollars for it. Paolo later explained that his mother and father had bought most of the mountain land, opting to build a new house, rather than trying to make an old one livable. I didn't quite understand what they meant by 'livable'. Zia Maria straightaway said, '*Vieni a vedere la mia casa.* Come and see my house.'

Later, after café latte, biscuits and a long chat, Zia Maria and I walked out of the Consumis' front door. About thirty paces away we found ourselves at the bottom of the old Rossi house. It was built in the style of most of the old farmhouses in the Casentino district. We walked up two small flights of stairs that had been worn into smiles by hundreds of years of scuffs from work boots, before reaching a small stone *terrazzo* that led to the front door. Underfoot were gigantic stones, flagging that hadn't been touched since the house was built.

'How old is this house?' I asked, fascinated by the lilt of

the floor and the aged wooden beams that supported the terrace roof.

'About five hundred years. I've had parts of it restored, but I've retained many of the original materials because they were sound. No point in ripping up the floor if it still works, eh?'

Zia Maria opened the heavy wooden door so that I could duck my head and walk through it into a kitchen that was swathed in darkness, except for a fire.

'Every farmhouse entrance is into the kitchen,' she explained. 'We used to keep the cattle under the kitchen and their heat rose through the floorboards. It was the warmest room in the house.'

'And the fireplace? It's so big!' Across one wall, the fireplace measured two metres by two metres, its grate at knee level. There were two chairs in the large spaces on either side of the hearth, so that whoever sat beside the fire was literally inside the fireplace.

'Nonna Angiolina's favourite place in the world. She's down in Florence, though, this weekend. Said it was too cold to come up.'

'And she had all six girls here, in this house?'

'No.' Zia Maria smiled cheekily. 'She had all *seven* girls in this house. Actually, she delivered Dina and Gina at another farm, but Anita, me, Gemma, Argentina and the second Anita were all born here. The first Anita died of diptheria when she was eighteen months old.'

'She had *seven* daughters? I thought it was amazing that she had *six*.'

'Ha! And she fostered two boys as well. We needed the money.'

'They worked on the farm?'

'No, Mamma was paid to breastfeed them.'

I was confused. 'Was she a wet-nurse?'

'No. We were very, very poor. There was no cash, but women with breastmilk could take in abandoned babies for breastfeeding. Sometimes it was the only money we had.'

I must have looked perplexed, but she brushed it aside. 'Come, this is the original sink, too.'

Carved in the same stone as the walls, the sink was about a metre long, five fingers deep, with another narrow, slightly tilted stone water run-off area attached to it. It was underneath the only window in the room, which accounted for the kitchen's darkness.

'How come all the windows are so tiny?'

'The smaller the window, the warmer the room, but it also means the old houses are very dark. That's one of the reasons why Gemma and Giovanni decided to design and build their own house, so that they could have large windows with sunlight.'

Along the top of a heavy, wooden cabinet beside the sink, Zia Maria had placed a collection of terracotta and copper pots. When she saw me looking at them, she pulled one down.

'There was no steel when we were growing up. These are the pots my mother used. She only cooked in terracotta. To boil the water or make the polenta, she used this big copper pot.'

'But didn't the terracotta pots crack on that stone sink all the time?'

'*Lo stagnigno* – a handyman passed by every few months and wired all the pots back together again. He'd put some kind of glue into the cracks, then wind the wire tightly around the pots till they stopped leaking. We threw nothing away, fixed everything – not like nowadays, when if something breaks you throw it away.'

Zia Maria led me out of the kitchen and through all the rooms. Remarkably, almost all were still furnished with their original pieces dating from the 1930s to the 1950s. 'This is my real home. Though I have an apartment in the centre of Florence, this is where all my memories are. I like to keep things just the way they've always been.'

The only new addition to the old Rossi home was a bathroom, as bathrooms didn't exist when Maria was a child. Zia Maria explained how, every day, the girls collected water from the stream, heated it and poured it into the terracotta bowls for washing their hands and faces. Until only several years ago, *la fontana* – the mountain spring from where they daily drew their water – used to be a one-kilometre walk. But the water had been brought up now to a community well that all four houses shared. For centuries the families had made the trek to the spring, which was really the beginning of the Arno River, Zia Maria explained.

'The Arno that you see in Florence starts here. No matter how freezing it gets, our spring has never been known to freeze over or run dry. It's diuretic, you know – makes you pee. Well, that's it . . . better get you back to your boyfriend!' And she took my arm and led me back to Giovanni's house.

While I was being brought up to speed on the finer points of old-fashioned Tuscan mountain domesticity at Zia Maria's house, Gemma had been busy. A steaming pot of *porcini* risotto sat in the middle of Gemma and Giovanni's long dining-room table. She had defrosted some of her mushroom stash (they are found in summer, when the optimum growing conditions are lots of heat, then rain) before finely slicing them with loads of garlic and parsley. Gemma had cooked the *porcini* mixture slowly in thick, smoky green olive oil before adding seven fistfuls of rice. The witch's brew over the fire was a *bollito*, a mixture of beef and bone together with carrots, onions, potatoes and a bouquet of fresh herbs. The wonderful broth these ingredients produced was added slowly to the risotto. Finally, a cup of *parmigiano* was added.

Sizzling over the fire now was a pan of lightly battered zucchini and cauliflower strips. The rest of the broth, Gemma explained, would be eaten for dinner with little pasta bows. The boiled beef and vegetables would follow the broth with her own brand of *salsa verde* – a green sauce of blended garlic, parsley and oil.

Looking back, this first lunch at Pratiglioni was the meal that initiated my love of Tuscan cooking. Gemma's risotto had a cream-like quality that was delicate, yet strong because of the *porcini*'s unusual flavour.

I was intrigued by the way she used fresh and dried herbs, garlic and oil, rather than bottles of pre-packaged spices, to create different flavours. Gemma tended to 'capture' the essence of her ingredients, she enhanced rather than drowned. Following that delicious and typical mountain meal, I became like a hawk circling the skies above her kitchen on the lookout for any movement below.

My newfound attentiveness in the kitchen was accompanied by a deep curiosity about the Rossi family. What was their mother, Nonna Angiolina, like as a girl? How did she meet Nonno Armando? How did they live up here in the snow with no central heating, apart from the cattle? I knew so little about the Rossi family, yet here I was with Gemma and her sisters, the focus of their hospitality. I felt a strong need to know more about them.

As the story of Nonna Angiolina and her life unfolded, we settled our full tummies contentedly around the fire.

Nonna Angiolina was born in 1893 in the bedroom of an archway house that straddled the main road of the tiny village of Borgo alla Collina. The house was like the town's welcoming banner. It stretched across the lonely mountain road that led from Florence to Consuma to Stia, in the heart of the Casentino district. Ten small stone houses were then clustered around a piazza before the road once again entered open country.

Every spring, Angiolina would put a change of clothes into a square of cloth, fold up the four corners to make a knotted handle, and walk to the Casentino farms to help sow the wheat. By the time she was twenty-seven, in 1921, she was still unmarried, an unusual situation for such a spritely and intelligent girl. That year she walked all the way to Pelago, well past Consuma, almost down into the valley of Florence. It was a twenty-five-kilometre walk and the furthest from home she'd ever been. While she was working in the fields, she became friends with a young shepherd who had come from across the Alps in Romagna to help with the lambing. Twenty-two-year-old Armando Rossi was to sleep in the attic with the other farmhands, while Angiolina was given a bed in a spare room on the ground floor. But even the most well-intentioned sleeping arrangements sometimes go awry. By the summer, Angiolina found herself pregnant to Armando. By Christmas, they were married with a baby, Alessandrina (known as Dina).

At first the young family took on a small farm at Villa, a few kilometres from Pratiglioni behind Giovanni's house, beyond the wood stacks where the mountain drops away. But after Armando had paid his landlord fifty per cent of all his earnings, there wasn't enough money left to feed his growing family. Gina had arrived shortly after Dina, and Anita was on her way. When word came from the Badiola that the Catholic Church had land with a larger holding open for tenure, Armando decided it was time to move his family over to the isolated plateau. By road (he had no horse and cart to use or borrow), Pratiglioni was about twelve kilometres of mountainous curves away. He decided to move house on foot.

Using a stretch of rope and a blanket, Armando fashioned an enormous sling with which to tie the kitchen cupboard on to his back. He then made his way down the slope in front of Villa and up the steep mountainside to Pratiglioni. He repeated this trip over and over until he had moved the Rossis' bedroom cupboard, clothes trunk, table and chairs, linen, kitchen utensils and farming tools. Finally, the pregnant Angiolina followed with the two babies. Till this day, no one can imagine the strength it took for Armando to move house from Villa to Pratiglioni on foot.

The tiny farm brought in little or no cash, compelling Armando to abandon the land in winter and go south to Calabria as a woodcutter. Angiolina was left in the mountains alone to care as best she could for the girls, the animals and the land. One way to make ends meet was to wet-nurse abandoned babies. In 1929, when Gemma was three months old, Angiolina hitched a ride on a cart down to Florence. Gli Innocenti – The Innocents – was the state's orphan group and paid good money for wet-nurses for orphans – three lira a month. In today's terms, that's three cents a month. Angiolina's first foster child, Raul, grew so big that when it was time to take him back down to the orphanage, he was too fat to walk. It was the same in 1932 with Roberto, taken in after Argentina's birth.

Once an orphan was taken in by Gli Innocenti, their surname was automatically changed to Innocenti. Subsequently, they could never shake the stigma attached to being abandoned or orphaned. They were known and recognised as an Innocenti for the rest of their lives.

Maria and Dina both sighed and said that they loved having Raul and Roberto around.

'We used to roll chestnuts across the floor for them to crawl after,' Maria said wistfully. 'We didn't have any toys. There was very little play. We always worked around the farm, just to survive.'

The flames continued to draw us into their warmth. Paolo put his arm around my shoulders and gently touched the back of my neck. He had grown up with these stories, but still he seemed to enjoy hearing them. I could tell that he was happy I was so interested in his family's past.

'You're the eldest, Zia Dina. When did you leave the farm?' I asked.

I learned that Dina's sisters used to call her 'the little penguin', because of her precise way of walking with her toes slightly turned out. Of all the girls she was the tidiest, and she was smart. '*Sveglia*,' they said, which means quick and 'awake'. She was a good girl with a genuine desire to please. Maybe that's why Dina didn't cry when at age eleven, in 1932, she was sent down to Florence to work as a maid.

It was rare to send eleven-year-olds away to work, but that year had been particularly hard. She was put into the back of a horse-drawn cart and taken into town. Upon seeing her new charge, the signora who was to be Dina's employer apparently cried, '*Oh mamma mia, ma sei solo una bambina!* Oh, my goodness, but you are only a baby!'

Dina had taken all she owned with her; a pair of underpants and one other dress. From that point on, her new signora would buy all her clothes and shoes. It was Dina's job to do the washing by hand, dry and iron everything, make the beds, and sweep and dust. She recalled that the signora's family was kind to her, treating her almost as their own daughter.

In cash, she was paid almost nothing. 'Not enough to buy anything with, but then I rarely left the signora's home,' she smiled ruefully. 'If I bought anything, it would have been a ribbon for my hair or a present for my sisters. My signora took me to the markets sometimes, where she would buy me pastries or sweets.' They were things that little Dina had never seen or tasted before.

Dina was permitted to go home and see her family at Pratiglioni for one week at Christmas and Easter, with perhaps some time in the summer if her employees didn't need her. Gemma explained that when Dina did come home, all the girls would sit around her while she spun stories about the food, the beautiful houses and glamorous people. None of the other Rossi sisters had been further than Consuma or Stia.

At age twenty, Dina was sent to work for a Dr Caroti, an opera lover. He introduced Dina to her greatest passion in life, music. Several times a year, the family would include her in trips to the theatre. All the sisters remember the doctor with great fondness, because he had saved Maria's life. Up at the farm she had been gathering the hay when a long piece of grass, the kind that you can't pull out because it has a sharp point at one end with feathery blades running down it, pierced her in the armpit. After a few days it grew into an infected lump and Maria developed a fever as the lump festered. By coincidence, Dina was visiting, so when Maria became delirious, Dina insisted that she be allowed to take Maria to see her employer in town.

After a forty-three kilometre journey, Dina and Maria reached the doctor's house in the early hours of the morning. Dr Caroti took them straight to hospital, where he operated to remove Maria's septic lump. Penicillin was newly available but out of the girls' financial reach, so Dr Caroti paid for the treatment while Maria recuperated in his house.

Not all of Dina's employers were so kind to her. One Signora routinely made Dina wash and iron all the clean linen over and over, just so she would be very busy all day long.

When the Second World War began, Dina moved to her last family before being called back to the farm where Armando wanted all his daughters safely together under his watchful eye for the duration of the war. Most doctors had already been called away to the war, so when Dina's last employer went into labour, it was Dina who delivered the baby. Tears flowed down Dina's cheek as she recalled the past.

'You see,' said Gemma gently. 'Dina was everyone's mother.'

We sat quietly. Then Maria thoughtfully went to fetch some handkerchiefs for Dina to fold. I now understood Dina's folding obsession. Twirling off into the kitchen with a call of 'Who wants a coffee?', Maria then added: 'I was sent into domestic service, too, you know.'

'How old were *you*?' I called after her.

'Twelve, though I was sent to Rome,' she called back.

'I can't comprehend you all as little girls being sent away,' I said, throwing up the palms of my hands in a gesture I knew they would understand.

'Lisa,' said Giovanni, 'you must try to understand life in Casentino before, during and after the war. We were all dirt-poor. Everything you see now is a result of many, many years of hard work.'

'There was no money, and with a farm so small, no way that we could make it. We made and used everything ourselves,' Gemma chimed in.

'But didn't you barter your cheese for meat, or sell your eggs at the market or something?' It didn't make sense. How could they have had a farm and not had any money?

'Because there were nine mouths to feed. Eight when Anita died from diphtheria, then seven when Dina left. The only goods we ever bought were salt, sugar and wine,' said Gemma.

When the girls were children, the Rossi family owned and milked about thirty sheep. After collecting the day's water, the girls' first job of the morning was to get the sheep out from under the house (they were kept under the larder next to the kitchen) or release them from their little holding pen and take them to the spring to drink, then on to the mountainside to graze. One or two of the youngest girls stayed with the sheep all day, taking their lunch with them in a sack – usually bread and pecorino (sheep) cheese. At five years old they were considered well and truly capable of this task.

Ten pigs were kept in a pen behind the house. One girl tended to them while another took the four steers out to water and graze all day on another part of the mountain. The cattle were used to pull ploughs or transport goods, not for food. They had a dozen or so chickens for eggs, and rabbits whose offspring were eaten once they'd been fattened up. The cornerstone of their diet was chestnuts. Throughout Casentino the chestnut tree thrives, with millions of chestnuts falling to the ground every October, November and December. The collection and preparation of their chestnuts was a long and arduous affair, but it was also a social event, akin to the process of killing and seasoning a fatted calf for a festival.

Once the chestnuts – anything up to three thousand kilograms worth – had been collected from the forest floor, they were taken to the *seccatoio*. Every farm had its own *seccatoio*, or drying house. These little structures look like rustic miniatures of the farmhouses, as they are constructed using the same grey stone blocks and slate roofs. Usually they are some distance from the house, closer to the forests. Along the inner walls are wooden slats that make wide shelves on which to put all the chestnuts. A fire is built underneath them, and every day for a month the fire is moved around beneath the chestnuts.

The month of the *seccatoio* fires is a month of great social interaction. Everyone goes daily to the *seccatoio* for a chat. Or they visit a friend's *seccatoio* to catch up on the gossip. Girls meet boys there, wives take time out for a rest there, and husbands have been known to stay there all day, 'Just watching that the fire doesn't go out, dear.'

Once the chestnuts are totally dried, they are taken from the *seccatoio* still warm and placed in enormous baskets. The men, women and children put on special boots that have nail-like stubs on the soles so that they can stomp on the chestnuts and split their skins. Then everyone sits down and peels them. The chestnuts end up looking like white, rock-hard raisins. They are then hauled off to a local mill to be ground down. Or in Nonna Angiolina's case, she would gather the girls to ground them down by hand. The girls would pack the chestnut flour tightly into wooden boxes so that the flour would keep its flavour. The almost-airtight containers also kept the weasels and mice at bay.

Breakfast every morning was a pot of chestnut polenta. It has a smooth texture with a smoky, sweet taste that doesn't really compare to anything. Angiolina would add fried bits of pork with lots of fat. Sometimes she would crumble pecorino cheese into the steaming polenta and then drizzle the pork fat over the top. If there was any fresh ricotta or preserved jam, they would sometimes add that. Angiolina would pour any leftover polenta on to a tray and top it with oil, rosemary and walnuts before baking it into a rubbery sweet called *castagnaccio*.

Vegetable minestrone with bread and cheese was the staple lunch every day, apart from Sundays when Angiolina would make fresh pasta or ravioli. Dinner was also *minestra di verdura* – vegetable soup, but with more potatoes or beans or bread. They would invariably finish their meal with apples from the orchard, which were stored in a coolroom at the back of the house. They would eat the apples with pecorino, bread and walnuts. Sometimes they would kill a chicken or rabbit, but this was rare as they had to keep enough to breed with. The chickens' eggs were used for the pasta or were beaten into a minestrone. Mostly they lived on homemade cheeses, and the vegetables and fruit that Angiolina grew around the house.

Their 'coffee' was made from ground barley. The girls never knew any other kind of coffee existed until they left Pratiglioni. They grew their own wheat, ground their flour and made their own yeast. Once a week the bread oven, built into the external wall of the storeroom behind the kitchen, was lit. On baking day they would produce a dozen or so loaves of bread, each weighing about a kilogram. When the bread became stale, it was cut into cubes and drowned in goat's milk for a snack. There was never any cow's milk, because they had no cows to milk. When I asked if they drank sheep's milk, they all looked revolted at the suggestion. Sheep's milk, they said, tastes like sheep poo. Apparently, it's only suitable for cheese.

Once a week was washday. All the girls had one or two changes of clothes for the working week and one special outfit for Sunday church. The girls would make their way down to the spring with their dirty clothes, linens and rags, and start scrubbing. Nonna Angiolina made all their soap. Zia Maria says it wasn't so cold while you were washing, because the action kept you warm, but once they started home their woollen mittens would literally freeze to the handles of their buckets. They would hold their hands and the buckets up to the fire to melt the ice. Once the day's work was done and the animals were settled into their pens, the girls would spin the sheep's wool into spools. Under candle and oil lamplight, they would knit their own stockings, jumpers and skirts.

I asked the women about the kind of shoes they used to wear. Gemma replied, '*Zoccoli.*' I was confused, as *zoccoli* means 'hooves', until Paolo, who I thought had gone to sleep, chipped in with: 'What the Dutch people wear.' Ahh, clogs.

Nonno Armando would find the softest tree trunks, chop them down to smaller pieces and then carve wooden soles from them. He would gather the old worn shoes and cut the soles out of them, leaving only the leather top part of the shoe. Then he'd stretch the leather over the rim of the wooden sole and hammer lots of nails around them. The girls wore thick, handmade woollen socks or tights and slipped their whole foot into the shoe. Here they now sat, forty years later, nodding to each other about how much more effective *zoccoli* were when compared with the shoes of today. The wooden soles, they agreed, kept their feet as warm as a roasted chestnut. When they skipped across the snow, frost or stream, the wood kept their feet dry. Much better than the rubber-soled shoes of today that become damp when wet, they concurred.

As Paolo's parents and aunties shared their stories with me, I listened, wrapt. They had Paolo's full attention now, too. He would add a bit of information or help to jog their memories. When he reached up on to the fireplace's mantelpiece to get down all the old farming tools, the others decided to leave their places on the sofa and armchairs to get on with their afternoons. Paolo told me he'd saved the scythe from being tossed out. It meant a lot to him because he could still see his grandfather using it in the fields. His grandfather had left him all his knives and hammers. They were relics of the past; tangible proof of how hard life was up here.

When Zia Maria waltzed out the door with a wave and a '*Ciao, a dopo*. Bye, see you later,' I realised she hadn't told me about going to Rome at age twelve.

I'll ask her tonight, I thought, when the other Rossi girls are here for dinner. But the opportunity didn't arise and when the last two sisters arrived together, the women's attention turned to them.

Anita was quick and birdlike. She had a ready smile and a nose that was just as prominent, if not more so, than her sisters'. If you followed the sheep path through the mountains, Zia Anita's farm was only a forty-minute walk away. If you drove, it was a thirty-minute, fifteen-kilometre drive from Pratiglioni to Campi. She'd picked up Zia Argentina along the way. Zia Argentina and her husband had bought a holiday home at Prato Vecchio (the Old Field), a village close to Zia Anita's farm. This was to be about the only time I would see Zia Argentina without her husband, Quinto, at her side. The pair gave the word 'togetherness' a new meaning. They rarely left each other's side. Zia Argentina was fuller, rounder and slower than her sisters, as though she'd led a much more sedentary lifestyle. She was also much slower to smile.

The five sisters stood around the table clapping their hands with joy over a wicker basket laden with farm goods that Zia Anita had brought. Eggs, pecorino, ricotta and a whole leg of prosciutto. She was the only Rossi girl to still live on a working farm.

'Ahh, *buonissimo*,' they cried, crowding around the table prodding and smelling.

'I can't stand the shop-bought ricotta of today,' said Gemma, with a very serious expression. 'It's such a poor imitation of the real thing.'

They all clicked their tongues at how mass production had changed the flavour of their favourite food.

'Right, if anyone here would like to take my place and spend all day making this stuff, let me know!'

'Oh, no, no, no,' they all backed down lightheartedly.

'It takes too much time to make the cheeses,' said Argentina. 'We'll have to be happy with what we can buy.'

I gathered that the women preferred their easy lives back down in Florence. Apart from Anita, none of them wanted the backbreaking life of farm work.

In groups and couples, the Rossi girls began to twitter and chat about their children's well-being like excited sparrows at a birdbath. Then it was time to lay the table and prepare dinner. I thought about Armando, so isolated on this farm surrounded by seven lively girls, and couldn't help but feel a twinge of pity for him. I'd heard that the old plough-scarred farmer was an austere man with no patience, incredibly strict and bossy. Anita told me later that he treated Angiolina like a servant, ordering her around with a rude voice. I thought of Giovanni's bossiness with Gemma and a cold feeling gripped my stomach. I hoped like hell that Paolo wouldn't grow to be like his father and grandfather.

'What kind of work does your family do in Australia?' asked Argentina. Seven pairs of eyes turned towards me.

'My mother has model agencies,' I replied.

'What kind of models does she sell?' enquired Argentina, looking perplexed by my response.

'Fashion models. Girls in magazines or on the television. My mother supplies the girls to do photographs for fashion work.' I stumbled, surprised at how badly it was all coming out. Mum was sounding more and more like a high-class madam every second.

'Oh,' was all she said. 'What about your father? Does he sell models, too?'

'He is in security. He supplies armoured vehicles and security guards.'

Her face lit up with understanding. '*Si, si.* My friend's son is a security guard. It's a good job. Terrible hours, but a good job.'

I decided to move the conversation along.

'What did Nonno Armando think about having seven daughters?' I asked.

'*Mamma mia*!' exclaimed Anita. 'He never lived that one down, not with how they tease around here. I am the youngest and he was so angry after my birth he refused to come to my baptism.'

'You must be joking!' I gasped.

'He was furious with Nonna Angiolina,' Gemma laughed. 'But our mother would say that the sex of his children was his fault, because he made only girl seeds.'

The next day after breakfast I rugged up and went down to the spring to fill a five-litre glass flask with the day's drinking water. I had claimed the daily water collection as my job, because no one would let me do anything else. Zia Maria was there, too. Her hair was in rollers under a scarf, at odds with her old men's padded jacket and work boots.

'No one dresses up on the farm,' she giggled, indicating her attire. She then settled back on to her haunches so as not to get her bottom wet while her water container filled.

I pointed to my own flapping boots, lent to me by Paolo, and laughed at my own gracelessness. With no prompting, as though she had read my mind, Zia Maria began to describe the early years of her life.

Born in 1927, Maria worked as a maid while living with a nearby family for the whole of her eleventh year. When news came to Consuma that a high-ranking Roman police officer was looking for a young girl to help with domestic duties, Maria's parents put her forward for the job immediately. She said the rich Romans knew that they would find a girl from the Tuscan Casentino mountain area, because it was well known they were poor. Though her sisters had routinely been sent down to work in Florence, none of them had been sent so far away from home. She said she was both excited and terrified. Her eyes took on a faraway look as she remembered exactly what she was wearing the day she said goodbye to her family.

In 1939, the country's leader, the dictator Mussolini, had been pushing a cheap, rough, blanket-type material on to the market. Many people had made dresses, pants, jackets and pinafores from the red-brown fabric, even though it was infamous for turning rock-hard when wet. Maria's was a simple dress with two big pockets at the side. Her hair had been braided into two long blonde plaits that were tied with two red ribbons. On her feet were plain black shoes and woollen tights, spun from the farm's lambswool and knitted by herself. Maria's suitcase was a square piece of cloth tied into a bundle and attached to the end of a stick. Inside the bundle was one other change of clothes and a spare pair of underpants. Her mother had also given her some rags and an explanation as to how to use them. Maria was not yet menstruating, and Nonna Angiolina knew it would happen soon.

It was mid-morning on a crisp November day when it was time to go. Nonna Angiolina was out working in the fields. Maria called out 'Mamma!' and put her hand into her pocket to find her white handkerchief so that she could wave goodbye with it. Maria didn't know that her new employer's address in Rome fell out with her hankie.

By the time the horse-drawn cart arrived in Arezzo, Maria was brimming with excitement. She'd never seen a big town or a train before. But halfway through the train journey, her world came crashing down. She realised she had lost her address in Rome.

At first I didn't understand why Maria had started to cry at this point in her story. Her face had twisted into a deep sadness as she recalled her long-ago terror.

'I had no money to go back to Arezzo and no money for when I arrived in Rome. All I could remember was the name of the man I was to work for, Commissario Terni. I was so frightened.' As I began to imagine her fear, tears sprang to my eyes, too.

'Babbo had told me to only ask a policeman for information if I got into trouble. I wasn't to trust or talk to anyone.'

Maria said she was sobbing by the time she got off the train in Rome. She walked around looking for a policeman, until finally she saw a uniformed man with a funny hat standing at the end of a long stretch of red carpet. She walked the length of the red carpet, crying. She told him she was lost and begged him to help her find a certain Commissario Terni. But the man wouldn't even look at her, let alone speak to her. Maria was devastated that she could be so ignored. She didn't know that he was a Royal Guard, unable to break his silence. Still, Maria didn't leave his side, staying by him until a change of guard arrived. The new guard did speak to her, though she could answer few of his questions.

'I didn't even know I was from Tuscany. I could barely even write my own name, as I'd left school at age eight. But I did say I'd come from Arezzo to work for Commissario Terni,' said Maria, wiping the tears from her face.

The Royal Guard took Maria to the police station nearest the railway. From there they rang police headquarters and located Commissario Terni, whose driver duly arrived to pick up Maria. She stayed in Rome, earning six cents a month, until the war broke out more than a year later.

The Consuma cold was now biting into our bones and our water containers were full. As she stood up, Maria shook the sadness from her long frame with a sigh. 'It was such a hard life,' she said. 'I'm glad that era is long gone.'

Then she kissed me on both cheeks and walked back up the hill to her house, the house where she had been born, the house that held so many memories for her and her sisters.

As I made my way back up to Giovanni's house, I thought about what this family had achieved in one lifetime. It had been hard to grasp just how poor the Tuscan mountain people were, only one generation ago. Paolo can easily recall visiting his grandparents and having to go to the toilet with everyone else into the sheep's manure trough so that the human excrement could be used as fertiliser in the orchard. At five years old, he too was sent out all day to stay with the sheep.

Eventually, all the girls married and moved away and there was no one left to help on the farm. Apart from Anita, the whole Rossi family now lives in Florence. Eventually, Nonna Angiolina and Nonno Armando were forced to sell the sheep, pigs and cattle and come down off the mountain, too.

It dawned on me that, to lift themselves out of their poverty, Gemma and Giovanni had worked hard and saved every day of their lives. But more importantly, I realised that that they did it mostly for Paolo. Giovanni had repeatedly said he only wanted one child so that he could give him everything he had never had. The one-child choice is echoed across the country, giving Italy the lowest birthrate among the world's industrialised countries. All Paolo had to do was study and become a doctor. They asked no more of him. He never had to help around the house, prepare food, wash his own clothes or think about the supermarket shopping. He just had to become a doctor. That was the fulfilment of his parents' dream.

The next day was New Year's Eve and the women made fresh pasta for lunch. They stretched it out over the dining-room table so that it looked like a soft, yellowing bedsheet. Gemma folded teaspoons of spicy mashed potatoes into it, cutting them into little square sacks called *tortellini con patate*. The tortellini are Casentino's speciality. She told me that every trattoria, restaurant and pizzeria serves its own variation of the dish. In winter, people drive up from Florence and Arezzo just to eat them with wild boar or rabbit sauce. We fried chicken over the fire and finished our lunch with Anita's pecorino and apples.

Well fed and content, Paolo and I packed our bags into the car, ready to lay two hundred places at Zio Franco's restaurant for his annual New Year's Eve dinner dance. During the drive there, my mind was full of *zoccoli, seccatoios* and lost Roman addresses. I felt that my time with Paolo's family had changed me. I had grown older and wiser. I understood so much more about the Consumi family's attitudes and behaviour. The Rossis and Consumis were from the traditional, old world but were living in the new world. It explained Giovanni's (and, to some extent, Paolo's) bad table manners. No one held any store by etiquette up here. Life was about the battle of getting food on to the table, not about how you ate it.

The way Gemma acted around Giovanni also now made sense. All the women here acquiesced to their husband's authority. Gemma's mother had been her role model. She knew no other way.

Paolo, on the other hand, had his feet in both camps. I wondered how he would cope with my family's expectations. Both my mother and father had modern attitudes towards sharing the housework and cooking. They were also sticklers for good manners. What would they think of the way the Consumis ate? Would Paolo always speak to me so sweetly, or would he take on the rude Tuscan tone of voice of Armando and Giovanni?

'Have you noticed how much your Italian has improved?' asked Paolo, as we pulled up outside the Trattoria La Baita.

'It must be the full immersion,' I laughed. 'There's not an English speaker for hundreds of miles.'

'Try rolling your Rs. I bet you can do it now.'

He was right. Out of my mouth came a perfectly rolled 'Rrrrr'. I could finally speak Italian fluently.

12

I stood in front of the rows of handbags, ready to attack them with a feather duster. There were dozens of them; shoulder bags, clutches, briefcases, duffels, all on glass shelves that lined long rooms and corridors similar to a series of underground, interconnecting rabbit warrens. Loraine had already started dusting down the back of the shop in the gloves and shoes section. As soon as she'd finished wiping the dust off the counters and shoeboxes, we would take out the tape measure and check our hips and thighs to see if we'd dropped any weight. Assessing our thighs was the highlight in an otherwise monotonous morning. We had to be quick, for soon another Contiki group would arrive for its talk on how all these leather goods were made. Then the group would be let loose in the shop and we would have to serve them.

I found my job as a sales assistant at Leonardo Leather Works just after New Year. It came through my contacts at the Red Garter. The owners of the two businesses had joined forces many years ago to offer tourist groups the complete service – shopping and drinking. Leonardo's is right around the corner from the Red Garter on Borgo de' Greci, a tiny street that connects Piazza della Signoria with Piazza Santa Croce. Thousands of tourists passed the shop every day. When not selling to them or dusting, a Florentine shop assistant passed the time of day by watching the myriad of nationalities and guessing where they came from. Rumpled Germans in their sandals with socks; the English, lightly dressed in the cold weather; and the Americans, the loudest and always in T-shirts that had something emblazoned on the front.

The clientele at Leonardo Leather Works was more varied than at the Red Garter, so I often found myself being mimed at by elderly American women trying to find jackets in their size. Some were on such whirlwind tours that my offers to help were brushed aside with, 'I'd rather wait and buy my purse in Florence, thank you.'

'But this *is* Florence,' I'd say.

'Oh heavens, no! Friday is Firenze, so we must be in Firenze.'

'But Firenze is "Florence" in Italian.'

'Well, whadaya know about that! Okay, whatcha got?'

I was in no position to judge their ignorance.

The same kind of shopper often asked if we sold anything by a fashion designer called Vera Pelle (which means 'real leather' in Italian).

'Ma'am, I've got the bags, jackets, wallets – you can have the whole Vera Pelle *set*!' I exclaimed.

Florence hadn't lost its magic. It was like living inside a sepia postcard. Winding through the maze of alleyways that led down to Piazza Santa Croce and Leonardo's, I loved the constancy of the earthy colours, the way the streets couldn't make up their minds as to where to go, so that you appeared to be meandering aimlessly, only you'd end up popping out on to a famous and lively little piazza.

Loraine and I were promised work until the end of the following summer, with a reassessment for next winter when Leonardo's could confirm the number of tour groups coming through. But Loraine was toey. She had a dream and she knew she never again wanted to live in England. For her, immigration to Australia was her future and a way out of Europe. Already in contact with the embassy in Rome, Loraine was in the process of applying for Australian residency.

Not so for me. I was going to go back to my home, only I didn't know when. No matter how much I loved it, staying on in Florence wasn't a consideration. My adventure was part of the travel experience, something every young Australian did before they settled down to their real lives and real jobs back home.

Paolo's family's stories, and how they had shared them with me, had touched a deep chord, but I had no feeling of obligation towards them because of it. I would be leaving them one day and didn't think about the impact that my leaving would have on them. A bit like Scarlett O'Hara, 'I won't think about that today. I'll think about that tomorrow.'

There was my career to consider, too – that is, once I'd decided what it was that I wanted to do. But the vocation could keep, because right now there was Paolo. Our love affair was fun. We were learning from each other, and giving each other what we needed. While I took refuge in his generous, caring love, he enjoyed being with a girl who loved him in a relaxed, easy-going way. He felt I gave him a unique insight into how another culture can live and love. Unlike an Italian girl, I asked very little of him. He didn't have to deal with my mother or father, nor did he have to share my time with my girlfriends. We shared the present without pressuring each other with thoughts about the future.

Paolo taught me the difference between saying *'Ti voglio bene'* and *'Ti amo'*, two very different ways of saying 'I love you' in Italian. A child, uncle or aunty, mother or friend can say *'Ti voglio bene'*, because it means I love you in a fond kind of way, but *'Ti amo'* can only be used between lovers. The Italians make a big distinction between the different kinds of love felt for your mother and for a partner.

In those days, the Italian language didn't make provision for the word 'girlfriend'. There was only *fidanzata*, which means fiancée. As the country became a little more liberated in its approach to young people having girlfriends or boyfriends whom they didn't intend to marry, the language adapted to accommodate them. Nowadays, someone can have a *ragazza* (girlfriend) or *ragazzo* (boyfriend). Paolo's friends and family only ever referred to me as Paolo's *fidanzata*. The title gave me kudos and security, but no feeling of responsibility towards him. Marriage to Paolo had never been discussed. We were still so young. It was unlikely that he was 'the one'.

A year in Italy can change a young woman. The anonymity makes you more interesting than you were at home, where everyone knows all about you and your family – and that improves your confidence. But for the daughter of a well-known personality, being anonymous let me become my own person. No one here watched the Australian media and saw

June Dally-Watkins tell the nation how to sit, stand, walk and eat properly. Therefore, no one had preconceived ideas as to how *I* should behave. I became, and was allowed to become, myself.

But it was also a battle to overcome the constant harassment from Italian men. What was novel at the beginning of the trip, especially when with the models, had become unnerving. Sometimes walking down the street was like running the gauntlet. Young men would whisper as I passed or refuse to make way. It felt like there were male eyes everywhere, watching. In cafés they stared shamelessly, as if girls were the most interesting object at hand to observe. Old men would put their hands in front of their faces, steeple their fingers under their noses and fix me with a concentrated gaze, like a judge contemplating the accused. Another man would lean back, his arms folded behind his head and look at me from under heavy lidded eyes. The staring was constantly intrusive, so that it was difficult to feel comfortable when out alone.

But, perversely, there was also a positive side to Florence, with all its flirty men. It made me feel beautiful for the first time in my life. When boys on motorbikes raced by and called out, 'Hey, *bella*. Dancey, dancey?' it was as though my femininity was being celebrated. In Italy, it is natural to compliment, desire, woo and pursue. In Australia, mateship and romance were confused and the dating rules were blurred and off-centre. My Florentine male friends stopped talking dirty and swearing when I was around, and they treated me as though I were a lady. In Australia, girls were expected to be tough and to take care of themselves. The sexes were so equal, it was hard to feel and develop any femininity.

As my faith in myself as a woman matured, so too did my taste in clothes. More and more, I started to acquire the Euro chic look. I loved my vintage cardigans (always will), but they no longer expressed who I was. The key to Italian fashion is simplicity, quality and strictly adhered-to colour selection. I now owned simple shoes and tailored trousers, which looked good with my new clean-line, dark grey and black jumpers.

Sure, I missed Sydney, but Mum and the boys were due to visit shortly and Mary McGlinchey, a dear friend, was already on her way over. There was my fluent Italian to show off, guided and knowledgeable tours of Florence to be conducted, and introductions to the boyfriend to be made.

Mary visited during her 'gap year' trip before starting law studies at university. When she climbed pillion on the Boxer, we hooned down the tiny alleyways and yelped with close calls and laughter. We went out for pizzas, and ran away from good-looking, lusty Italian boys who ogled and threw their phone numbers at us on folded bits of paper. Often we ate at the Consumis', where Gemma would force-feed Mary with commands to '*Mangia, mangia*! Eat, eat!' Mary's Anglo-Saxon protestations were far too mild for Gemma to understand, which forced me to intervene.

'*Non vuole piu, basta!* She doesn't want any more, that's enough!' I said loudly, until Gemma stopped putting food on Mary's plate.

'Who are you calling a bastard?' asked Mary, incredulous.

'No, it's *basta*! Not *bastard*.'

'Oh, thank God . . . I thought you were calling Gemma a bastard for overfeeding me,' and we'd crack up.

Until Mary's visit, Paolo and I had had a dream run with our relationship. Never a short tone of voice or a sharp word. So, when he came over one night and grumpily asked to speak to me alone, my skin crawled with dread.

'I never see you by yourself anymore. You're always with

Mary,' he complained, with his arms folded.

'Yeah, but Mary's visiting and she's one of my best friends and I haven't seen her for a year.' It seemed incredible that he could have a problem with that.

'*Si*, but you should not ignore me when one of your friends is here.' His voice had a childish tone I'd never heard before.

'True, but we've got a lot of catching up to do. Nothing's changed between you and me. When she goes, we'll still be together, but who knows when I'll see Mary again?'

He was jealous of Mary. And I was outraged at his proprietorial behaviour. The conversation ended badly when neither of us would give ground, resulting in a storm-off, then a standoff.

Over the next few days, I felt like there was a worm eating away at my stomach. I'd wake up in the morning feeling awful without knowing why, until I remembered that Paolo and I weren't talking. The sick grip on my stomach wouldn't let up until I went around to see him. I crept down the tunnel to his bedroom after Gemma let me in, knocked on his door, and then opened it to see him studying at his desk by the window. My entrance had broken the room's stillness, Paolo's immersion in an intense moment of study, his head and body bunched over his books. His head jerked back in surprise when he saw me.

'I don't want to be without you,' he said levelly.

'Me neither.' Our first fight was over. It was a long, long time before we had another one.

Mary went home with a bang after Paolo organised a secret visit to see the restoration of the Duomo's ceiling. Like in a scene from *Mission Impossible*, we darted in through the cathedral's back door to meet Paolo's friend, Luigi, so that he could smuggle us up on to the scaffolding while all the other painters and art historians were on their long lunch break. We climbed the four hundred and sixty-three steps to the top, then crept through a hidden door on to the makeshift wooden boards that skirted the circumference of the inner dome. Vasari's frescoes, *The Last Judgement*, were centimetres from our noses. Mary and I treaded around the boards softly, speaking in hushed tones, feeling as though we were in the presence of something holy and sacred.

Climbing back down, Mary thanked Paolo and Luigi profusely for giving us such a privileged viewing of the frescoes.

Mary whispered in my ear. 'Paolo is so *gorgeous*.'

I smiled contentedly.

'How on earth are you going to *leave* him?'

I looked back at her blankly, as though the thought had never crossed my mind. 'I don't know,' I said.

Hearing Mary say it out loud almost made me want to hush her, because by saying it, talking about it, she was making my departure inevitable and real. Unwittingly, Mary had planted a seed in my heart that from that moment onward grew bigger every day. Perhaps I should stay on here with Paolo. Or maybe it would be best to go now. Cut my losses before I got in any deeper than I already was. Perhaps my destiny is to stay on in Italy, after all. Surely not. I never planned on living here; I only ever wanted to visit.

It was as though I had ten different voices with twenty different opinions swirling around in my head. I shoved the voices into a box, put the lid on it and then placed the box in the back of my brain, until I couldn't hear the voices anymore.

Spring brought many surprises. Paolo the medical student became Doctor Giampaolo Consumi, the dentist. The radical change in his career path followed the passing of his exams and a toothache. The same dentist who had operated on Giovanni filled a cavity in one of my teeth and offered Paolo a job. The dentist was really an orthodontist and until now had been allowed to perform surgery himself, despite not having a medical degree. But the laws on who could practise dentistry in Italy had changed. This dentist needed a partner with a medical degree if he was to continue practising. So, while I sat with my mouth open in the dentist's chair, Paolo and the dentist struck an extraordinary deal that saw Paolo become an equal partner in the business, start work and earn good money immediately. My boyfriend was now a dentist, rather than a doctor – a change that offered limited sex appeal when compared with medicine. But he was employed, and that was the main thing.

Mum's visit was another change. Finally, my family was going to meet Paolo, and Mum was anxious about it. Our recent phone calls had been punctuated with delicately phrased questions about Paolo. When I'd left Sydney, Dad had told me not to fall in love with an Italian, or if I did, to at least make sure he was enormously wealthy or titled, preferably both. Mum had nodded in hearty agreement. They were both worried about their daughter's deep involvement with a man from the other side of the world and concerned about my future. Mum was on a mission now to find out whether Paolo was an Italian stud using her daughter as a plaything or a good boy with honest intentions.

The platform at Florence's railway station was already full of pushy passengers disembarking in a hurry. I tried to tell Paolo that Mum is always the last to get off any train or plane (manners = let others go first at all times), but I'd lost him in the crowd. When I next spotted him he was in the arms of my mother, who was crying and laughing and shaking her head as if she couldn't believe she finally had a hold of him.

'Mum, this is Paolo!' I said stupidly, as if she didn't already know that.

'We recognised each other,' she said, still laughing but standing back to look at the two of us together.

Later, back home with a glass of wine and our feet up, she told me that she liked the look of Paolo very much. 'He's clean cut, neat and handsome,' she said. 'He also seems very kind.'

Grania and Terry flitted in and out of the room and the conversation, adding comments like, 'He's a really nice guy, Mrs Clifford. You don't have to worry about him.'

Mum seemed content – and I was, too. Sitting in my Florentine living room with my mum was wonderful. As we chatted, it felt as though we'd reached a new level in our relationship. The talk was more adult, less mother to child, than it had ever been.

The next night, she was due to meet Gemma and Giovanni. 'I'd like to have them over here,' I suggested. 'They've never been to my place.'

'Great idea,' Mum agreed. 'More intimate than a restaurant.'

'But we can't cook Italian, because Gemma does it way better than we ever could. Hmmm . . . and Australian or English food is so boring – what about Chinese?'

'Indian?' said Mum, picking up on my train of thought.

'Yes! That's it! They've never travelled, so let's do something really interesting!'

It seemed like a good idea at the time.

Early-evening sunlight poured in through the French doors on to the table that Mum and I had set with any and every kind of Asian crockery that Grania had in the kitchen. Grania had also provided most of the ingredients for our Indian feast, as Florence only had one poorly stocked ethnic food store and its shop assistant became increasingly angry as we kept asking for things (cardamom, coriander, fresh ginger and garam masala) that she didn't have. It was probably just as well that we couldn't put more in our plastic bags because it was mighty difficult juggling Mum and all the shopping on the Boxer. I was worried about Mum riding pillion, but she rode like a trooper, at one stage almost wetting her pants she was giggling so much.

As we surveyed the table, we thought we'd done extremely well in view of the limitations of our ingredients. Lamb curry with coconut cream, spicy dry chicken curry and dhal. We'd kept the curry mild to mildly hot using fresh hot chillies from the markets. There were three kinds of condiments.

The balmy evening and recent daylight savings changes provided the extra daylight needed for Gemma and Giovanni to bicycle over to Poggio Imperiale, an all-uphill feat that greatly impressed my mother. When they arrived, sweating and happy, there was so much babbling and gaiety that I was hard-pressed to keep up with all the translating. I guessed they were just as relieved as Mum to be meeting 'the parents'.

We sat down and Mum, like a cooking teacher, dished everyone up, explaining as she went how this mango chutney should be eaten with the chicken and how to take some of the heat out of the curry by mixing it with the condiments. Mum finished and with a flourish of her hand said, 'Please start'.

There was silence at the table. Paolo had thrust forward his jaw and was absentmindedly scratching the stubble under his chin. Gemma looked like she wanted to ask a question (maybe something about the Indians in America?), only she didn't know which one to ask. Giovanni looked down at his plate with his eyebrows pushed so high he looked like he had a stack of pancakes on his forehead. A rumble started to emerge from Giovanni's throat, a deep smoker's raspy cackle. Then he was laughing, coughing, blotting tears from his eyes with the heel of his hand, his nostrils flaring like a set of bellows. Paolo caught the convulsions like a contagious disease, and then Gemma caught it, too. Mum and I looked at each other and started doing the 'heh, heh,' kind of laugh that showed we were missing the joke.

'*Ma siamo in Italiaaaaa,*' said Giovanni, recovering long enough to say, 'But we're in Italy,' with a lot of inflection on the *a*. '*Qui si mangia Italiano.* Here we eat Italian,' he went on.

'*Scusa, scusa,*' said Paolo. 'But my mother and father have never seen this kind of food and I think they're a little surprised.'

This was all before they'd even *tried* the curry. According to Giovanni, it was really the condiments that got him going. The yoghurt with cucumber was just beyond the pale. The bananas with desiccated coconut inconceivable. Even the plain rice was difficult for him to comprehend. The fact that there was not even a loaf of bread on the table was pretty much sacrilege.

From the Consumis' point of view, it was as though we'd played a practical joke on them. A very good one, too. Men like Giovanni are not interested in trying other foods. They want to eat, and eat well. He couldn't understand why we would want to eat anything else but Italian, so it was all highly amusing to him. The men then began to eat quickly, slowing down once the spiciness of the food registered.

'Pah!' went Paolo, to cool down his tongue with an airy exhale.

The third condiment, a small bowl of finely chopped fresh tomatoes with basil, disappeared immediately. To make Giovanni feel more comfortable, I made some more and also brought in some *parmigiano*, oil and bread. Gemma's curiosity bubbled over and her questions started to flow freely. Mum and Gemma shared their love of cooking and talked animatedly about Asian food. Every now and then, Mum would dash into the kitchen for an Indian spice to wave under Gemma's nose.

All my silly fears about Gemma and Giovanni being alienated because of their table manners dissolved. No one noticed how anyone ate. Etiquette was the last thing on everyone's mind.

Giovanni kept breaking into cackles. It seemed he had some excellent new teasing fodder.

'Wait till I tell Zio Franco what the Australians made us for dinner. Will you give him the recipe for the yoghurt dish? He might want to include it on his menu at the Baita. Ha ha!'

Mum saw the humour in it all and once the shock of the chilli and the condiments was over and the ice broken, everyone got along just fine. The three of them were such different people – Mum happy in the social pages, Gemma and Giovanni content in their vegetable patch. Yet, they seemed to click, maybe because they now had Paolo and me very much in common.

When we waved goodbye to them from the door, Gemma and Giovanni were riding off down the hill side by side on their bikes with Giovanni's arm slung affectionately over his wife's shoulders.

'Now, there's something you'd never see in Australia,' said Mum.

My brothers arrived the following week to find a fully planned itinerary had been worked out. Mum, a superb planner at the best of times, had outdone herself. We stood underneath the stars in Piazza della Signoria and listened to a huge orchestra play the '1812 Overture', using booming cannons for effect. Giovanni gave us tickets to the opera at Teatro della Pergola. Paolo drove us to Siena and San Gimignano on day trips, and took the boys on his motorbike to the hills, searching for the best views of Florence. Marc and Tim said they liked Paolo very much.

'He's a really nice guy,' said Tim after returning from a ride in the countryside with Paolo. 'He only has one problem,' he went on.

'Oh?' said I, all ears.

'He lives in Florence.'

After I waved Mum and the boys off, it took me days to shake the sadness that had settled around my heart. Their visit had reminded me of how easy it was to be with fellow Aussies in a conversational sense. Talking with my brothers was relaxed, the joking natural, the connection comfortable. Never was a word or phrase misunderstood. Never was there a reference to a famous person or political figure that I hadn't heard of. Never was there an anecdote that I didn't understand. I realised that my conversations in Italian were hard work and often superficial, because my vocabulary could only go so far. I had missed communicating with Australians, but I hadn't realised how much until now.

This new, unsettled feeling began to affect the way I related to everything around me. Italy was now tinged with constant comparisons to Australia. Instead of being different and exciting, it wasn't as good as back home. The siesta time started to bug me and I wished I could work through until five in the afternoon and then go home for a swim. The way people drove just made me angry. The way they spoke seemed impatient and rude, instead of kind and well mannered.

My impatience with what I saw around me started to filter into my relationship with Paolo. He (and the rest of Italy) had the terrible habit of throwing his garbage out of the car window or dropping it on to the footpath. Rather than gently teach him about the importance of taking care of his environment, I became angry, called him selfish, and went on to accuse the whole country of being filthily irresponsible. He never took my ranting personally, but rather would say, 'OK, you're right. I'll try to remember. Though I'm sure if I forget, you'll remind me.'

He was patient and thoughtful about my endless comparisons of Italy with Australia, even agreeing with most of my negative observations. Italians are often the first to put down their own country, so embittered are they by years of systematic corruption and abuse of their laws. Whereas I would jingoistically defend Australia, outraged by any suggestion that my country was anything less than the best place on earth to live.

However, we still loved each other. The sight of him walking towards me made me catch my breath and think, 'Wow, I can't believe he's mine'. Paolo bundled me up in his own special brand of secure love and accepted me for what I was. Regardless of our differences and my growing impatience with Italy, as a couple our harmony was strong. It was only when he was around his friends that our different wavelengths clashed.

Much of our weekend time was spent on the motorbike. Paolo had printed 'LISA' in big gold letters across the back of my black helmet. Every Saturday we joined Paolo's best friends, who all had powerful bikes, to ride out in convoy to an isolated, ancient little village. The group had made a nickname for themselves – the Gruppo FIST, taken jokingly from an old Sylvester Stallone movie that I had never seen. We'd roar into town, park our bikes and then line our helmets up along the windowsill of an out-of-the-way restaurant.

On the way home, images of rustic olive groves surrounded by medieval stone walls, or of cypress trees rising along luscious green hillocks, flashed by. Little piazzas where old women bent over their needlework or hung out their pasta to dry made indelible impressions on my mind, as did the niches on the sides of the roads with their shrines to the Madonna nursing a baby Jesus in front of a shelf of plastic flowers.

It was all beautiful, but something was changing inside me. I had started to crave the familiar.

This was my frame of mind when, in July, Paolo suggested we both take a week off work and go to the seaside holiday town of Rimini. It sounded like balm for my blues. A beach lover and walker from way back, living away from the sea had been unnerving at times. It felt weird not being able to see the sea, smell the tide going out or jump into the waves after a long, hot day. I felt like a kid who wasn't allowed to go to her favourite playground. I'd tried to explain to Paolo how water is a big part of a Sydneysider's life and that being without it had taken a lot of getting used to. He knew I'd been suffering from *malanconia* – melancholy thoughts – and felt that some time out at the beach might help. The gesture was typical of him. If I had a problem, he always tried to help me resolve it.

On the day we were to leave, I was sitting at the garden gate with my backpack when Paolo's motorbike roared up the street. But instead of allowing me to jump straight on to leave, Paolo motioned for me to wait for him while he carefully propped the bike on its stand. With his hands shoved deep into his jacket pockets, he walked over and smiled broadly.

'I wanted you to have this so that you could wear it while we're away,' he said, passing me a little brown box with gold writing on the top. As I flicked if open, my heart skittered with emotion. This was the first time a man had bought me jewellery. Inside was a small, simply cut, dark-blue sapphire and gold ring. While looking up to thank him, I gingerly tried to put it on my right hand.

'No, it's to go here,' he said, pointing to my wedding finger.

My eyes widened as I tried to figure out what the ring meant.

'I want everybody to know that you're mine.'

We never discussed whether the ring signified that we were engaged.

While clinging to Paolo's back for two hours at high speed, my mind wandered away from Italy and saw what it wanted to see. There were images of being a kid in a red one-piece Speedo on Bondi Beach, getting dumped so badly I had sand burn on my elbows. Of my little yellow plastic kickboard with the handles on the side for catching waves. Of how Dad would wipe the sand off my feet before he lined the towels across the back seat of the brown Valiant, which could easily have doubled as a fine pottery furnace in summer. Of the itch inside my T-shirt as the sea salt dried on my fresh sunburn. And of how we were all hosed down on the front lawn before we were allowed inside the house.

Rimini was the seaside antithesis of these memories. About one hundred and forty kilometres east of Florence, Rimini is on the Adriatic Sea, directly opposite the coast of Croatia. Though you can't see it, you know it's there. A sandy stretch of at least fifty kilometres, this holiday destination isn't one of the tiny inlets that are featured in glossy travel magazines. There are no exclusive cafés with colourful awnings over tables in flagstone bays. There are no wealthy Milanese wearing fabulous tans, chunky gold jewellery and white linen as they stroll Rimini's beachfront road. There are no luxury marinas with rich Romans dining off the back of expensive yachts. Rimini isn't the Italy that the world imagines when they think of the Italian seaside; yet, it is indeed one of the country's most popular beaches. This is where the real Italy, the blue-collar and blue-singlet set holiday for one week to two months every year.

Mostly families, they drive down from their crowded northern industrial towns to spend as much time as they can afford in the same *pensione* every year. It's the only time they'll see the sea all year and they savour every salty breath. The traditional Italian holiday has always been to travel within Italy to the same place. The children come with their mums and dads, then grow up and holiday with friends until they marry, have kids and come back to Rimini to holiday again.

Paolo's family had been staying at Rimini's three-star Rolex *pensione* since he was a child. There are photographs of Giovanni looking distinctly uncomfortable on a deckchair in his trousers, singlet, and shoes and socks, as he could never bring himself to don a swimming costume. His bricklayer's T-shirt tan strikingly obvious, Giovanni also had a hankie with the corners knotted on his head. Other photos show Paolo in rubber jellybean beach shoes (there were crabs in the sand) and a hat (to prevent sunstroke), cuddling a collie or a Shetland pony, both animals supplied by a professional photographer on the beach.

Rimini's beachfront is a maze of cafés and entrances to the many different *bagno*, or bathing areas. The beach itself is divided up into one hundred-metre stretches of sand, each millimetre owned and managed by a *bagno*. Each *bagno* includes dozens of *cabinas* – little changing rooms next to showers, playground areas, zones with tables and music, or bowling areas for the oldies. Every *bagno* has a different theme, like the 'Sirena', which is all white with blue and silver mermaids on the walls. Or the 'Oasis', which has lots of perfectly manicured grass lawns with loads of plants and a waterfall. The 'Mirage' has a mirror theme with everything painted in light blue, navy and white stripes. The 'Maestrale' look has polished wooden decking with a red-and-white-striped colour theme. From the road down to the sea, the beach is lined with umbrellas and matching deckchairs. Towering above the *bagnos* are loudspeakers that pump out advertisements for local businesses.

'What a profound invasion of privacy,' I said to Paolo as I

tried to relax in spite of the ceaseless ads for restaurants, hair salons and bikini shops.

'*Rape* is a profound invasion of privacy. Stop exaggerating.'

'Harrumph.'

There is no public space on the beach – the *bagnos* own the sand down to the sea and each one rents out umbrellas and chairs for a fixed seasonal price. For example, today, an umbrella and a chair (the minimum available) for the weekend would cost around twenty euros (forty Australian dollars) – plus another five euros for a stretcher-type cot. In July, a place on the beach will cost you around fifteen euros (thirty dollars) a day. And Rimini is cheap. At Viareggio, northeast of Florence on the Liguria Sea, it's thirty-five euros (seventy dollars) a day and at Forte dei Marmi up to fifty euros (one hundred dollars) a day. The beaches open on 1 May and must all close on 30 September.

It's a long walk through the slime until you can put your head under water. Rimini's beach was eroded by the wash of the sea, so the council decided to dump piles of large rocks about fifty metres from the shoreline to stop the sand being swept away. The move saved the sand, but caused the water to stagnate, which formed the algae. Consequently, a swim means dodging large floating clouds of green slime. The sand, imported from elsewhere, is so fine it sends up dust plumes when you walk. Not that your feet ever have to touch the sand. The *bagnos* come complete with little plastic runways that make a comfy (and squeaky) pathway to your umbrella and the sea.

There's always plenty to do; windsurfing lessons, paddle-boats and canoes to hire, beach volleyball, and the *bagnos*' outside bar areas always have music and, now, electronic games. With so much entertainment on the beach, one wonders when there is time to relax. But the Italians have this all worked out, too. You relax when you eat, and you eat often and *a lot*.

The fact that your *pensione* is only a three-star establishment means absolutely nothing when it comes to food. Ninety-five per cent of all Rimini's hotel accommodation is three-star, which will provide you with breakfast – bottomless cups of juice and café latte, a selection of fresh pastries, fresh mini-rolls with a tray of hams, salamis and cheese. No one has heard of muesli in Rimini.

Lunch at the Rolex was buffet style. A typical midday meal included three types of pasta dishes, followed by meat (steak or roast beef or chicken), roast potatoes, spinach sautéed in garlic, and salad, followed by cheese and dessert. No prizes for guessing why the Italians drink such tiny cups of strong coffee after lunch. Then it was everyone up to bed for at least two hours. All this costs around twenty-five euros (fifty dollars) a day. But what you save on the hotel, you spend on the beach.

At around four in the afternoon, people start to reappear on the beach, in fresh swimming costumes. I was the only bather who appeared to have only one costume. Even the children had five or six pairs of togs, which were changed regularly throughout the day as they became sandy and salty.

Dinner was served at eight and always started with a soup or broth with little *pastina*. It was marginally lighter than lunch in that you could have mozzarella and tomatoes or an omelette instead of the veal *parmigiano*.

By day two of our holiday, I felt myself complacently slipping into an overfed stupor. There was no burning hot sand to compete with on a five-kilometre walk back to the car, no disappointment in finding that there's not a shop or tap within a ten-kilometre radius that offers water. Here there were chairs in the shade, fancy fountains to cool my dehydrated feet, showers at the water's edge to rinse under, cafés at every turn. It was all so easy, so pampering. Yet, niggling away underneath my almost vacuous brain was guilt. Where were the trees? Where was the space? The clean water? Where was the beach, dammit? The contrived scenery and cosseted people were getting to me. I believed that beaches should be natural environments and, above all, free. I felt like a hypocrite, a traitor to the cause. To try and explain it all to Paolo seemed ungrateful, even churlish. He was paying for this trip (he never let me pay for anything, ever), so it seemed wise not to complain. Sometimes he did appear to understand my exclamations of shock, such as when a boat with loudspeakers passed by spruiking in competition with the loudspeakers on the beach. But when I launched into a description of what beaches are like in Australia, he started to look weary.

The most beautiful time on the beach is sunset. The water laps calmly underneath a pink sky, streaked with orange. But this is the precise time that you'll find the streets and beach of Rimini empty. Everyone is indoors eating or getting dolled up for their evening *passeggiata*. No one seemed to notice the special peace that had descended upon the beach after its busy day, because, like cows ready to be milked, they all followed each other home for their rigorously adhered-to feeding schedule. It all conspired to make me long for familiar ways of living. Only the longing was manifesting itself in more than just impatience now. This was unhappiness – ridgey-didge, true-blue homesickness.

Another winter passed before my need to leave became as glaring as a set of headlights on high beam. There wasn't much discussion about it with Paolo; there wasn't any room for it. My lack of fulfilment in Italy was stifling our relationship, getting in the way of its growth. Paolo offered me commitment, security and financial generosity. But I felt we were too young for all that and besides, it was time for me to develop a career. Italy was holding me back.

On the surface, Paolo took the news well, but he had been expecting notice for some time. I had a sneaking suspicion that his masculine pride wouldn't let him express anything more than mild disappointment. Anything more would have been a sign of weakness, in his eyes. In the weeks leading up to my departure, he fell into the swing of our impending goodbye and was almost cheerful. After almost two years of absorption in our love affair, we were both excited about the prospect of a free future. Paolo had become one of the fastest amateur motorbike riders in Tuscany and had wanted to spend more time out at the professional motorcycle circuit, Mugello. It's more than likely he harboured secret dreams about turning professional and wanted to dedicate himself to his hobby. Whereas on sunny Saturday and Sunday afternoons, I dragged my heels about going out to Mugello to track his time and sit around in the greasy pits. Maybe I was holding him back.

'Hi, Mum. I'm coming home in two weeks.'

'Darling, that's wonderful. But what about Paolo?'

'He's fine about it. Actually, I think he's even looking forward to being single again.'

'Are you leaving each other for good?'

'I don't know.'

'Is Paolo upset?'

'A little bit.'

'Do you still love him?'

'I think so.'

'Oh, dear.'

Frankly, I was too selfish to care about any sadness that Paolo may have been feeling. Thoughts of Sydney sent me into breathless spins of excitement. I was bursting out of my skin to get back home. I had my new look, my gorgeous new Italian clothes, handbags and shoes, and I was dying to show it all off. In the end, Paolo and I held each other tightly, kissed, promised to keep in touch and never to forget each other. Then we wished each other luck and joked about what our futures would hold, sort of celebrating our separation as if it were a new awakening in our lives. But we never mentioned the possibility of either of us being with someone else. That's where we drew the line – other boyfriends or girlfriends. No, no, no. That didn't bear thinking about.

Gemma and Giovanni were just about to leave for a weekend up at Pratiglioni when I stopped by to say goodbye. Paolo had already told them I was leaving, so they were expecting me.

'*Ritorni in Italia?*' said Giovanni, standing by Gemma's side at their front door. His question, 'Are you coming back to Italy?' made me feel uneasy.

'Don't ask her that,' said Gemma, seeing me hesitate. 'She needs to see her family, that's all.'

Giovanni reached into his breast pocket for a cigarette, lit it, inhaled deeply and surveyed me. I didn't know what to say.

'She'd know whether she was coming back or not. It's not a tough question.'

Under his scrutiny, I felt like a child who had failed her

father. Giovanni looked like he wanted to admonish me, but was holding back.

'Maybe one day I'll come back, Giovanni.'

'Don't forget us,' he said, with a gruff kiss. He stepped back inside with Gemma and abruptly shut the door.

13

The good thing about having a mother who runs her own business is that you can always come back from a long overseas trip and walk straight into a job, especially if that mother wants to pass her business on to you. Training began immediately, with the model and deportment schoolteachers taking me under their well-groomed wings to show me their classes. The afternoons were spent in Dally's model agency learning how to negotiate deals for the models and book them into their jobs. It was no secret that Mum had earmarked me as her successor. She even had a new nametag made up for me – Lisa Dally-Watkins. Wearing it was out of the question. I am very attached to my name and felt that my identity was being challenged enough under the weight of the charm-school business.

Before long all the deportment, modelling, photographic posing and television-commercial classes fell to me. Nobody questioned this, or my return. It was the natural order of things. Young Australians travel, and then come home to settle down. The business would one day be mine and, goodness knows, with my Italian wardrobe, largely paid for by Paolo and Mum, I looked the part.

My friends greeted me with excited hoots and screams and hugs. Having been without their special acceptance for so long, talking for hours over white wine or coffee was enormous fun. One forgets when travelling that true old friends rarely judge. When you say something silly, they know you well enough to know that you may not mean it tomorrow. Years of knowing each other have created a deep bond of understanding. In the end, going home is all about the welcome and security of old friends and family.

The girls wanted to know everything about Paolo. Yes, his English was good. Yes, he was kind and generous. No, he really was very Italian in the way he thought and acted. No, he's not coming out here. Hmm, I don't know how I feel about him now.

Yes, the ring is from Paolo. No, it wasn't an engagement ring, more of a friendship ring, that's why it's on my right hand now instead of my left. No, I don't miss him, I'm too busy learning how to run Mum's business. It's time to get on with life in Australia, not Italy. No, I don't think I can be the next June Dally-Watkins, it's just that I can't think of anything else to do at the moment.

Carel and I shared a bright and airy apartment in Bellevue Hill. Her own model agency, Models Worldwide, was in the same city building as Dally's and doing well. Together we lived and breathed our mother's business.

Only, in the long run, what's right for your mother isn't always right for you.

Most Saturdays while we were growing up were spent at beauty contests. Marc and I were too young to stay at home alone, so Mum would take us along while she picked the winner in the Miss Grace Bros, Miss Beach Girl, Miss Showgirl or Miss Australia quests. Miss Roselands was always my favourite because it was held under a fabulously huge fountain that stretched from the ground floor to the top floor with water that dripped down thousands of fishing lines.

In the 1970s, most of Sydney's malls and shopping centres had some kind of beauty quest. There were always lots of Misses waiting to be discovered and set on their path to stardom with a June Dally-Watkins modelling career – her course was their prize. Mum, the main judge, model spotter and sponsor, would sit up on a podium at a table with the other judges. A long catwalk, usually lined with red carpet, would connect the changing room to the stage. The girls would model in their high heels and swimming costumes before coming back on stage to twirl in their evening or daywear clothes. Marc and I would whisper our thoughts on each girl to each other, then get bored and wander around the shopping centre. Towards the end, Mum would always call us over to ask our opinions. We were so proud as we made our way, embarrassed but thrilled, behind Mum's table so that she could confer with us on our choices. Now the audience knew she was our mum and we beamed with happiness.

During the school holidays, we would go with Mum on her Asian fashion tours to Manila, Hong Kong, Singapore and Bangkok. Travelling with a bunch of beautiful girls always opened doors, so there were many privileges and special invitations wherever we went. At home, models with bandaged faces and black and blue eyes would recline on our couches while they recuperated from nose jobs. Gay fashion designers swanned around the kitchen preparing 'drinkies for Mummy' upon her return home from work. Mine was a sophisticated and modern upbringing, well before it became groovy. But through a child's eyes, these were people and things that I had to compete with for Mum's attention. So, in a selfish way, I started to resent my mother's business from a very early age. It was like living in one big strongly female-oriented family, a matriarchal society in which Mum was the matron and the point of everyone's convergence. In view of how jealous I was of the business, I should have known that Mum's path wouldn't be mine.

When Mum accepted an invitation to debate feminism with Germaine Greer on Channel Nine's *Mike Walsh Show*, which subsequently became *The Midday Show*, my brother Marc and I were thrilled to be included in the live audience. This television appearance was more exciting than usual, because twelve-year-old Marc was desperate to get Mike Walsh's autograph in his brand-new autograph book.

We were seated in the third row of the studio audience when the lights were dimmed and the 'Applaud' sign flashed. Everyone clapped as Germaine Greer, an international identity who is greatly respected for her analysis and promotion of sexual equality, walked on to the set and took her seat. Germaine didn't have a high celebrity rating in my ten-year-old mind. It would have been *really* cool if Mum was being interviewed with Moonface-Bert Newton, Paul Hogan or, better still, Strop. All I knew about Germaine Greer was that she had published a book called *The Female Eunuch* and that Mum strongly disagreed with it, but I didn't know why.

When Mum was introduced, applauded and seated, the cameras rolled and Mike started the debate off by pointing out the different attitudes that both women had towards feminism. Then the gloves were off . . . and, ready for a good intellectual sparring, Germaine ripped into Mum about the June Dally-Watkins creed that rejects feminism in favour of 'femininity'.

Miss Dally, with her usual grace and poise, barely had time to collect her thoughts before she was under attack with another pummelling of pro-feminist punches. Mum had some good rebuffs in defence of her argument, but she was mincemeat at the hands of Germaine, whose sheer force of aggressive energy made Mum's polite reasoning sound ineffectual. Germaine believed that women were living in a male-driven world and that there were massive inadequacies for working and married women; that women were slaves to their men, were overlooked and under-cared for.

Miss Dally: Women should highlight their feminity and get to the top using it.
Germaine: There is no top to get to, because men bar the way.
Miss Dally: I've achieved my own goals without burning my bra or putting men down.
Germaine: You're an attractive woman. Not all women have the same advantage. It's time for all women to seize equality and write their own destinies.

They were two women dedicated to the same goal – promoting women. Yet, they were the antithesis of each other in how they went about it. Their antipathy was evident during their televised appearance.

The harsh studio lights shone down on to my perfectly

groomed mother, her pale pink silk shirt and smart corporate jacket, with her long legs superbly folded at just the right angle under a skirt that was just the right length. Germaine, in comparison, had no makeup and a mane of long, tussled brown hair. She wore simple black pants and a nondescript red shirt that looked messy.

But I could see that *what* Germaine said was more important than the way she looked while saying it. My heart began to skip quickly because maybe, just maybe, Germaine was right. She made sense to me. Oh, no! I was on her side and not Mum's! The conflict about who to root for in this debate made my stomach lurch. I had a fiercely protective loyalty towards my mum, but Germaine had twigged a realisation in me. I knew then, with a squirming discomfort, that I was a naughty feminist. I doubted I would burn my bra and couldn't wait to shave my legs, but I knew at that moment that I was going to grow into more of a Germaine than a Miss Dally.

All in all, it wasn't such a good day because, during the rushed ad break, Mike Walsh ended up dedicating his autograph to *Dear Marcia*. Marc was devastated.

Ironically, I was up on the dais judging a beauty contest for June Dally-Watkins when I found my true vocation. Feeling sorry for the downcast losers, who were giving half-hearted, disappointed smiles on my right while the winner gave a delirious-with-joy, sparkling smile on my left, I made the 'Every girl's a winner' speech. Afterwards, one of the other sponsors of the Wollongong Miss Beachgirl quest, a director of the WESGO radio network, approached me and told me I had a good voice for radio.

Oddly, radio was an industry that had always fascinated me, especially radio news. The WESGO man's timing was perfect. With his encouragement, the idea boiled and bubbled until I knew without a doubt that radio journalism was the perfect career choice for me. Yes, I would learn the ways of the wily world then personally communicate the truth to the people, carry the message across borders, infiltrate corruption, and break news stories that would change the system. I had a very honourable attitude towards journalism. I wanted to save the world.

When I resigned, Mum took the news well. 'But what are you going to do? You only know the modelling industry.'

'I'm going to be a radio news journalist. First I'll get a job doing volunteer work at my local radio station 2RES FM, then I'm going to apply for a scholarship at the Australian Film, Television and Radio School,' I told her confidently. That's what the WESGO man had said, so I followed his advice to the letter.

By Christmas that year I'd won a scholarship to study at AFTRS. It was a compact six-month course and on graduation I was hired by radio station 3BO in Bendigo, a goldrush-era mining town two hours north of Melbourne. One year after leaving Paolo, I was off to Victoria to start my career in journalism.

Dubbed The Centrepiece of Victoria, Bendigo burgeoned in the 1850s when tens of thousands of hopeful gold diggers from all over the world flocked to the area to make their fortunes. Some of the town's architecture is original, giving it a cosy, Victorian-era feel. It's a thirsty town, with a country pub on many street corners, some of their entrances shielded from the sun and rain by red bull-nosed corrugated iron. In the early 1980s, Bendigo's coffee shops hadn't yet become trendy cafés. They were homely restaurants run by middle-aged women who served homemade relishes, jams and chutneys with tea and damper or scones.

It was a terrific town for a young journalist to work her way through her early errors in broadcast news. The people had a forgiving sense of humour (3BO is nicknamed 'The perspiration station' and 'The armpit of the network') and took kindly to a city kid sent to the bush to learn the basics of radio. Every green journo makes mistakes; it's to be expected. Only, some young journos make the standard mistakes and then go on to invent a whole new, previously unheard-of set of bloopers, faux pas and on-air stuff-ups. I'm sure that when the peeps went off and the evening news started with Lisa Clifford, the Bendigo listeners turned up the volume and settled back for their nightly ten minutes of comedy.

First I pronounced the names of nearby towns such as Tatura, Nagambie and Moama with an Italian accent, where the emphasis is on the first syllable, and all vowels at the end of the word are duly pronounced. Second, I was so keen to do a good job that the DJs often took advantage of my enthusiasm. Like when I was doing the live Saturday morning news preview.

DJ: Lisa Clifford's coming up shortly to tell us all about the Bendigo news of the day. What's happening around town, Lisa?
Me: Well, the Eaglehawk Dahlia and Arts Festival promises to be a real feast for the eyes this year.

DJ: We'll look forward to hearing all about that . . . and Lisa, do you think you could do a traffic report for us?
Me (sounding excited and honoured at the prospect): Of *course*. I'd *love* to.
DJ: Great, when a car goes by, you'll let us know.

I may even have been responsible for 3BO's radical increase in telephone calls. When the Bendigo Neighbourhood Mediation Centre opened to help and handle all those arguing neighbours, a simple spelling mistake saw my announcement read out as the Bendigo Neighbourhood Meditation Centre. In retrospect, they may have done a lot better getting the bickerers into meditation rather than mediation.

At night, putting a pre-recorded news tape to air was permissible if I had to attend a council meeting or press conference and couldn't be in the studio to read live. On one particular occasion, I managed to pass the wrong recording on to the DJ so that halfway through the bulletin 3BO listeners were treated to a loud 'POO, BUM, WEE' before going on to Take 2. That was a far sight better than a young journo before me who had made the same mistake; only he had said, 'FUCK, FUCK, FUCK.' The last time I saw him he was a reporter on Channel Nine's *A Current Affair*, so it couldn't have harmed his career too much.

The only way I managed to get through my stuff-ups was because my editor, whose nickname was Turps (there were only two journalists in the newsroom), was the kindest man ever to grace Australian radio news. Graeme Turpie stood by my every mistake and encouraged me to persevere.

In the 1980s, Bendigo had a rural and city population of around seventy-five thousand. (It's now around ninety-two thousand.) There were enough people to keep the police force, a team of detectives and the courthouse relatively busy. It was all good for learning about crime and court reporting, essential beginner's knowledge for any reporter. On occasion, high-profile politicians would come through and make themselves available for interviews. Turps usually provided me with a list of questions 'to get them on', but for some reason when Jeff Kennett, the Victorian Premier, came to Bendigo I had no prepared question list. No matter. I had formulated a question all by myself that would really pin him down.

As the Melbourne media that had followed the Premier to Bendigo crowded around him in what's called the scrum, Mr Kennett answered the questions of state importance while I waited my turn.

'Mr Kennett,' I yelled, my heart pumping with adrenalin. 'Why are you here?'

His eyes searched the scrum until they found mine.

'I was invited, so I came.' Then he smiled hugely, turned to his minders and said, 'That girl's got a big future ahead of her with hard-hitting questions like that.'

Life as a young journalist learning the radio ropes in Bendigo wasn't all about stuff-ups. With endless patience, Turps taught me how to reduce the number of words in a story down to three or four short, punchy paragraphs. How to cut out the fluff and leave in the important facts. He helped to sharpen my on-the-road interview skills and demonstrated how to dub on to cartridge tape for on-air use.

One of the biggest issues for a young radio journalist is overcoming the fear of being live on air. While you wait for your cue to read the news, the studio is deafeningly quiet, as still as a padded cell. The 'thump, thump' of your nervous heart is so loud that you're sure the audience can hear it down the microphone. It takes months of practice to learn how to control your vocal wavers and tremors while you deliver the news live. There are times when things go wrong, causing a blind terror to rise behind your eyes and tighten your throat. Live news reading was a nerve-snappingly hard slog for me. But it was also tremendously stimulating and fulfilling. Being a journalist had to be the best job in the world. No one else was at every important event in town. Be it the yearling sales or a murder hearing, every day was interesting. Gradually my news delivery improved, and listeners heard less stumbling and misfiring audiotapes and more professional news bulletins.

The same couldn't be said of my Bendigo social life. It never progressed. I felt as if I'd have to run naked past a construction site to get the boys to notice me. In clubs there were no invitations to dance, and in pubs no one, except workmates, ever bought me a drink. Essentially, I had nothing in common with Bendigo men. I guess they weren't into the Euro-chic look which, in the end, only served to make me look different from the Bendigo girls.

Most nights I'd tumble on to my bed, exhausted. There was a sliding glass door in my bedroom through which I could see a paddock complete with white-trunked eucalyptus trees with long sinewy branches and rustling leaves. The grass was green, cropped low by the cows that grazed there during the day. As the sun set over the bush on the horizon, the cow pats started to look like deep black holes in contrast with the white clusters of dry, hard, long grass that were like the sharp spears that had pierced Zia Maria's armpit. A weatherworn, rickety old fence surrounded the paddock. It closed with a lilting gate and a large link chain to a hook on a post. The paddock was country Australia, and I loved it.

Then, when it was dark, I would curl up and feel alone. Painful aches would squeeze my heart as I thought of Paolo. The hollowness of missing him was like a secret layer of my true self that no one knew about. At the end of the day, I peeled off the professional and social layers until a private and painful layer of longing was exposed.

Images of his face or body would loom before me then flash away again, as though he was haunting me. I missed watching the way his fingers were drawn to his brow for a massage when there were important issues to think about. I missed his rumbling, deep voice and his take on the world and what was happening.

But underneath the layer that missed Paolo was a tight level of pressure. The voices that I'd put in the box at the back of my brain when Mary was with me in Florence clamoured for release. Australia or Italy? If you have Paolo, then you can't have Australia. If you live in Italy, then you can't have a career. If you can't have a career, then you'll be financially dependent upon Paolo for the rest of your life. That was the reality. And those equations would never change. Missing Paolo made me feel pressured to give up Australia and all the opportunities that my own country provided.

I hadn't uttered a word of Italian in more than two years and rarely spoke of the time I'd spent in Florence. Talk about Paolo always made me feel uncomfortable. So, like a treasured memory that had no bearing on my current life, I kept him to myself. He seemed familiar but distant now, like a favourite character in a much-loved movie. What was he up to? Was he seeing someone? We were writing letters, but at a rate of about one every four to six months. His letters were humorous, fondly expressing concern for my well-being. But he never said 'Come back', and to telephone each other would have been tantamount to giving in, backing down – almost like saying, 'I want to get back together again'.

Then came a call from Mum.

'Darling, my dear friend Shirley Wakefield has just come back from Florence. She saw Paolo while she was there. I didn't think you'd mind if I passed on his phone number.'

My breath caught. 'How is he? What did Shirley say?'

'She said that Paolo talked constantly about you. Apparently, he still loves you very much and wants you to go back to Italy.'

A feeling of total resignation washed over me. To know that he still loved me made me feel like giving up the fight. It was as though a wave of emotion was washing away the layers of pretence. I gave in to the tears and let them stream down my cheeks.

'I think about him a lot.' My voice was small, tired.

'Well, then, why don't you give him a call? He was such a nice boy.'

'Yeah, but he lives in *Italy*!'

'Just call him.'

So, I did.

14

We stood hand-in-hand at Santa Maria Novella train station, smiling shyly at each other, feeling awkward and self-conscious. My phone call from Bendigo, only one month before, had put us back on a lover's footing immediately. Our voices had been soft and tender with affection. We'd decided that I should quit my job immediately and come over as soon as possible.

When I stepped off the train we'd hugged for the longest time, silent, not moving – just holding each other. But then we became hesitant and unsure of what to do or say next. With no phone-call distance to hide behind, we found ourselves giggling nervously at each other. As we carried my bags back to his car, I stole peeks at him and caught him doing the same. It was as though we couldn't believe what we'd done. We were back together again, which made us look at each other and break into almost delirious laughter.

Paolo had changed in the two years that we'd been apart. The hair at his temples was grey. He had lost his boylike, carefree look and gained more of a mature, manly appearance. His skin was drawn more thinly over his cheeks as if he'd dropped puppy fat that I'd never noticed he had. He was fitter, though not broader. I found him very attractive in his black leather bomber jacket, black jumper and jeans. He had that European casually well-dressed look that in those years the rest of world was trying to copy, but never achieved with the same panache.

'Like your jacket,' I said.

'Like your hair,' he replied. 'It looks good longer.'

'You're going to have prematurely grey hair, like Giovanni.'

'*Si,* but I can always dye it.'

'Yuk. Don't you dare.'

It felt strange to be sitting in his little car again. As Paolo negotiated his way through the tiny streets, an unexpected surge of joy made me smile at all the city's familiar sights. Being back in Florence felt good, which was odd because while in Australia I had thought that I hadn't missed it at all.

*Bumpety-thump*ing along the cobblestones past the breathtaking beauty of the Duomo and on past the clay-coloured houses, I felt a surprising sense of ownership towards it all. So much of my past had been shared with Paolo here. Perhaps Paolo and Florence were a package, after all, so that when I longed for him, in some ways I was actually missing Florence, too.

On the way over on the plane I had done the soul searching I should have done before I spontaneously threw in my job. Leaving had been a manic, mad rush, with little thought given to the consequences of moving in with an Italian man that I hadn't seen for two years. No one was particularly surprised at my farewell; in fact, most of my family and all of my girlfriends were breathless with encouragement and excitement. They all thought the rendezvous with Paolo was swooningly romantic. It was as though they were living their fantasies through me. 'You'd be mad not to take a chance on a Florentine love,' they said. Buoyed along by the fluttery fairytale, level heads never asked questions because dreamy hearts were in control. Once we were in the air though, there was time to think. Was I crazy to give up all my plans to become a successful journalist for an Italian lover? He was a trustworthy guy, but would he really look after me while I was so far away from home? By the time the plane was descending into Rome, quitting Bendigo and 3BO appeared to have been the right decision. If things didn't work out with Paolo, there was always a return ticket home and time to start again. Youth was on my side and the moment to follow my heart was now.

'You've been going to the gym a lot. You look really fit,' I said to break the silence.

'I've taken up karate.'

'Wow, I'll have to watch myself.'

'Don't worry. I'm not lethal yet.'

Silence. More silence.

'Amore, tutto bene?' said Paolo, sensing the strain of uncertainty in the car. We weren't talking much, the giggling had stopped, and our conversation was starting to sound stilted. But, ohh! Just the sound of that word, *amore*. My

heart ricocheted out of my chest. *Amore*, the way he said it with his soft rolling R's – 'My love, is everything all right?' It melted me so fast I almost slid off my seat.

'I'm fine. It all feels a bit funny, that's all. Culture shock, I guess.'

He reached over to hold my hand. His touch was incredibly reassuring.

It was lunchtime and Gemma and Giovanni were waiting for us at what was to become my new home – Teatro della Pergola. Paolo wouldn't hear of me staying anywhere else. The idea of living at the theatre with his parents didn't make me feel uncomfortable. On the contrary, it gave me a sense of security. Gemma and Giovanni were my Italian mum and dad – they were home base. A couple living with a boyfriend's parents is practically unheard of in Australia, whereas in Italy it isn't uncommon. Florentine rental apartments used to be as rare and expensive as hen's teeth, making it nearly impossible for many young couples to set up a home. Anyway, it was far too early in our relationship to become a de-facto couple. We were like the thousands of other young Italian couples forced through lack of money and available space to live in the parental home, only we were different in that we weren't yet married.

Italian parents like their children to be close by, so these living arrangements suited Gemma and Giovanni just fine. It's not exactly spying, but by 'living in-house' they would know exactly how their son's relationship was progressing. No doubt they thought we were at a prelude to the marriage-and-grandchildren stage, a most desirable prospect for them, though they would never have pressured us into wedlock. Paolo would have been furious at any intrusion into his pace and plans. He had always been protective of his private life, in stark contrast to many young Italian males who rely on their mothers for advice and support. In Italy, there is a name for the male behaviour of hanging on to a mother's apron strings – *mammismo*, and men who practise it are called *mammoni* – mummy's boys. Fortunately, Paolo had never exhibited any *mammoni* qualities. He was quite unique in this respect, because a recent study showed that one in three Italian men sees his mother every day. Almost all felt it was their duty to telephone their mothers every day, and almost every man interviewed wanted to eat with her more than once a week.

In respect of Paolo's mother, I had also appeared to pull another lucky card. Gemma appeared not to encourage *mammismo*, and this too was out of sync with the rest of Italy. This is the only country in the world that runs successful schools for mothers on how to 'let their sons go'. The courses have titles like, 'What will become of my darling son?' Italian mothers and their interference with their daughters-in-law are the cause of relationship breakdowns in more than a third of marriages. Hopefully, Paolo's mother wouldn't drive me to the same distraction as many other Italian girlfriends and wives.

When I walked through the Consumis' door, the last two years seemed to dissolve away into nothing. Familiar smells floated along the corridor. From out of the kitchen came Gemma, nervously wringing her hands just like she had on the first night we met. She was flushed with excitement and I felt a rush of love for her as we hugged. She'd spent the morning making *nudi* (the naked spinach and ricotta balls) and *spezzatino*, my favourite beef and potato stew. It was her way of saying, 'Welcome back'.

Giovanni was already in position at the table. He'd opened a new flask of red wine and had a cigarette in his hand. He hugged me warmly but stiffly, in the way that gruff men not comfortable with physical displays of affection do. Then he put his teasing into top gear – *his* way of welcoming me back.

'*Come si sta in Italia, eh?* Life is pretty good in Italy, isn't it? *Non potevi stare senza di noi!* You couldn't go on without us!' he joked.

Giovanni's ribbing helped to dispel a weird feeling of déjà vu. I'd been a part of this lunch scene many times, though the pictures that I had replayed in my mind were two years old. Here I was again, and nothing had changed. It was as though someone had taken a faded photo and computer-digitalised the image to give it a fresher look. Gemma and Giovanni also acted as the extra parties that Paolo and I needed to take our nervous focus off ourselves.

It felt wonderful to speak a foreign language again. Stumbling through my sentences in an Italian that was rusty but still good, I told them I was now a journalist. They didn't seem to think that journalism was anything special. It was as if they didn't know, or want to know, what becoming a journalist had entailed. They seemed only to care about the here and now.

After lunch, I followed Paolo to his bedroom. The room was the same, apart from one change. His single bed had been replaced by a big double bed. I fell on it, exhausted.

'Have you been doing a lot of entertaining on this new bed while I've been away?'

'No, no. I bought it for you.'

'Your parents are being so lovely. Do you think they mind

that we're sleeping in the same bed together under their roof?' I was concerned that I may have been compromising them in some way.

'No, no. We always slept together at Pratiglioni, remember? They don't care. It's not as if they're both at church confessing their sins every Sunday. They're Catholic, but not *that* Catholic. They've missed you. Now go to sleep and I'll wake you for dinner.'

Paolo pulled the shutters closed while I changed into my pyjamas. It was winter in Italy, a rotten time to come back. But as Paolo snuggled in beside me, I loved the feel of the thick, warm doona over us while the freezing wind rattled down the street. There was a pleasant thread of thought running through my mind as I drifted into a peaceful sleep: Paolo would be there when I woke up.

15

The winter symphony season of Teatro della Pergola was in energetic *allegro* mode when I settled into my new home. There was rarely a time when the walls of the Consumis' apartment weren't pulsating with the uplifting crescendo of a classical performance or rehearsal. Every night from eight, the floors fluttered with Vivaldi, Cimarosa or Mozart. Banal Saturday morning showers became waterfalls of rhapsodies when the orchestras rehearsed the great concertos of the masters. On Sunday afternoons in front of the TV, our coffees were rippled by matinees of romantic piano by Chopin.

Built between 1652 and 1657, the Theatre Pergola is one of the world's most romantic theatres. Similar to the one depicted in the film *Moulin Rouge*, the Teatro della Pergola has sixty-six gilded gold and beige private boxes, on three floors. The boxes line curved walls that sweep from the thick red stage curtain to its spectacular entrance, a fourteen-metre-high glass and wrought-iron doorway. An ornate glass chandelier with thirty-three bulbs hangs over the foyer through an elegant line of marble columns.

Behind and around the elegantly polished theatre is an ancient rabbit warren of corridors and tunnels. Off from these passageways are the changing rooms, hot water and heating systems, storerooms and custodians' apartment. The Consumis' tunnel-like corridor ran from the kitchen down the length of the backstage area. At one end of the corridor was Paolo's bedroom and at the other end was his parents' bedroom and the bathroom. It was only this corridor, with its dark, low-vaulted ceiling, that separated our bedroom from the opera and ballet performances. A door directly opposite Paolo's bedroom led into the enormous off-stage area where ropes and massive spotlights hung from beams across the stage. The Consumis' home was almost inside the stage.

Every night before showtime, elegantly dressed theatre-goers would gather under Paolo's bedroom window. Their happy chatter made me want to stick my head out of the window to look at them all. Lying on our bed, I could hear the audience murmur while they sat in their plush red-velvet seats waiting for the show to start. Then the orchestra would begin and our room would swell and sway with violins and cellos.

Not that we bothered to listen, or even to see many of the shows. We were so totally absorbed in ourselves and the new music that I'd brought over from Australia. While classical music hovered in the corridor, we shut our door tightly and turned up Neil Young's *Harvest* or Alan Parson's Project's *Pyramid*. We lay on our bed, with the stereo speakers above our heads, and talked. It was like we were living in a void where no one else existed. Our world was only us, Paolo and me, in our inner sanctum; kissing, feeling, listening and singing to the guitar. I had never felt more loved or protected.

Every day, Paolo had to go to his surgery and work. He came home for lunch and siesta from one until three. Then he came home for dinner at seven-thirty. I spent the days walking around Florence, visiting the museums, looking at Michelangelo's *David*, exploring the Uffizi, checking out the food and clothes markets, cooking with Gemma or reading. I had no friends of my own in Florence. Loraine had gained residency in Australia, Terry had married and moved to Perugia to open a bookshop with her husband, and Grania had moved to warmer climes in Greece. My days were structured around waiting for Paolo. I couldn't wait to hear him zip up the road, my ears specially tuned to singling out the sound of his *motorino*'s souped-up engine. By the time he'd parked, I'd be at the window waving. He'd run up the stairs and I'd be at the door ready for him to swing me into the air as if I were Nonna Angiolina.

Always in the background were Gemma and Giovanni smiling benevolently at our antics. As with everything in their lives, they were happy if their son was happy. Giovanni, however, was adamant about one thing. He wanted me to go to the police station to register myself as a foreigner living in their home. That was the law. Only, Paolo and I were too lax to bother. When finally the days turned into weeks and Giovanni could stand it no more, he knocked on our bedroom door after Paolo had gone to work.

'*Vieni con me dalla polizia.* Come with me to the police,' he said in his sternest voice. 'If Paolo won't take you, I will.'

I pulled on my jeans, grabbed my jacket and passport, and headed out the door, scampering to keep up with Giovanni. He liked to shove his hands into his jacket pockets and whistle or smoke while he walked.

The *Questura* (police headquarters) was about a two-kilometre walk away. There wasn't much to talk about on the way, as Giovanni didn't have much conversation. Up to now, our conversations had revolved around him taking the mickey and what it was like growing up at the farm. It wasn't that we didn't like each other; we just had nothing in common, apart from his son.

A compound that took up a whole block of the city's centre, the *Questura* sat behind thick stone walls. When we arrived, a queue of foreigners snaked down the road for at least thirty metres. In anticipation of their long wait, the Filipinos had brought thermos flasks and picnic baskets, the Arabs sat or slept on colourful cushions and rugs, and the Somalians and Tunisians made themselves as comfortable as possible on ripped-up cardboard boxes.

'Oh, no,' I moaned.

'That's not our queue,' said Giovanni. 'Not unless you want to apply for residency and a work permit?' He looked at me curiously with no hint of a smile. In his heart Giovanni may have wanted me to, but he wouldn't have tried to influence me.

'No, not right now, thank you.' I felt like I was declining a cup of coffee.

He grunted and continued past the queue, through the *Questura* doors to a desk where a military policeman gave us a form. Written like a questionnaire, the form asked my intentions in Italy. Three months into my stay in Italy, and though very much in love, I still had no idea as to whether I wanted to live in Florence permanently. Marriage with Paolo was a distant possibility, but I felt far too young to embark on that course of action.

I ticked the boxes that indicated I was to live with the Consumis for six months while I studied Italian. I handed it back to Giovanni to sign.

'Apparently, you can stay legally for six months. Then you either have to re-register or leave,' said Giovanni, as we walked back past the long line of hopeful immigrants.

'Right.' I honestly didn't know what to say, so I didn't say anything until we got home. Then I said, 'Thank you'.

'No, don't thank me. In Italy, we don't thank family.'

It was such a kind thing to say that I thanked him again. He shook his head, lit a cigarette and walked down the corridor back into the theatre.

I was now truly under the Consumi family's wing. I thought about mentioning rent. Australian children often pay some sort of a rent when they live with their families. But a gut feeling told me that the Consumis would have been very offended if I mentioned it. The months slipped into more months while I stayed on at the Theatre Pergola. They never asked me how long I planned to stay or when I was going home. I was grateful to them for that.

Any hopes that Paolo had harboured of becoming a professional motorcyclist had been dashed during my time back in Australia. He wasn't fast enough, and his dentist's surgery was doing far too well for him to quit on a whim to race. However, his love of speed hadn't diminished with the dimming of his racing star.

As had been the case several years back, our social life was largely conducted on the back of his motorbike. His Gruppo FIST mates were still his best friends and the group's main activity was still motorbike riding. Time, however, hadn't made these daredevils more responsible on the roads – they were crazier than ever.

After several espressos on a Saturday afternoon, a destination that involved a route full of curves for maximum corner consumption would be chosen. Then we would head off into the countryside where all the men competed with each other. Not for first position, but for speed, style and grace on the road. These trips were beautiful, and I enjoyed them. But if we ever had to go further afield, to places such as Bologna, Arezzo or Viareggio, the Gruppo FIST would take the autostrada, the Italian highways. Along these unbroken stretches of roadway, the one hundred and twenty-kilometre speed limit was posted for convention rather than adherence.

When Paolo started to top speeds of one hundred and ninety kilometres an hour, I was terrified. At such intense velocities the wind force was so strong I couldn't even hold my head up. Feeling like I was on a suicide mission, fear and fury erupted and I would scream at Paolo to slow down. The Gruppo FIST's speed addiction had to be put down to cultural ignorance, because no one else seemed to mind the danger. In any case, motorbike riding had lost its appeal. The bright side to this was that Paolo started to enjoy my preferred mode of leisure transport – horses. Once he stopped mistaking the reins for handlebars, Paolo found that galloping gave him the speed fix he craved. On Sundays we'd often make for San Casciano, a village south of Florence in the rolling hills of Chianti, near Siena. A riding school at Ponte Rotto (Broken Bridge) would hand over their horses and we'd canter off on to a hillside so perfect it looked like the plasticine landscape of a child's train set.

At night we'd go to the Red Garter, where a different group of friends partied until early in the morning. They were mostly English-speaking expatriates with whom I felt on more common ground. At two in the morning we'd pop into the bakery behind the Red and buy hot pastries, before moving onto the Yab Yum, the city's hippest disco.

Above all, I liked to go up to Consuma and have lunch at Zio Franco's restaurant. Everyone hugged me warmly and said how pleased they were that I'd come back. That's when I really felt like I belonged in Italy. We'd walk in and sit down beside the roaring fire at the table reserved for family. If it became busy I'd pitch in with Simona, Zio Franco's daughter, and help to ferry the *tortellini di patate* back and forth from the kitchen to the tables. Zio Franco's sister-in-law, Zia Piera, would be in the kitchen pink-faced from stirring the steaming sauces and pastas. Her lovely smile looked like it was reserved just for me.

When early summer rolled around, Paolo and I escaped more often to Pratiglioni where the air was fresh and clean. We went for long walks through the woods, spying deer, wild boer and pheasants. Paolo's parents owned the woodland on one side of the gravel road that led down to the farmhouse; the land on the other side was state forest. There were hectares of protected pine forests full of *porcini* mushrooms and wildlife. We'd walk to the spring for water and sit by the stream for hours. Then it was back down to Florence on Monday, ready for Paolo to start his working week.

One day I came home and was surprised to find Paolo hanging around the front door, waiting for me.

'Go into the dining room and see the new dining-room table that Mamma bought,' he said oddly.

'I hope you turned the heater on or I'll freeze in there,' I said, joking about the room that was used as a coldroom/larder during the year and a dining room once a year at Christmas.

There was no new dining-room table, but there was a beautiful piano sitting in the corner.

'Where did you get this?' I cried.

'I rented it for you. Maybe you'd like to start having lessons again.'

I couldn't believe his thoughtfulness. But as I hugged him in thanks, I also knew he'd intuited that it was time for me to get busy.

As wonderful as my life with the Consumis was, boredom was starting to itch at my feet. The last months had been carefree, like a prolonged holiday. But it couldn't go on forever.

'I also think you should do an advanced Italian course. Clean up your grammar and increase your vocabulary.'

Paolo was right. It was time to fill up my days with activities that gave me a sense of accomplishment. He knew that if I didn't, it would only be a matter of time before boredom got the better of me.

Soon the watermelon and coconut carts started to appear in Florence, heralding the arrival of the very hot and humid months, July and August. My Italian course had come to an end, leaving me once again to wander the medieval streets and ponder my life and its future. One day, after trudging through the crowded streets, I came back to the Consumis' house complaining about the number of tourists.

'You can't even walk down the street!' I wailed. 'The tourists don't make way to let you pass. They're everywhere!'

'*Si*, even living in our own home,' said Giovanni with a cheeky grin.

It was difficult to make out what they felt about having a potential Australian daughter-in-law. They only ever tried to make me feel like one of the family. But as the summer months heated up, so too did Giovanni's jokes. His bantering took a new turn, as if he was trying to tell me something.

'*Devi stare li.* You have to stay there,' he said to Gemma, pointing to the stove. Even though his tone was in jest, everyone knew he was serious. He wanted good food twice a day, and to get it his wife had to be at the stove.

'I'll buy you a chain, Giovanni, so you can keep her there,' I said in defence of Gemma. But Gemma would dismiss my defence and defend her husband.

'Ah, Lisa, if you want to keep your man happy and at home, you have to cook well.'

Was there a message here? Or was I becoming overly sensitive?

The longer I lived at the Theatre Pergola, the more I saw potential problems for a future between Paolo and me. Paolo did nothing to help around the house. When he came home from the gym, he left his bag at the door so that his mother could clean, wash and dry its contents before repacking it with fresh workout clothes. When she didn't do it right, he complained like a petulant, spoilt ten-year-old.

'Mamma, where are my gym shoes?' he would yell angrily.

'They're on the windowsill drying,' Gemma would reply meekly.

'Go and get them, or I'll be late,' Paolo would growl and off Gemma would trot to fetch the shoes that he could so easily have retrieved himself. Perhaps it was his way of shaking off any potential maternal clinginess. By being rude to her, he kept her at a distance and could never be accused of being a *mammone*. Or perhaps his behaviour was just another brand of *mammismo*, because she kept him childish by never scolding him as a mother should. In any case, his behaviour was making me lose respect for him and his mother.

I also found it difficult to understand why Paolo and Giovanni never complimented Gemma on her delicious cooking, even though she always produced something marvellous for their lunch and dinner. When I asked Paolo why no one ever said her food was good, he explained that his father felt that complimenting Gemma would have stopped her from trying harder. Giovanni didn't want Gemma to become complacent in the kitchen, so he never praised her.

Giovanni ate like a caveman, and Paolo wolfed down his food like his dad. If there was a potato or a slice of meat left in the pot, Giovanni or Paolo would snatch it up before anyone else could get to it. In Italy, it's the men who are served first, receive the finest cuts of meat and are offered the last morsels in the pot.

Immunity from Giovanni's manners was perhaps possible, but I could never ignore the way Paolo ate. He was on the fast track to eating like his father. Perhaps it sounds petty or snobbish, but I knew enough about love to know that meals with your boyfriend are important and if his table manners disgust you, love can't last. Attraction becomes revulsion.

The best solution was to tackle the issue head-on. So, I started to tease Paolo about his table manners, hoping that by using Tuscan humour he would get the message and clean up his act. It worked for a little while, because Paolo had been educated by, and eaten meals with, some of the country's top doctors, so he knew that his behaviour at the table was unacceptable. But his bad habits quickly returned, because he had no family standards to adhere to. Nor would he make any changes for me. He thought my fussiness was typically 'female' and culturally based.

For the moment, I had to overlook Paolo's tantrums and table manners. It was too hard to retrain him with his mum and dad around. Rising above these sticky situations would require a de-facto relationship, a living arrangement that was gaining appeal. Though Gemma didn't intrude upon us, neither did she allow me to help around the house. And though she didn't walk into our bedroom unannounced, she did do her fair share of snooping.

Our room was our haven, and I regarded it as a private place that only I would tidy and clean. Not so Gemma. Every morning she would sneak in to remake our bed with tight hospital corners. No amount of protest worked. Any attempt at putting our clothes through the washing machine was met with, 'No, no. I'll put the colours in this batch and the whites in that batch,' or 'Eek, don't put the washing machine on that temperature, you'll shrink everything!' Life was like a home economics class and I was failing. I took to hiding my used underwear so that I could at least wash those myself, but she burrowed deep into the cupboard and found them. They reappeared the next day washed, ironed and prettily folded. I gave up the fight at maintaining domestic duties, because I realised that Gemma actually enjoyed doing them for us. Even so, I found it intrusive. My privacy felt compromised.

By the time Paolo started his annual August holiday break, we still hadn't made up our minds as to what to do about 'us'. For Paolo, there was no urgency. His life wouldn't change, so it was easy for him to cruise. For me, a decision had to be made. To stay or go? I loved him, but as time passed my heart reeled with uncertainties that undermined my love for him. When we left for our holiday by the sea, there was a gnawing feeling that I was in an adult relationship and it was time to think seriously about marriage and children. But I was scared witless about the whole children thing.

16

The Italian seaside did nothing to increase my maternal confidence. Mothers lined the shoreline holding out terry-towelling robes for their children, ready to bundle them up into their warm arms, even though it was forty degrees. They often carried their children back to their deckchairs so that their little feet didn't get sandy. Some children screamed hysterically and demanded they be carried. Kids as old as ten stood immobile while mamma changed them into dry swimming costumes three times a day.

I made it my business to listen in on their conversations and watch how families behaved, and I was shocked to discover how little the children did for themselves. Mamma did everything. I could see why Paolo spoke so badly to his mother. All the children did. The mothers made themselves so available to their children's every whim that the children had no respect for them.

At the beach playground, mothers ran after their children, calling out '*Amore, non correre, sudi.* My love, don't run, you'll sweat.' When I asked Paolo what the women meant, he said that if the children got too sweaty they might catch a chill. I laughed out loud at this and then poured out my worries to Paolo. My way of mothering would be completely different from the Italian way. The children here were too spoilt, coddled and over-protected. Australians tended to let their kids run free and sweat as much as they wanted.

'Just bring the children up your way,' Paolo said, giving me a hug.

'But everyone will think I'm a freak.'

'It doesn't matter what everyone else thinks. The most important thing is that *we* agree on how to bring up our children,' he said.

The actual process of giving birth in Italy also gave me the willies. There were loads of stories about sturdy midwives jumping on contracting stomachs to push babies out. As for the care of the babies themselves, Paolo's own cousin's child had been dropped on its head during a caesarean delivery. When the bruising and swelling on little Francesco's head became apparent (they weren't told of the fall), the hospital denied any knowledge of an accident. Only when they went ahead with legal action did the hospital staff admit to letting Francesco slip through their fingers. The maternity hospital staff was prepared to put Francesco's life at risk rather than admit to a mishap. Paolo himself was paranoid about his baby being mixed up with someone else's, because of the media hype surrounding past neonatal confusion. Then, going through the birth and the period of looking after a tiny newborn baby without the comfort of having my sister or mother around was the icing on the cake.

'Have the baby in Australia without me,' said Paolo, looking so mournful that we immediately dismissed that option.

My resistance to having children in Italy went even further. What if my child got sick? I was worried about not understanding the language if something really went wrong with my kids when Paolo wasn't there. The thought of having a tiny sick baby, being stressed and stumbling through a poor explanation of symptoms to a doctor and risking my children's health chilled me.

Paolo held my hand and listened carefully to my concerns.

'I'll always be there to help you,' he said.

His reassurance didn't bring me much comfort.

The indecision and fear of the future surrounding my impossible love affair had brought on another emotion, one that I'd never before experienced: depression. In theory, I was the luckiest girl in the world; a handsome, loving man who lived in one of the world's most beautiful cities was willing to care for me for the rest of my life. In reality, there was nothing to do in Florence except wait around for him, learn Italian and visit museums. So what if Italy housed seventy-five per cent of the world's art treasures? I wanted action, not Botticelli.

The depression always followed the boredom, and loneliness accompanied the depression. A happy wake-up mood was sustainable until Paolo left for work. Then the whole day loomed ahead like an empty cinema screen. The pictures to fill in the blanks couldn't be found because the depression locked me into lethargy. Going back to selling handbags was an option, but my career snobbishness made a lifetime spent working as a sales assistant look exceedingly unappealing. I wanted to be a journalist; in fact, I *needed* journalism for my self-worth and self-identity. But how could I report *here*? I didn't have the experience to file radio stories from Italy. I was a 'no one' with one year's experience at 3BO.

One of the strongest messages that my mother had given me as a child was about work. A woman, she would say, must have a career. 'If he walks out and leaves you with nothing, you'll survive if you have your work. If you have no career, you'll be left with nothing.' Her advice was part of my programming. I felt insecure and beholden relying on Paolo for money. Then there were my expectations. My upbringing had trained me towards taking over a large, successful female-oriented business. I was too ambitious – a stay-at-home life would never be for me.

Towards the end of the year, I could take it no longer. There was no purpose to my existence in Florence, apart from a man. Italy was devoid of anything else – there were no friends, no family, nothing that belonged or represented the essence of me. There was always a pain in the corner of my heart, and the ache was about being so far away from the people I loved most and having to decide on whether or not to leave them permanently. A love affair was no longer a good enough reason to stay. The dilemma was that I wanted Paolo, but I didn't want Italy. And I felt too young at twenty-three to decide either way. Sometimes I didn't even think I knew what love was.

As I lay on our bed, seeped in a black mood while waiting for Paolo to come home, unfamiliar sounds would come from outside the window. At these times I felt like a powerless outsider, unable to break through a barrier that separated my world from the foreign activity outside. The buses roared by with a different engine noise; the motorbikes and mopeds whined, wheezed and whizzed. The sounds were different from home, and my depression prevented me from rejoicing in the difference. I felt dislocated and at odds with my surroundings. Only the comfort zone of my home and family could banish the bleakness I felt inside.

When Paolo bounded into our room, he was happy and voluble about his day, while I was sad. He resisted asking what was wrong. He didn't want to know. My mood swings were difficult for him. Whenever I told him what was wrong, it sounded as though I was criticising everything about his life. It made me feel guilty and him helpless.

When finally I told him I was getting too depressed to feel as though I could ever be happy in Italy, he threw himself on the bed.

'Well, go home then, and I'll come as soon as I can. All right?' He propped himself up on his elbows and leaned closer to gauge my reaction to his suggestion.

'That's a *fantastic* idea. God, that would be *great*,' I said, leaning over to kiss his face.

'We'll work out what to do when I come to Sydney.'

As soon as I knew that I was going home, the weight of my confusion lifted from my shoulders and I felt as light as a bird. It was as though someone had switched on the light and the brightness flooded in. I was instantly happy.

While Paolo and I sat holding hands talking about when he could come to Australia, the orchestra across the corridor started to tune up, sweeping off-key violin and cello notes into our bedroom. The musicians' chairs scraped on the wooden stage as they settled into position before their sheet music. My spirits soared with their concerto as I realised our relationship no longer depended on my permanent relocation to Italy. Now there were other possibilities. Paolo might like Sydney very much and decide to move there. Maybe we could live between Australia and Italy.

'*Si mangia,*' Gemma yelled down the hall. Dinner was on the table and Paolo's parents were already seated, impatient to eat and get off to work.

Sitting down at my place across from Giovanni, my face beamed with good cheer. I chirped, '*Buona sera, a tutti.* Good evening, everyone.'

Gemma placed her hearty minestrone before me. She and Giovanni weren't fooled. They hadn't missed my recent lack of humour and Gemma's eyes were examining my face. Only this morning she had insisted I help her prepare the *topini* for lunch. *Topini* means 'little mice', and they are a lighter, Tuscan version of the classic gnocchi.

Gemma had knocked on our bedroom door soon after Paolo had gone to work. '*Su, su! Oggi non si legge a letto. Vieni ad aiutarmi!* Up, up! No reading in bed today. Come and help me.'

Her cure-all for listlessness was a flurry of domestic activity. We'd stood in the kitchen, side-by-side, and mashed and rolled the potato mixture into little sausage shapes while she'd prattled gaily away to a morosely silent audience.

Bluntly, Giovanni now asked why I was so bouncy. 'Is there good news?' he said with a hopeful edge to his voice.

My enthusiasm about leaving evaporated. I suddenly felt terribly guilty. For a year the Consumis had treated me like their daughter. They had accepted me unconditionally, with warm and generous care. They had never pressured me into staying or going, and had never enquired as to whether there were any marriage plans afoot. For all their giving, they had never asked for anything in return. I felt so ungrateful. I looked sideways at Paolo and hoped he would be the one to tell his parents that I was going.

'*Lisa ha deciso di tornare a casa,*' said Paolo, looking squarely at them both. 'Lisa has decided to go home.' As still as stones, Gemma and Giovanni looked at me.

'Paolo's going to come to Australia next summer,' I said, feeling this would lighten things up. There was a burning need to make things better.

'Are you coming back?' said Gemma. It was the question they all wanted an answer to.

'Sure, I'll *always* come back.' It sounded so trite. As though they were children being absently waved away with a careless, 'Of *course*, silly.'

In truth, the future was a mystery – open-ended. They probably sensed that, because they asked no more questions, leaving everything to Paolo. Too stricken by a sorry conscience to say much to them, we finished the evening meal quietly, planning only to meet up at Consuma the following weekend for goodbyes to the rest of the family. I would depart shortly afterwards.

Just as Consuma is the hub of the Consumi family, the little town of Stia is hub to the Rossi sisters. Stia is in the heart of eastern Tuscany's Casentino mountain area, about twenty kilometres on from Consuma. Its woodland and farming fields are dotted with sixteenth- and seventeenth-century castles, monasteries and fortress-like abbeys. Stia's population thrived throughout the harsh winters by harnessing the power of the Arno River to run textile mills. The town is buttressed by thick stone walls that run alongside the Arno, with several ancient bridges to link the two banks. In summer, the river's rock pools are open to the public for icy, invigorating swims.

On Saturday afternoon, we met Vani, the son of Zia Anita (the aunty still living on the farm) and his wife Adriana, in the crooked, sloping Stia piazza so that little Francesco could safely waddle beside the old fountain. As happens in Italy's piazza system, which can be likened to Australia's bush telegraph, word of my departure was out. Zia Anita's daughter Daniela soon arrived with Zia Maria's daughter Claudia, and as we left the piazza café to convoy our cars up to Zio Franco's for dinner, more distant cousins came out of their houses and shops to say farewell. Each auntie and uncle asked if there was a plan to return to Italy, and to each of them I said, 'Yes'. They were happy with that and thought that Paolo's plan to visit Australia was the next logical step in our relationship.

On Sunday, the Rossi aunties and Nonna Angiolina came up to Pratiglioni for lunch.

'Oh, your mamma will be so happy to have you with her.' They nodded and patted my hand, full of sympathy for a mother who had been separated from her child. Nonna Angiolina sat huddled beside the flames in the huge grate. She gazed at her daughters silently before passing me a plastic shopping bag. Inside was a pale pink shawl, soft, long and tasselled.

'I made it for your mamma. You tell her I hope to see her wearing it up here soon.'

She let her gnarly, arthritic fingers linger on the shawl, then turned her face back to the fire before drifting off into her unassailable world.

After lunch, Giovanni settled on to the couch as the women cleared the table and moved into the kitchen to wash up. As was Paolo's habit after lunch, he slipped away up the stairs for his siesta. As I moved to follow him, Giovanni called me over to sit on the couch next to him.

'Do you see the family crest on the wall?' he asked, pointing to an old painting of a maneless lion that was dancing on his hindquarters in profile. Written underneath the lion in bold black italic print was:

Famiglia Consumi
Nobili di Ferrara ai tempi di quel Ducato,
1482,
La Consuma

I nodded and wondered about the significance of the lion's unnaturally long, pointy tongue. It flicked audaciously out of its mouth, while above the lion was a five-pointed crown.

'When my family came to Consuma, there was nothing here except trees and snow.' He shifted on the couch to turn and face me. Never had I seen Giovanni's face look more serious. It felt strange to be so close to him, to have such one-on-one attention from him.

'We were a noble family from Ferrara. That's where Paolo's blue eyes are from. We have northern Italian blood. In 1482 the Duke of Ferrara declared war on Venice. The Duke sent the four merchant families that did business with the Venetians into exile. There were two hundred and fifty people in all. There were the Romeis, the Bandinellis, the Alberonis and the Consumis – each family ordered to leave their homes and businesses because of the wrong affiliations. The families decided to travel together to Florence. Along the way they decided they had three main priorities: find work to survive, stay a united force, and watch and wait until the crisis was over so that they could move back to Ferrara. But the war went on for years and they knew then that none of the families would ever return to their homes. The expulsion was permanent. The Bandinellis and Alberonis decided to stay in Florence and continue as merchants. The Romeis bought a castle at San Gimignano and farmed. But the Consumis wanted to own more than just arable farming hectares. They wanted to possess land as far as the eye could see. Land that could never be stripped from them.'

He paused to look at me to see if his words were sinking in. They were. Paolo had never told me this story. Giovanni went on.

'The Consumi family went as high up into the Tuscan mountains as they could, where no one before had dared to settle. Up here my ancestors knew they were safe and would never again be exiled.'

The women in the kitchen were putting the coffee on trays, starting to filter back into the room. Giovanni looked away from my face to the doorway into the kitchen before going on. He lowered his voice, as if he didn't want anyone to hear what he was about to say.

'Giampaolo is the last in the line of men that came from Ferrara. There are no more Consumis from Consuma after him. I want you to think about that when you return home and when you come back. Giampaolo must have children. Give my family the respect it deserves. Don't waste Giampaolo's precious time.'

'*Si*, Giovanni,' I said, my heart pounding. Now wasn't the time to ask about the meaning of the lion's flicking tongue.

The women broke our silence with chatter and coffee.

Giovanni kept his head turned steadfastly to the fire. I stood and went up the stairs and lay down on the bed where Paolo lay sleeping. Everything Giovanni had said churned inside me. He was right. The Consumi family didn't deserve to be picked up and dropped by an indecisive Australian girl.

If ever I returned to Italy, I'd have to marry Paolo.

17

Whirr . . . screekle . . . screeech!

The sound of the voice tape rewinding always made me think of secret satanic messages. I listened for them a lot, sometimes rewinding songs on a slow speed to find the allegedly hidden verses that were meant to subversively influence our thinking, but I couldn't pick any out. Mucking around with songs on tape while gazing dreamily out the window was my favourite pastime during the slow news moments over my weekend shift.

When radio station 2UW hired me, it had a leafy outlook on to Rangers Road in Sydney's Neutral Bay. From day one, the newsroom's vibe felt custom-made for me. Landlines and two-way radios that connected us to Perth, Melbourne and Brisbane chattered away in every corner of the room. Tapes ran over international news bulletins that buzzed with British BBC accents and American CNN reports. Phones rang and the journos typed. I felt important just being there. Everyone would jump up with serious expressions on their faces and run with much urgency into the padded recording booths to put down their stories. It felt like the centre of the universe – a thought echoed by one of the journalists who, on my first day, said sarcastically, 'Welcome to Sydney's nerve centre'.

Before 2UW changed its name to Hits FM, it was an AM station with a 'Classic Hits' or 'Hits and Memories' format. Short, thin men with surprisingly deep voices introduced 'all your old favourites' during the day. At night the lines were open to melancholy callers who rang in to dedicate their choice of romantic love song.

The 1980s were the years of plenty in Australian broadcasting. The 2UW network had the money to throw resources at its newsroom, enabling it to grow into a well-respected information source with a Sydney staff of about twelve. Every hour we relayed bulletins across New South Wales to the smaller country stations that didn't have newsrooms of their own. 2UW's news director, Pam MacKay (at the time, Australia's only female news director), hired me on the strength of my voice. She planned to train me in police and court reporting, as well as weekend news reading. That meant weekdays spent out on the road covering the evening's unfolding crime stories before following them through to their conclusion at court during the day, and weekends spent writing and reading the hourly news bulletins on my own.

Ecstatic at being employed, I'd go down to College Street Police Headquarters early every morning with a merry skip in my step to hear all about last night's violent events. Journalists representing almost every Sydney radio, newspaper and television station straggled in at the same time to morosely share the reports. Joviality wasn't a common characteristic among the journalists at these 6 am press conferences. Usually in a better mood was the police public relations person, who sat behind a table happy to dish out details of the previous evening's horrors – perhaps an appalling murder, a stabbing, sexual assault, shooting or armed robbery – upon request. I would either send a thirty-second voice report down the phone, or write a script for the newsreader to read out.

My greatest professional challenge at this point in my career was learning not to colour in the facts. For instance:

Police Media Officer: A thirty-five-year-old Blacktown man has been charged with malicious wounding after an attack in Sydney's west overnight. It's alleged the man set upon a group of people outside a Wentworthville hotel shortly before midnight. Three people were taken to Westmead Hospital suffering multiple stab wounds to the chest and arms. The man is due to appear in a Sydney court later this morning.

Early Lisa Clifford report from Police Headquarters: A group of partiers was viciously attacked by a knife-wielding man outside a Wentworthville pub last night. Police say three of the terrified people were stabbed in the arms and chest as they desperately tried to ward off the attacker's knife. They were ferried by ambulance to Sydney's Westmead Hospital shortly after midnight. The attacker, a thirty-five-year-old man from Blacktown, has been arrested and charged. He will appear in a Sydney court later this morning.

A very swift reprimand pointed out that:

A. The people outside the hotel (it may not have really been a pub) may have been Salvation Army officers and not partiers.
B. The victims may have been karate experts and not at all scared.
C. The victims may have laid down on the ground and let the man attack them, rather than "desperately" try to ward off the knife.
D. Their friends may have driven them to hospital.
E. NEVER ASSUME THE STORY. DELIVER ONLY THE FACTS, YOU GOOSE!

The media room at Police Headquarters was probably quite nice immediately after its refurbishment. But it soon looked shabby, because most of the crime reporters were transient and no one really respected it. Partitions lined the walls so as to give each news outlet its own little cubicle. The journalists had stuck up brightly coloured radio logo stickers, car bumper adhesives or other media promotional material to identify their workspace. Old newspapers and yesterday's media releases covered most of the other surfaces.

From the ceiling hung a king-size TV. A garbage bin with last week's half-drunk cappuccinos and toasted ham, cheese and tomato sandwiches usually occupied the middle of the room. This bin also doubled as a goal during quiet news moments when the boys played 'shoot the crumpled ball of paper'. The game was later made more sophisticated by the 2WS journo who attached his son's toy basketball hoop to the wall. The blokes would whoop it up, with score sheets that lasted weeks. The girls (there were two of us) would watch the game or read the newspapers. An invitation to compete was never extended. No offence was taken on my part for the lack of inclusion in this basketball game. Pam MacKay had prepared me well for the PHQ press-room. The men were renowned for their boys' club antics.

By nine o'clock, which story to follow for the day would have been discussed and decided upon. By ten, I would be in one of Sydney's local, district or high courts, ready to send stories back to the station. The case may have been about a ten-year-old due to appear in the children's court over some scandalously antisocial behaviour. Or it might be a bail application by a paedophile with repeated convictions. Mostly, the stories revolved around vile killings. The more shocking or peculiar the crime, the more media attention it attracted. The spotlight always belonged to the men and women who showed the least regard for human life. They gave us our 'best stories'.

Despite the horrors involved in matters of murder, manslaughter, assault and arson, I adored my job. It took surprisingly little time for me to develop a macabre fascination for the details of felonies. Though I cringed at the more gruesome particulars, I took to the position like a duck to water.

My job was to get a voice report back to 2UW for each hourly news. The general idea was to report back before anyone else. Consequently, there was always an undercurrent of competitiveness with the other stations to 'break the story'. The race to be first often resulted in my feeling like a spy on a covert mission. You would never let the other journalists know what you were up to, while you always tried to find out what they were covering. A normal day was a buzz; a good day was one big adrenalin rush.

I particularly enjoyed radio news, when compared to print or TV. There was something noble and honest about radio. There's a saying in TV news: if you don't have the pictures, it didn't happen. Television can only run a story if they have the pictures to go with it. Once a story breaks, the station has to send out a cameraman, who has to transmit the pictures back to the station after waiting for a window in the satellite for the station to receive them. The pictures then have to be edited into a running story in time for the six o'clock news. With radio, I was a mobile communications centre. All that was needed was a mobile phone. And radio is immediate. It requires only a flick of a switch to go live to the location of a breaking story. When there's a big disaster, such as a fire or a train crash, people turn to their radios for the news and for current updates.

During these nine months that I spent apart from Paolo, I thrived on radio. 2UW was a steep learning curve that demanded concentration and effort. Early starts and weekend work burned big holes in my social diary, but that was fine because I had Paolo in the back of my mind. He was coming for his August holidays and had already booked his ticket.

Paolo and I often telephoned each other. He also wrote long letters telling of how much he missed our 'long talkings'. He drew funny caricatures of us with big lips hugging and kissing. He said that during the day his memories of what I looked like faded, but that every night I appeared clearly in his dreams. In these dreams, I was always leaving. He wrote that he hoped his dreams would soon change into me always staying.

18

The week before Paolo's arrival I was feverish with excitement at the thought of my Florentine finally being in Sydney. My girlfriends teased and joked about the countdown to P-day. My family, too, was in overdrive. Dad wanted to come and meet Paolo at the airport. It took all my powers of tactful persuasion to convince him that it would be better to meet Paolo after we'd had some time alone together. Then Dad's mum, Nanna Jess, called to say she was arranging a big family get-together at her house on the Sunday after his arrival.

'What would Pedro . . .?'

'It's Paolo, Nanna,' I interrupted.

'Yes, dear. What would Pablo . . .?'

'It's *Paolo*, Nanna.'

'Yes, dear. What would, ahem, Paulo like to eat? A roast leg of lamb and pavlova?'

Celebration was in the air, with my whole family looking forward to his arrival. But along with the excitement I felt some apprehension. I was afraid that once Paolo was actually in my own country, I would feel differently about him. Maybe being in Australia would highlight how very Italian and foreign he really was. Maybe that would turn me right off him. Maybe he would discover I was changed and unfamiliar when at home and decide the attraction was no longer there.

When Paolo finally did step out of Customs at Kingsford Smith Airport, he looked deliciously dishevelled after his flight. He was wearing jeans, a white T-shirt with a denim shirt and a navy jumper draped across his shoulders. He didn't see me at first. It wasn't until he was trundling his suitcase trolley down the ramp that he spotted me weaving through the crowd towards him. When our eyes met, his expression brightened with warmth and love. I hoped he saw similar feelings reflected in mine. With airy sighs of relief that he was finally here, we hugged each other closely. Any anxieties about how we would feel about each other were replaced by a sure feeling that we were once again hooked.

Even so, our brakes were on. I would have loved to jump all over him, but the large chunk of time that had separated us still had to be bridged. I held back from him also because he seemed more fragile than when on his own home turf, as though his usual strong sense of self was off-kilter. Anyone would be tired after the twenty-four-hour flight from Rome to Sydney, but he seemed truly disoriented. It made me want to mother him, but I knew he hated that.

'God, this country is a long way away,' he said, slumping on to my shoulder.

'I know. It seems like the flight is never going to end,' I said, leading him outside to the car.

'My legs feel like wobbly guillotine,' he said.

'I think that's *gelatine*, Paolo.'

As we drove through the southern suburbs towards the waterfront apartment that I rented in the east, the joy of having him with me was almost matched by the thrill of showing him my country. I felt a strong sense of pride in Australia. He'd been to America so he had experienced space and modern architecture, but I felt the beauty of our land, beaches and bays would blow him away. It was early morning, and Sydney had never looked better.

These were Paolo's first impressions:

'The sky is very big here.'

'The colours are brighter, clearer.'

'The air is clean. It smells different.'

'The drivers are too obedient. Where is the fun in driving like this?'

'The harbour is magnificent. Are there sharks? Can we swim anywhere?'

Once home and recovered from the shock that he would have to sleep with the sunlight streaming in through the gauzy curtains because there were no shutters on the windows (every house in Italy has shutters), we tentatively began to relax. After a long walk around Rushcutters and Elizabeth bays, I took him home to fall into the deep slumber that only jet lag and a general anaesthetic can induce. I tucked him in, put the kettle on, and felt sort of warm and cosy knowing that my old companion was only a room away.

The wind had risen and whipped up the sea. I sat on the couch listening to the moored sailing boats tinkle as they rocked back and forth. I realised then that it would take time for us to find our harmony together here. There was no doubt that our physical attraction was still strong. That wouldn't change no matter where we were in the world. There was something else. It was a reversal of our roles and it had already impacted on our relationship.

In Australia, I was the boss. I decided where we went, who we saw, when we saw them and why. I drove the car, gave directions and organised his day. Not easy for an Italian man used to doing everything his way.

As his holiday moved into its first week, my instincts turned out to be well founded. His loss of control made him feel disempowered, so that he often became sullen and frustrated. I ignored his moods and ploughed on, feeling that it was my right to drag him around Sydney and introduce him to my extended family and friends. I only had two weeks off work, so when friends threw dinner parties especially for Paolo I was happy to chat until late. Our mornings and afternoons were spent with more friends in cafés in Bondi and Bronte. In the early evening my brothers and sister would drop by after work. Then it would be another dinner party or restaurant. Eight days into his trip, Paolo cracked under the pressure of the social whirl with its perpetual interest in him. He complained that he felt on show and stressed.

'Enough! I've come here to be with *you*,' he said. 'I can't even remember who I've met or what they're called.'

I was deeply offended by his refusal to spend any more time with the people close to me, but I also felt that he had a point. Our time together was precious and his holiday had become frenetic. So, we called a moratorium on socialising and dedicated our time solely to each other. Only then did he truly relax, which enabled us to find our footing as a couple again.

By the time my two weeks' holiday leave had finished, Paolo was into exploring on his own. He loved to take the car and discover the long stretches of deserted beach in Sydney's north. Driving further north to Peat's Ridge, near the Central Coast, he hired horses at Glenworth Valley and rode through the bush for hours alone. Though he had loads of people offering themselves as guides, Paolo was the kind of man who needed to absorb Australia's uniqueness independently.

When he started to feel comfortable with the idea again, we ventured back out to dinners and parties. This time around Paolo was more confident, having learned a few lessons to keep him in good stead. Such as eating dinner before dinner. In Italy, guests arrive and immediately sit down to eat. In Australia, guests arrive, have a few drinks and then a few more drinks, before finally sitting down for their meal. By that time, Paolo was so ravenous he would be almost face-down on the floor. He'd signal surreptitiously to me and whisper, 'Do you think we'll eat soon? Is dinner almost ready? I'm going to have to finish off these peanuts, OK?'

Once the guests were seated, he would inhale the pasta or risotto dish only to hang his head in disappointment when he learned that a salad and dessert were the only courses to follow. It's not that Paolo ate a lot, it's just that Italians eat far more than Australians. Italians follow pasta with a meat dish and two vegetable dishes. *Then* there's salad and dessert. To rectify the dinner-party problem, he would cook up a big bowl of spaghetti and leave home with a semi-full stomach.

Towards the end of his trip, I finally felt that Paolo had settled into Australia's ways. He had become accustomed to minding his manners at the table, though he still gobbled his food down three times faster than anyone else. At least now he looked up from his empty plate as though embarrassed at having once again succumbed to a dreamlike state of gorging.

'Likes his food, doesn't he?' Dad would say.

My father didn't know it, but Paolo *was* making an effort. Paolo would even fill my mother's wine glass with an exaggerated flourish, and then wink at me. He also got the hang of getting his shopping done between nine and five and doing without his siesta.

One Australian custom that Paolo really found an eye-opener was having a big party in your own home. Because ninety per cent of Italian families live in small apartments, often with a grandparent, young Italians never have parties at home. They socialise outside in the piazza, bar or disco. Paolo thought the Sydney habit of having a big bash in a house rented by four young people was terrific fun. The music was loud, the drinks flowed and the girls danced. He was gob-smacked that these parties were often almost entirely populated by women.

'But where are all the men in Sydney? There are so many beautiful girls to dance with!'

'Gay or down at the pub, love,' my girlfriends replied, swarming around him.

'My friends in Florence will not believe it when I tell them that I danced with five girls at once,' he laughed happily.

'Tell them to come to Sydney!' the girls joked. (At least, I *think* they were joking.)

In the end, Paolo loved Sydney and felt comfortable with my family and friends. They all seemed to like him, too. But on the whole, his time in Australia hadn't been what I'd imagined. In many ways it had been difficult. I had been crushed when he insisted we stop spending time with my family and friends. Many times his desire to be alone with me made me feel torn, as though I had to choose again between him and my family. I resented him for not taking my family more into consideration. After all, I had left them for long periods of time because of him. Didn't he understand that they needed to, in fact deserved to, know him better? But he wasn't accustomed to sharing me with others. Nor was he used to sharing more of himself. I had tried to keep everyone happy, but it had been difficult.

The tone of his holiday Down Under also made me realise that Paolo was unlikely to move to Australia to be with me. Our relationship thrived in Italy but felt stunted in Australia. More often it's the women who can adapt to the demands of a new country, not the men. It's easier for women to pick up on the nuances of a new culture and bend themselves to fit in. If Paolo emigrated to Australia, rather than me move back to Italy, happiness would have been an uphill battle. The harmony we achieved so naturally in Florence would almost certainly have eluded us in Sydney.

The windows on to the harbour were open to let the sun and cool air into my apartment. It made no difference. The room felt like it was shrouded in a dark, heavy blanket. It was the day before Paolo was to leave and I was sitting on his lap in the armchair. My legs dangled over the armrest, my arms were around his neck. There were dark splotches on his T-shirt where my tears had fallen.

He had asked me to marry him. Though my heart had swelled with tenderness, I softly shook my head. We kept our heads burrowed into each other's necks. We couldn't look at each other.

'I can't live in Italy,' I said. My voice was muffled, ashamed. 'I would be so unhappy it would destroy what we have now.'

'Do you think you'll ever change your mind?' His voice had a cracked edge.

'I don't know.' I hated myself. Love and guilt merged painfully. He merited so much more than vague references to a possible future.

'Then, now we must break away from each other,' he said quietly. 'I would not be happy in Australia and you the same in Italy. What is the point in us continuing?'

So, this was what had been on his mind. I had dreaded this goodbye with a gut feeling of impending doom, and now I knew why. His proposal wasn't the surprise, his suggestion to end our relationship was. Evidently, he had given our future far more serious thought than I had. He must have known that he would finish our affair if I turned him down.

'You want to break up?'

'Lisa, we *have* to break up.'

That night our hearts were squeezed more tightly than I had thought possible. I lay on my side, melded into his back like a spoon. Tomorrow Paolo would catch a taxi alone to the airport and fly back to Florence. We would try to forget about each other. We decided together that it had to be a clean break. No phone calls, no letters. That was the deal. Hot tears pooled on the side of the bridge of my nose and plopped on to my pillow.

Paolo said nothing. He wasn't outwardly angry or hurt, just quietly sad. He accepted our break-up on the grounds that I was Australian and wouldn't leave my country.

For me it was so much more complex. Paolo had many of the qualities that I wanted in a man, but that didn't seem common in Australian men. He was solid, capable of commitment and able to provide for an eventual family. He was also extremely emotionally giving. Italian men are brought up in an environment where it's OK to talk about love. Paolo wasn't ashamed or afraid to express how he felt, which in turn made me believe in him and our relationship. Australian boys our age seemed to have a different way of going about love. Sydney girls never felt too sure of their boyfriends. Everybody left everybody because they had found someone else or because they just wanted to be friends.

Was Paolo irreplaceable? Would I ever again feel like this towards someone? I was once again caught up in a confusing web of analysing Paolo, us, the future, and life in Australia versus life in Italy. I consoled myself with the thought that maybe we were young enough to replace each other.

The trouble with being in love with a Florentine is that everyone thinks you are completely barmy not to want to live in Tuscany. There was such a total lack of understanding as to what it is really like to leave your homeland and family for Italy, that it was impossible for me to talk about Paolo with anyone apart from my very close friends. The idea that one could move to Italy and find eternal happiness was firmly planted in many people's minds. Books, magazines and movies make living in Tuscany seem like a dream come true. 'Live in Italy and be happy for the rest of your life!' the story goes. For a while I tried to explain the reality of moving permanently to a foreign country. When I saw that most people had no idea what I was getting at, I shut up and stopped talking about Paolo.

On the surface, I now had everything I wanted. A great

job with an exciting future, a terrific flat, and I was meeting loads of new people. I was single and free to do as much market research on Australian men as I wanted. But no one compared to Paolo. That was half the problem. I was dating, comparing and ditching at an alarming rate. After two years, and even though we'd had no communication, he was still very much on my mind. The other half of the problem was that, even if I *did* contact him, I still wasn't sure that I could live in Italy. My friends suggested I try writing a list of the pros and cons.

The pros of living in Italy	***The cons of living in Italy***
Paolo + love	Miss family and friends
Financial security	Nothing to do except make babies
Children and my own family	No journalism
La 'dolce vita' – great food	Communication in Italian tough (hard to crack jokes)
Gorgeous clothes, cheap too	No Thai or Asian food
	Depression
	No beach

And on and on it went. The comparisons, the confusion, the thinking about it . . . always the bloody thinking about it. The lists didn't work, dammit! On the contrary, they only exacerbated the restlessness that was constantly pricking at my consciousness. The whole situation was driving me crazy. Then it struck me: I really must *be* crazy. That's it! I needed psychological help. I was having a mid-youth crisis and it was time to sort it out. Everybody else was on the psycho-babble train, I might as well jump on it, too. Professional counselling would surely be the answer.

Dr Wanda Rose (not her real name) was recommended by a close friend who had heard her address a prominent women's business network on confidence and self-assurance issues. Her office was in Sydney's inner west in a freshly renovated townhouse, tucked away behind a back lane. It also appeared to be her home. All morning at work I had felt excited at the prospect of nutting out my problem with a proper shrink, but as I gingerly walked up the steps and rang her bell, I felt my courage retreat.

Pushing back a wiry, grey cowlick, Dr Rose welcomed me into her hallway. Adorned with Indonesian jewellery that was at odds with her corporate pants and jacket, she ushered me into a large study, then seated me in front of a heavy desk before going around to the other side to sit down and face me.

Dr Rose pushed her cowlick back from her face at the beginning of every sentence, which made her ornate bracelets tinkle.

Hair back. So, what's the problem?

I explained my quandary. I wanted to live in Australia, but every time I settled down to a steady life with a secure job, I started thinking about my Florentine boyfriend.

Hair back. Ha ha, that's not a problem. I would *love* to live in Florence.

Yes, that may well be, I said. But I don't. Still, I can't seem to let him go and I can't seem to go to him. I'm caught in a vicious cycle.

Hair back. I see. What would happen if I put some Italian music on now? How would you feel?

I'd rather you didn't. It would almost certainly make me cry.

Hair back. Are you in love with Italy or the man?

Hmm, the man (sniff). Though I think I miss Florence a bit as well. To some extent I think they go together, yet I couldn't live permanently in Florence.

Hair back. Is he in love with you?

He might even have another girlfriend by now. We haven't contacted each other for two years.

Hair back. How much guilt do you feel? Did you let him down?

There's quite a bit of guilt. Towards his parents, actually (crying now). They took me into their own home and treated me like a daughter. I feel as though I've let the whole family down.

Hair back. Why do you feel the need to talk to me about this?

Because I want you to tell me what to do.

Dr Rose fixed me with an intense stare. I can't tell you what to do. But I can tell you what I think. And that is that you are still in love with him. Would it be the end of the world if you simply wrote him a letter to find out how he feels about you now?

When I had gathered myself together, I told her that if Paolo and I started writing to each other then I'd more than likely quit my job and go back to him. In a halting, teary voice I told her I was scared of getting depressed in Florence. The depression would end up with me coming back here again. I was trapped.

Dr Rose stood up and came around to my side of the desk to pass me a tissue.

Then she aggressively pushed her hair back. 'For God's sake, Lisa. Love is something that you can't fight. You can't battle it for the rest of your life. It will always follow you. Live it, follow it. At least go through with love, get into it, go through it and give yourself a chance to get past it and over it.'

I dried my tears and thanked her with fifty dollars. She'd helped me make up my mind. I would send Paolo a letter, though it didn't feel good to be the one making the contact again. Nor was I sure as to what to say. I'll just let the letter flow, I thought, and see what comes out.

On a Sunday afternoon the 2UW newsroom was so peaceful it had an almost surreal atmosphere. I settled into my workstation and enjoyed the peace, such a contrast to the mind-numbing cacophony that normally infiltrates my concentration during the week.

The weekend on-duty journalist has a series of duties that involve mooching about in a tracksuit or jeans while checking for something new to lift off the newspapers. An idle flick through the computer for some Australian Associated Press national or federal political stories is a good idea, as is a couple of taped BBC voices to give the broadcast an international flavour. Once Police Media has given an interview on the overnight crimes, and the ambulance and fire brigade have backed the police up with any further information, your shift is usually set. When Melbourne and Brisbane have sent in their stories, a few rewrites between bulletins is all that is needed to keep your news sounding fresh. The afternoon stretched ahead with most of my work already done. I was thinking clearly and feeling confident. The newsroom and its familiar computers was the perfect place for my delicate operation. It was the right time to write to Paolo.

Rather than use the computer's busy 'Bulletin File' for my

letter to Paolo, which was used for all the stories that went to air, I thought it prudent to write my very private letter in the disused file that was aptly called 'Dead'.

The only other soul in the radio station was the DJ, and the solitude helped me to write down my innermost intimate feelings. Once the letter was under way, I felt compelled to tell Paolo all. The letter spelled out how confused I was and how much I thought about him. I missed our friendship. No one had taken his place and I missed our easy, familiar sex life. I longed again for what we had shared. I didn't know how much I wanted all that back until I started to write the letter. How did he feel? Did he think we could spend a holiday together? How about meeting up for some fun international travel? I also wrote that our long stretch of silence had only increased my longing for him. Perhaps it would be better if we talked occasionally, or dropped each other the odd letter. Then the riddle of each other's existence wouldn't ultimately turn into a mystery that had to be solved. Of course, if he had a girlfriend, there was no problem. I understood. With an affectionate, but not too lovey-dovey sign-off, the letter was done.

The letter was honest and heartfelt, but not desperate. It felt liberating to at last share my feelings with him. Happy with it, I printed it off, finished my shift and went home.

The next morning my beeper went off at Police Headquarters. That was unusual, as the newsroom always phoned. When I glanced down to read the beeper message, my stomach lurched in fright. It was from the 2UW station manager, John Williams. The message read:

DUMP ALL STORIES. REPORT TO ME PERSONALLY AT 2UW. NOW.

I was in very, very deep trouble about something. The recall wasn't even from Pam MacKay, but from her boss, the big man himself. Like most radio-station managers, John Williams was a really nice guy, unless we were being sued. That was the only conclusion I could draw from such an urgent message. Oh, no. Something had been stuffed up and 2UW was now being sued over it.

As I hightailed it across the Harbour Bridge, my mind ran through every major story that I'd broadcast over the last few months. No obvious mistakes sprang to mind. I'd just have to front up and take whatever punishment was dished out. I sincerely hoped that my mistake hadn't aborted a murder trial. A television reporter had only recently done just that. He'd televised the legal details given in court while the jury was out. His mistake meant that it could take anything up to five years before the Director of Public Prosecutions could try the accused again. So much could change in the years between trials. Witnesses' memories could fail, and people might become unsure of themselves under cross-examination. I would never forgive myself if an oversight of mine had caused such a grave miscarriage of justice.

I tapped on John's office door, my heart in my mouth.

He jumped up from his desk and strode over, with a serious look on his face. John didn't mince words. 'You've been writing sexy love letters to your Italian boyfriend on the newsroom computers.'

'Oh, my goodness!' I spluttered, too stunned to admit to anything.

'This morning I received a phone call from 2GB's manager.' John looked stern. 'Apparently yesterday afternoon, while you *should* have been working on news copy, you were busy writing to a certain *Paulo*?'

'Yes, that's right.' How did he know this? My face was beetroot with embarrassment.

'Didn't you know that the "Dead" file is linked to our network stations and that the general managers and news directors read that file for network messages first thing on a Monday morning?' His voice had softened slightly.

'Oh, no! I had no idea.'

'Yeah, that's pretty clear. It's our network information file. 2WS, 2CC in Canberra and the whole Canberra Super Bureau and God knows who else has read your letter, Lisa.' He started to smile. His grin told me that the station managers had probably had a laugh over it.

'I am *so* embarrassed. Sorry, John.'

'I guess I don't have to bother telling you not to do that again,' he said kindly.

'Ah, no.'

Feeling like the joke of the network, I left his office and trudged into the newsroom upstairs where about five journos were on duty. When I walked in they all started shouting, 'Tell me if he has a girlfriend!' and 'Let me know when he writes back, I'm dying to know if he wants to go on that holiday with you,' and 'Lisa, love, didn't know you were lonely. I would have given you a cuddle!'

I mailed the letter later that same day.

Within a month, a letter with Paolo's familiar scrawl arrived from Florence.

Carissima (Dearest),

I'm thinking of you often recently and then you write. Now I find myself waiting for your call. I've realised you're the only woman my heart can beat for, even though I tried to put you out of my life, like you did in Australia.

Our breakdown was very confusing and we were not mature enough to get married.

We let it go too easily.

I have bought my own apartment and live alone. There is no one in my life. I've met a few girls but it didn't work. I can't fall in love with anybody.

I very much want us to be friends and don't want to lose you. You know I can't write well in English, so I will finish here. Let us see each other soon. Anywhere you want. Or come and live with me in Florence.

Here is my new number. Call me when you can.

Goodbye my darling,

Your Paolo

P.S. Life is long and anything can happen.

His words made my heart flip and filled me with pure joy. We were in this feeling together! With that knowledge, surely I could overcome any black moments of depression and find happiness in Florence? The boredom, the homesickness, the cultural differences between Paolo and me; none of it mattered. He loved me – that surpassed all. Not only that, there was a big change this time around. Paolo had left his parent's home to live on his own. I was so proud of him. He was a brave and unusual Italian man. In Italy, seven out of ten unmarried men over the age of thirty-five still live with their parents. But Paolo wasn't one of the numbers. He had the strength of character to leave his folks and look after himself. After two years without each other, we could share our lives again and plan for the future. And this time, there would be no live-in parents to deal with.

Life's direction was changed as I pulled out of Australia for yet another try at living in Italy. My resignation from 2UW was accepted by John Williams with a knowing smile. Notice on my apartment was given and the furniture and household goods put into storage. 'Honda for sale' advertisements went into newspapers. Mum and Dad understood and gave me their blessings. Good friends were more wary this time around, but still encouraging. Journalist friends thought my life was a wondrous tale of incomparable romance.

During the weeks before I left, Paolo and I talked long and often by phone. We shared an unchallengeable belief that we were made for each other. I would fly to Rome. He would take time off work, as it was not yet summer, to come to Rome airport and pick me up. I would move into his new apartment. We never doubted that we were doing the right thing.

19

Fresh from the Sydney world of sexual equality, the differences between Italy and Australia were already apparent. Standing in the Customs area of Rome airport, after scrabbling with the Italian passengers for their beloved exit pole position, I found myself being inspected by the men and women alike. Here, though, there was social permission to do so. Unlike Australian women, Italian women don't mind being perved at. This is a country where serious political TV talk shows have the men discussing the issues, while near-naked women lounge on tables in the background as decoration. And no one complains.

After a while the women dismissed me, but the men acted as though I had a scent and they wanted to pick it up. They seemed to find me far more attractive than Australian men did. It wasn't just my foreignness, either. Italian men have a way of being aware of, and attentive to, women that most Anglo-Saxon men don't have. The uniformed military policeman who stamped my passport had a sexy gleam in his eye as he matched my photo to my face. This would be unheard-of conduct for an Australian Customs officer. Quite simply, I felt desired in Italy and ignored in Australia.

I had also forgotten how confident Italian men are with their masculinity. They swaggered about the luggage collection area so self-aware and sure of themselves. I put it down to the Italian way of mothering. Mamma worships her *bambino* and the *bambino*, no matter how ordinary, grows up to believe he is totally desirable. Somehow, he infects you with it.

It had been ten years since my first trip to Rome. How much better I understood the Italians now. I no longer regarded their interest as harassment but, rather, as flattering attentiveness. I glided blithely through their stares instead of nervously avoiding them, and took this as proof of a new maturity.

There was a deeper confidence to my composure now, acquired through journalism and age. Even though Paolo was on the other side of the Customs barrier and my heart pounded with excitement, I controlled my nerves. My newfound decisiveness and strength was reflected in my face. Features formerly jumbled by girliness had been replaced by a womanly order. The Italians would still address me as '*Signorina*', but it wouldn't be long before that changed to '*Signora*'.

Drawing my breath, I pushed the trolley out into the chaos and tried to find Paolo's salt-and-pepper hair in the waiting crowd. Then there he was, almost unrecognisable, striding towards me with a full head of jet-black hair.

'Ahh, you're dyeing it!' I cried, as we hugged nervously. He was beaming with happiness, not trying to be cool and to hide his excitement. That was one of his disarming charms, his honesty about the way he felt. He held me at arm's length and then pulled me to him again, not for long, just time enough for us to remember the feel of our bodies so close.

'You are more beautiful than ever.' He said it so sincerely that blood rushed to my cheeks.

'Thank you. But why are you dyeing your hair?' There was a note of disappointment in my voice.

'Because grey hair is for old people. Does it look that bad?' he asked in a way that said he thought it looked good.

'No, no,' I lied, thinking that men with dyed hair looked fake and vain. But talking Paolo around to my point of view would take time. 'It makes your eyes look very blue,' I said encouragingly.

Apart from his hair, Paolo had changed little. Though he did have a more wholesome look, with luminous skin that shone with good health. His body seemed a bit leaner, more rangy.

'I've taken up cross-country motorbike riding,' he said, after I commented on his obvious fitness. 'A thinner body gives you better balance and speed.'

'When do you find the time to work?'

'Work is always there. I've had a lot of spare time to fill. Now I do gym, karate, cross-country and speed motorbike riding.'

'Why limit yourself? I'm surprised you haven't taken up sky-diving and rock-climbing, too.' Paolo had always been a keen sportsman, but this new list of hobbies was starting to sound obsessive.

'Actually, I was thinking about cycling. You know I love anything on two wheels.'

'No wonder you're single!' He laughed goodnaturedly at my teasing.

Our physical attraction still sparked, making the electricity of his proximity exhilarating. In many ways, it didn't feel too strange to be beside him again. We naturally fell into step beside each other. Our many phone calls had helped bring the past closer to the present, making our reunion easier. From the moment we saw each other, we picked up where we had left off in our last phone call. We also spoke in two different languages. Paolo had already explained that he spoke English rarely; it felt awkward and no longer flowed. The same was true of my Italian. So we continued to speak to each other as we had during our phone calls – in our mother tongues. We found that we understood each other perfectly and expressed ourselves easily this way. Our peculiar way of communicating in both English and Italian never changed.

Because we had shared this exciting moment of reunion before, we knew that our two years apart had to be annulled with 'go slow' time. We needed space now to talk and ponder. A little shyly, but feeling wonderful, we settled into his black BMW and caught up with the years as the road from Rome to Florence zoomed by.

My new address was Via Orsini, a well-known Florentine street on the Oltrarno side of the Arno River. It branches off from the big roundabout that leads up to Piazzale Michelangelo, one of the city's main tourist attractions because of its replica of the statue *David* and sweeping views. Chaos reigns supreme in Via Orsini, with cars parked wherever a spare metre of space is found – up on the curb, back-to-front (it's a one-way street) and double-parked across the corners. The woman at number 5 owned four cocker spaniels, so you can imagine the state of the footpaths.

A jumble of shops that catered to the working-class families living in the apartments above them competed with each other for space. A baker with trays of pizza, *schiacciata* topped with olives, and breads from Puglia, Rome and Tuscany, was next to the fruit and veg shop. The *ortolano* had his cases of blood-red oranges, crunchy *rucola* and iridescent eggplants heaped so high they took up most of the footpath, so that you had to squeeze into the doorway of the butcher. A deli, passionately dedicated to cheeses and salamis, was beneath us, next to a lingerie shop that was next to the poultry shop, electrician and plumber's shop.

Paolo's apartment had a spare bedroom and living room that fronted Via Orsini's rumbling roar, a noise so constant that peak hour seemed to last all day. On the other side and in the European style, Paolo's bedroom, bathroom and kitchen looked on to a quiet courtyard that every apartment on the block backed on to. His bedroom was peaceful and sunny, with high French doors that opened on to a small veranda running the length of the bathroom and kitchen. Gemma's embroidered linen curtains were on all the windows, giving the rooms a muted glow. The shutters, doors, windows and floors were all in polished, battered old wood. The kitchen had been renovated with terracotta tiles, pale-wood cabinets and marble-topped benches. The little apartment smelled fresh and new.

'Do you like it?' asked Paolo, panting after lugging my suitcase up the four flights of stairs.

'I do, yes, it's lovely,' I said, sticking my head into every room, feeling very content with the secluded, nestlike feel of the place.

'I've had a satellite dish hooked on to the roof so that you can watch CNN and the BBC.'

He seemed to have made every effort to ensure that I would be comfortable, and I was touched. There was only one peculiar aspect to it all. Every surface shone with good care. Time spent together at Teatro Pergola had taught me that Paolo couldn't give a toss about housekeeping. But then, maybe ownership of a home had changed him. That happens to some guys. Hope tugged.

'Your home is very clean, Paolo. Is that a cleaner or you?' I asked, puzzled.

'*No da vero*. Not likely. Zia Maria has been coming three times a week. I've been paying her to cook and clean. But she said now that you were coming, there was no more need for her. I thought you'd like the privacy.'

I wasn't sure if I was disappointed or happy that Zia Maria no longer helped out. It may have been nice to have her help. Still, her automatic retreat with the arrival of another woman was a very female Italian thing to do. The older generation like to serve their men, so the assumption was that I would, too.

Unpacking was fun. Pleasurable feelings of loving coupledom made lining up my toiletries in the bathroom next to Paolo's seem very intimate. The same with placing my pyjamas and books on my side of his bed. This was a real de-facto relationship, and the security of finally sharing a home with a man warmed a part of my soul that the years of being single had chilled.

His considerate gesture of clearing space for me in his

bedroom cupboard and chest of drawers compelled me to wrap my arms around him. 'Sweetheart, thanks so much for making all this room for me,' I whispered in his ear.

He was in the kitchen and had flicked on the TV while I pottered and settled. 'Hmm? I didn't do that. Zia Maria must have,' he said absently.

'Oh.' It was only a little thing. Never mind.

'Shall I cook up some pasta for lunch?' I went on.

'That'd be great. Zia has left some fresh tomato sauce in the fridge,' he said, looking up with a happy smile.

I cooked lunch, revelling in the nurturing role. This was another part of myself that singledom had never allowed to emerge. The caring, mothering aspect of the female spirit, preparing food in a kitchen shared between lovers. It felt comforting and came naturally. Paolo had the fridge well stocked with fresh salad, hams, cheeses and yoghurts. Rifling through the cabinets I found he'd bought pretty white porcelain plates and crisp tablecloths. Spreading out our feast on the round, country-style kitchen table in the corner, I looked out of the French doors on to the sunny courtyard and thought how lucky I was. Italian men tend to be very generous with their women. They share their money and possessions with their partners as a matter of course. The kitchen, the apartment and everything in it felt like it was mine, as though it had all been given to me simply by the grace of my coming back. I felt secure, blessed.

After our siesta we took a Sunday afternoon stroll down the Arno River to a favourite area in Florence. On the Oltrarno, San Niccolo is a tiny shopping and residential area that centres around the fourteenth-century gateway in the old wall that surrounded the city. An ancient tower underneath the winding garden stairway that leads up to Piazzale

Michelangelo heralds the way into San Niccolo. A thousand years ago, merchants who passed through the tower into the city had to pay a quota of salt for permission to sell their wares in Florence. Today, council lights flood the tower, and a stage and bar area is set up behind it. Jazz floats into the summer-scented night as enthusiasts enjoy the view of San Niccolo's tower with the Arno as its backdrop. Past the tower, down through Via San Niccolo, we stopped for a coffee and pastry at Il Rifrullo, a café with an antique feel to its dark green, maroon and gold décor. Its afternoon clientele were Italian gentlemen with cultured voices, neatly clipped grey beards, and hats like my grandfather used to wear.

We walked further on; up to the ancient San Niccolo door in the battlement wall itself. We stopped to touch its wood, rub the huge iron nails that studded the door into place and imagined marauders from another century trying to bash it down. We walked up the steep hill behind it and turned right into an exclusively lush residential area. Creamy sand and sienna-hued villas stood amid perfectly manicured lawns, their solidity made graceful by vine-covered terraces and arched doorways. Nature and architecture had never seemed so harmonised. The aesthetics of Italy, with Paolo's hand in mine, calmed any fears that leaving Australia for Florence would be difficult. For the first time, I felt it would be a privilege to live here.

That night, the BBC news made me feel part of the world, not just Australia. The British news service ran global issues, stories of national importance that impacted on the whole of Europe. I was struck by the significance of the stories and compared the BBC news to Sydney's smaller, provincial services. My consciousness of the wider world was growing.

No longer did I feel locked out of my own distant country, but rather admitted into a larger, international one.

During our first week back together, Gemma and Giovanni came over for an Australian dinner of shepherd's pie and apple crumble. Their smiles reflected a canny understanding of the reversal of our roles. This time they were the visitors. We took their coats and walked them into the kitchen where Paolo, instead of Giovanni, opened the wine and sat down at the seat with the best view of the TV. They were clearly thrilled that we were back together again and in such de-facto bliss.

'*Hai trovato l'Australia!*' Giovanni teased his son, distorting the Italian saying '*Hai trovato l'America*', which means 'You've found America'. For those who had lived through the war, the Americans represented health and wealth. His joke was to change the country, but keep the message.

Giovanni didn't enjoy the pie, gruffly pointing out that it was only a beefed-up bolognese sauce with mashed potatoes over the top. Gemma, on the other hand, the victim of years of criticism in the kitchen, praised it heartily. She kept trying to bob up out of her seat to help, but I kept a firm hand on her shoulder.

'Gemma, it's a pleasure to finally cook for you. *Stay down!*' I commanded.

'Tee-hee,' she giggled, like a child being given extra candy.

During the apple crumble, which was a big success, she finally relaxed and relinquished her role of lady-in-waiting on the men. When the water, wine or oil ran out, she gleefully watched me rise to fetch it.

'*Ora tocca a te,*' she laughed gaily. 'Now it's your turn.'

But I didn't see my *donna in comando* – 'woman in charge' of the kitchen – behaviour as a permanent arrangement. These were small gestures of care through which I could repay Gemma and Giovanni for their years of kindness towards me. Paolo sat oblivious to my efforts throughout the meal, not offering to help. Many times Giovanni had told me that his son had never lifted a plate off the table. So, not wanting him to lose face with his dad, I didn't harangue him to clear the plates or put on the coffee. He was the picture of the Consumi family host. Sitting back in his chair, telling jokes and offering his father Vin Santo or grappa. Let Paolo paint that picture for his family, I thought. There's time enough for him to pitch in.

The Consumis' lives were changing. Giovanni and Gemma were due to retire in six months, prompting them to buy their own apartment. Their retirement plan was to divide their time between summers at Pratiglioni and winters in Florence. They were excited about their new home and asked me to come and see it with them soon.

As they left, they hugged me and said how happy they were that Paolo finally had someone to look after him. Paolo shrugged off their comments with more banter: 'But I'm the one looking after her!' They looked doubtful and walked down the stairs calling, '*Ciao*, we'll call you soon.'

That night Paolo confided that he felt fulfilled for the first time in his life. He said that until now he had felt incomplete and that we'd been apart for far too long. With his brows deeply knitted, he said he was coming out of a tunnel of lonely solitude.

'It's a new beginning and I'm so excited.' He nestled close and looked into my eyes. 'I want you always by my side. Will you marry me?'

This time, his proposal was a surprise. His words provoked an overwhelming tenderness from deep within my heart. This man had been my friend since I was seventeen years old – which felt like always. All that I knew about trust, reliability, care and protection from a man, he had taught me. And no one else compared.

'Yes, I will.'

We set no wedding date, but we decided to immediately tell everyone of our intention to marry. Especially my family and friends in Australia. That way, they would all have time to save up for their tickets.

That week Paolo surprised me with a diamond solitaire ring, set in a thick yellow band of gold. The diamond's sparkle had just the right amount of glitter. It was big, yet not so big as to be garish.

'Darling, it's perfect, absolutely perfect.' Turning my hand this way and that, I was amazed at how treasured the sight of an engagement ring on a wedding finger could be.

'This matches it well, don't you think?' said Paolo, holding out his other hand. In it was a solid gold Rolex watch. Again, he'd made the perfect choice.

Swaddled in the soft folds of *amore,* I slipped into a cocoon of love. The outside world fell away, as if there was a conspiracy to leave us alone so that we could nest in peace. I felt fat with a cosy, homely contentment. Paolo worked while I looked after the house, shopped and cooked delicious meals. Without being conscious of it, I had taken over where Gemma had left off.

20

Drenched in the sweetness of our first months together, letters home spun humorous tales of housekeeping. To run your own home in Florence is very different from living at your mother-in-law's house and it seemed that Italy, with its weird shopping hours and long siesta, did all it could to thwart me.

Every time I set out for a shop, I found it closed. On Wednesday afternoons, invariably the time set for all our grocery shopping, my shoulders would sag with despondency outside the butcher's. Duh, that's right, all food shops close on Wednesday afternoons. On other days a venture down to the baker's at three resulted in a kick for not remembering that all food shops stay closed from one till five in the afternoon. Added to that was the mystery of the clothes, toiletry shops and hairdressing salons, all of which shut on Monday mornings. Several times the banks caught me out by closing from one in the afternoon.

It probably seems strange to Italians that in Sydney you can buy milk at a petrol station, whereas to me it seemed absurd that in Italy you could only buy milk at a *latteria.* Bus tickets were sold by the cigarette shop owner, who also had the licence to sell salt. Ducking down to the 7-Eleven for some bread isn't an option because 'open late' corner shops don't exist. Just like there are no bottle shops that sell alcohol after 8 pm. If you become sick at night or over the weekend and need to fill a prescription or find a painkiller you must drive around Florence to find the *one* chemist that's open until 11 pm. The chemists take turns in staying open until late. Nothing is open twenty-four hours.

Then, in June, just as I was becoming accustomed to the Florentine shopping timetable (having it printed on paper and stuck to the fridge helped), *all* the shops closed on Saturdays and stayed open on Monday mornings. On the upside, August was a piece of cake – *everything* was shut.

When I did manage to get it right, few shopping experiences compared to the delights of picking through my *ortolano*'s seasonal produce. Our Mr Fruit and Veg – Franco – always had a recipe to go with his vegetables.

'You know, my wife makes my favourite pasta sauce with those little tomatoes and you can't grow them all year round. Those ones come up from Sicily.'

'Really? What does your wife make?'

He moves forward to caress the tiny tomatoes that are unlike cherries and more like a flavour-packed pear-shaped neonatal San Marzano. The tomatoes are as big as his thumbnail.

'Ahh. Graziella cuts them in half, takes a bunch of this

basil, some parsley, lots of oil and *parmigiano* and tosses it all through some spaghetti. *Freschissimo!*'

He'd sold me. I'd buy the lot, plus the ingredients for his favourite *fagiolini di Sant'Anna* – knobbly runner beans that were as long and wide as a little girl's hair ribbon.

'Simmer them in garlic and tomatoes, *dolcissimo!*' he advised.

While getting a handle on shopping, there were also the eating rules to get used to.

Lunch is at 1 pm and must consist of pasta or rice, then a salad and maybe some meat. Salad is acceptable, but not optimum for dinner. Every evening meal must begin with a soup. Vegetables and meat aren't served together on the plate, but on different plates and eaten one after the other. My Aussie habit, which was difficult to break and seemed simpler, was to cook meat with three veggies and put them all on one plate. Bread *must* (no excuses here) be bought fresh from the baker's every day.

Italy was so quaint and traditional it would make me laugh. Except when, one morning, Paolo awoke to find there was no milk for breakfast. Not only that, there was no bread, no cereal, nothing bar some roasted chestnuts from the day before. He hit the roof.

'What do you mean, you missed the shops?' He hissed. 'You had all day yesterday to go shopping and you missed the shops?'

'I mucked up all the times and I missed the shops and I forgot – the lot. What's so bad about that?'

I was thrown by his anger. It was no big deal . . . so he would have to have breakfast out, so what?

'Look, Lisa. In my family, we all have to contribute.

I work, bring the money home. You are the woman – you cook, shop and look after the house.'

My mouth must have been on the floor, because he went on.

'Do you have a problem with that? Or don't Australian women look after the worker in the family?' His voice was rising to a yell.

'Australian women don't *have* to do anything. I've been doing the housework because I *want* to, not because I *have* to. What is this? Are there rules to living here?' I was spitting with fury. How dare he say I had to shop, clean and carry out all the household duties? It was the most chauvinistic thing I'd ever heard in my life.

'You don't work. What else do you have to do? The least you can do is look after our home!' This was our first ever screaming match and he was as florid in the face as I was. Paolo stormed into the bathroom to get ready for work. I paced the bedroom and thought how irrational it was to expect a woman to do everything in the house.

'We'll talk about it later.' *Slam!* And he was gone.

After so much time spent living with his family, any other woman may have seen this tantrum coming. But believing that Paolo wouldn't demand of me the same servile behaviour that he expected from his mother, I thought our domestic duties could, and would, be shared. How dare he demand that we play such old-fashioned wife/husband roles? Years ago, my brother Tim had thrown his creased shirt over my head and roared with a mock macho voice, 'You're a woman! Iron this!' It had been such a joke at the time because of the outrage he knew he'd invoke. Paolo had a retarded view of modern-day society.

I was also terribly hurt. I had done all the chores without complaint until this moment and I was disappointed that he didn't appreciate that. Not only was there no recognition of the work itself, but also he didn't seem to notice how much my way of life had had to change to fit in with his.

Then, slowly, as the day progressed, I capitulated. All my friends' mothers came to mind. (Not mine – she wasn't a good role model in this case.) They had done most, if not all, of the household chores while their husbands worked. I wasn't employed; Paolo was supporting me. Perhaps I was being selfish. Maybe there was a duty issue at stake here. It would be best if I accepted the inevitable. The homemaker's job would have to be mine. I gave in, but not without some demands of my own.

'All right, the home is my responsibility,' I said later that night. 'But Paolo, you have to try and understand how different the way of life in Florence is for me. Please make more effort to understand that everything here is foreign to me and it can be enormously difficult to adapt to even the littlest things.'

'*Va bene*. All right,' he chortled, happy that I'd consented to play the role he wanted for his future wife.

'And, I've decided to get a job at a radio station.' Surely, my having no money was giving him all the control.

'Terrific,' he said. 'Two people earning are better than one.'

'And there's one other thing. Who set up this house – the sheets, the plates, the tablecloths?'

'Mamma and Zia Maria, of course. They found everything and did it all. What's wrong?' He looked at me guilelessly.

'Nothing. I just wondered.' There was no point in explaining. He had absolutely no idea. As always, his mother had done everything for him. All he had to do was arrive at his new, fully kitted-out apartment to find all his clothes unpacked and everything in its place. He was like a king in his castle.

Oh, well. If I wanted this relationship to work, I'd have to try to be queen.

21

March 9 is a special day in Italy. Women gather for lunch, dances and parties, mothers take their daughters out to dinner, and sisters make the effort to meet with each other or their best female friends. Husbands, boyfriends, fathers and sons give their women a sprig of yellow mimosa flowers. Schools organise art sessions where the children paint or make collages of mimosa to take home to Mamma or Nonna. March 9 is International Women's Day, and for twenty-four hours women are honoured and uplifted. On this day it feels as though the universal sisterhood of women, with its special brand of female, nurturing love, is truly united and venerated.

Gemma and Zia Maria bustled me into their car with shouts of '*Vieni, vieni, Signora Consumi!* Come along, come along, Mrs Consumi!' before setting off to Consuma for lunch at Zio Franco's restaurant. I hadn't been back to Consuma in well over two years and found that the Rossi sisters and Consumi wives welcomed me back with hugs and clucks, all speaking at once.

'Eh, eh, eh, we knew you'd come back. Took your time, though.'

'And you're getting married? Wonderful! Will you have little kangaroos soon?'

'We think it's marvellous that you're having the wedding up here.'

I was beginning to feel like a member of their inner circle, a player on their team.

The Women's Day tables were covered in white tablecloths and yellow placemats. Sprigs of yellow mimosa sprouted from pyramids of smooth, white stones that had been placed in the middle of each table. Flutes of *prosecco*, with silky yellow string bows tied around the stems, greeted the seventy or so women. In contrast to the heavy Tuscan mountain food that Zio normally served, the menu today had been geared towards a woman's tastes. A light beef broth with angel hair pasta, then asparagus and *taleggio* cheese risotto, followed by stuffed zucchini flowers and grilled quails with garlic and bay leaves. For dessert, candied orange peels dipped into chocolate, and espresso coffee.

Beside me, the widow of Giovanni's long-dead brother, Zia Piera, turned to me and asked how our wedding plans were progressing. 'Will it be an afternoon or morning ceremony?'

'We thought afternoon, then everyone can walk back here to the restaurant for dinner and dancing.'

'You'll have to hire a bus to bring everyone up and then take them back down to Florence. How many people are you expecting?'

'It's hard to say, though we sent out two hundred invitations. We thought we'd invite everyone because so few Australians will be able to make the trip over.'

'*Mamma mia!* What about the dress?'

'Oh, I don't know yet. The wedding isn't for another year, so I'll wait a while.'

Zia Piera nodded and pointed to cousin Carla. 'Maybe Carla can help you. She's a wonder with a needle. Not as good as her mother, though. Sewing was Zia Dina's speciality.'

Zia Dina's face lit up when she heard her name mentioned. 'My mother, Nonna Angiolina, taught me how to sew, but it wasn't her speciality. It was sties.'

'*Si, si, si.*' They all looked down at their hands while sharing the same melancholy expression. '*Peccato, peccato*. Shame, shame,' they muttered.

'What's the shame?' I asked, perplexed.

'In the old days, every woman had some kind of a gift or skill that she developed and shared,' Zia Piera explained. 'We called her gift her speciality. But we've let all that go.'

'For sties, Nonna Angiolina would take a grain of barley, drop it into the eye, hold her fingers over it and pray. The sty would be gone the next day,' continued Zia Dina.

'My mother's speciality was ridding the children of worms,' said Giovanni's sister Beppina. 'Guistina would rub the children's bellies with oil, round and round while she cast a spell on the worms.' The other women at the table nodded as they remembered.

'Sounds crazy nowadays. But Guistina had the power over those worms, she bewitched them. I wish I could remember her spell, but she never passed her speciality on to me.'

'Ah, but we didn't care about those things when we were young. All the secrets have been lost,' said Zia Piera.

'Remember Nene?' asked Beppina. 'She was Consuma's midwife. Delivered me and all the locals.'

'Birthing was *her* speciality. We'd call her out in the middle of the night . . . freezing! She'd come and help our mothers while the men hovered outside. She was strict with the men; never let them near the women who were birthing. "Done your job – now out," she'd say. Nene had no training and the families would pay her with eggs or a loaf of bread, whatever they had,' said Zia Piera.

'Another speciality was making nappy rash cream. Ohh, how we used to swaddle those babies. It was terrible, really. That's why we needed so much nappy cream. How they must have suffered. We'd rip the old sheets into strips and bind the babies from under their arms down to their hips, then wrap their legs together down to their ankles.' Zia Beppina used her hands to demonstrate the binding technique.

'*Una cosa preistorica.* It sounds prehistoric,' I gasped. I had no idea that, only a generation ago, some Tuscans still bound their babies.

'*Grazie a Dio.* Thank God we don't do that anymore! Nonna Giustina kept Giovanni bound till he was eighteen months old,' said Beppina. 'Perhaps Nonna Giustina couldn't cope with so many toddlers running around the house.'

'Do *you* have a speciality, Lisa?' Zia Piera looked at me intently.

'Only if you count radio stories. I write news for radio and specialise in court stories. You know, murder, killings, things like that.' The ten women at the table looked at me with expressions that varied from alarm to blankness.

'But can you sew?'

'No. Actually, I hate housework. It's a bit of a problem for me. Paolo expects me to do everything in the house, and in Australia we tend to divide the domestic duties.'

'As long as he loves you and brings the money home, what more could you possibly want? You be *la bella signora a casa,* the beautiful wife at home. Forget your work,' said Gemma.

I was feeling it more often now, this knowing that an explanation would be useless. The traditions and habits that had moulded the thinking of the women at this table were set in centuries of stone.

'I'm hoping he'll change.'

'Ha, ha, ha. Darling, if your contractions start at lunchtime, you'd better hold the delivery off until after Paolo's eaten. He's a Consumi from Consuma. And you'll find the dishes in the sink when you come home from hospital.'

'Oh.' There was nothing more to say.

22

Tutto Radio, a middle-of-the-road music station, hired me to present their 'What's on around Florence' program in English, two days a week. Dressing up in my 2UW clothes to go to write and record in the studio gave me the social lift, mental stimulation and focus that I needed to feel as though I was contributing to society again. On those days, Paolo went to Gemma's house for lunch. Every other day I cooked a two-course meal, twice a day. That's Italy. We all love the wonderful Italian food, but someone has to cook it. Only, the incessancy of the 'home for lunch and siesta' ritual was locking me into a suffocating routine. Paolo didn't like it when I wasn't home for lunch.

Reheated leftovers were off the menu, and Paolo wasn't the kind of guy to whom you could say, 'How about something simple for dinner? Let's just have some toasted sandwiches and soup.' His extreme fitness regime called for food . . . and loads of it. This turned into a two-fold problem. One: I had to create an athlete's eating plan tailored to his needs – more carbohydrates at lunch, only protein for dinner and no fats at all. Two: he was rarely home.

This second problem was dire. Monday and Wednesday nights were karate, Tuesday mornings were gym, and Sundays were speed motorbikes. This schedule was manageable. It was the 5 or 6 am starts on Saturday mornings to spend the day competing in Tuscan cross-country dirt bike races that ultimately tipped the balance in our relationship. Sport was his priority. The lesser importance placed on my needs resulted in a growing feeling of resentment. I felt like a whining hag.

'When will you be home?'

'After I wash the trail bike and the trailer. Around six tonight.'

'But that means I'll be alone all day.'

'Why don't you go and visit your friends at Leonardo Leather Works?'

'I did that last Saturday.'

Within months of returning to Florence I became terribly jealous of his fun Saturdays, of his motorbike, of his motorbike friends, of his sheer activity. I cared deeply for him but began to seethe inside. How I hated his muddy, sweaty helmet, boots and padding gear, audaciously dumped outside on the terrace with the arrogant assumption that I would wash them. Finally, I cracked.

'I've given *everything* up for you – left my job, left my family, left my home, and you give up *nothing* for me!' I yelled one Friday night.

'This is the way I relax. I need it after a week's work. You have no right to ask me to give up dirt-bike racing for you.' His voice had a steely determination that told me he wasn't going to give ground.

'I'm only asking for more of your time.'

'You have me all week. This is my weekend.'

'But after all your sport you're always too tired to do anything with me.'

'Lisa, you need a sport, too. You might also make some friends of your own.'

That was his solution to my loneliness. The next morning at dawn, as he walked out the door to race, he turned back and whispered into the dark room.

'Tomorrow we'll go and see about buying you a horse.'

It was every little girl's dream come true. As a child, every year on my birthday I would walk home from school, praying that when I turned the corner, there in front of our house would be a horse float. Inside it would be my very own palomino, whom I'd call Honey, or a Welsh mountain pony whose name would be Star. The closest I ever came to having a horse was being given a copy of the *Horseman's Manual* for Christmas. After reading it avidly, I tried to copy all those fab 'working, medium, collected and extended' trots every Saturday morning during my weekly ride around Centennial Park.

Shine compared very favourably with Honey and Star. He was a superb seven-year-old golden-red gelding. It was his unique colouring and roundly arched neck that made me choose him over the ten or so other horses that were paraded before Paolo and me. The manager of the stables had advised us not to buy Shine, but to instead take an older, quieter mare that would pull no stunts when out riding in the hills around Florence. Shine had been brought down to Italy from Russia, where he had been ridden little and schooled hardly at all. But Shine's beauty (hence his name) far outshone his travel mates, so we disregarded the professional's advice.

Bella figura, with its imperative to look stylish at all times, played its part and Paolo, who very much wanted me to be happy and absorbed in my hobby, decked me out in full riding regalia. Long, black leather riding boots, beige jodhpurs, a helmet, a leather crop and anything else that took my fancy. Feeling very smart, I looked more like an Olympic Equestrian event competitor rather than a dinky-di Aussie used to jeans, a beat-up pair of R.M. Williams boots and a hired nag. Shine, too, was spoiled with an expensive new saddle, bridle, halter and lead reins, rug and a complete grooming kit.

Shine was then given five-star accommodation at La Fattoria di Pagnana stables at Pagnana, about fifteen kilometres east of Florence and only a twenty-minute drive from home. He had views of softly rolling hills, swaying cypress trees and olive groves. Well-maintained white picket fences marked the paddocks where he was turned out. It was a horse and rider's paradise. I thanked Paolo and felt fortunate indeed to be engaged to a man who threw himself so wholeheartedly behind my needs.

Mostly, Shine had to be schooled. The stable manager had been spot on – underneath Shine's golden exterior was a disobedient and headstrong mule. I had only an average amount of schoolgirl experience of riding, so handling him was a battle. Day after day, trying to tame his hard mouth and pulling head, we rode around and around the indoor and outdoor rings at the stables until we were both giddy.

Bored with the repetition, but still not fully confident about taking him out into the open space of the countryside alone, we joined another group of riders for an afternoon amble. The riders were nice, middle-aged men with reliable mounts.

As we saddled up, the bell from the little church on the hill above the stables rang ten times. It was an exciting moment. After this, Shine and I would be able to take romantic rides through the Italian countryside. Maybe even take a morning tea picnic and a book to read in a quiet field.

Once out of the gate, beautiful Shine shed his well-bred veneer and became a wild beast. He reared and bolted, finally throwing me after a hair-raising charge through a paddock. Shakily settling my sore rear end back into the saddle, I didn't breathe until we were safely back inside the stable gates.

'Same time tomorrow, then?' the men called as they brushed down their horses before leading them back into their stalls.

'No, I think I'll take a break tomorrow.'

Rather than breaking Shine's spirit, he had broken mine. From then on, riding him was an ordeal, rather than a pleasure. Shine didn't set hoof outside the stable after throwing me. I'd go up and groom him, ride him around the ring, then sit in the sun and doze. But I never told Paolo – I was too embarrassed.

Now, on Saturday nights, both our muddy boots and dusty pants lay heaped together on the terrace waiting to be washed.

'How is Shine going?' Paolo would ask.

'Fine, just fine.'

'I'll come up and watch you ride next week.'

'No, no. Don't bother.' I'd say quickly.

The idea of owning a horse was far more attractive than the reality. If we'd thought it through more thoroughly, we would have realised that tending a horse is a solitary activity and is no answer for loneliness. On weekdays I was often the only person at the stables. Shine soon showed himself for what he really was: a stopgap measure for a problem that was still there.

It is said that there are three distinct phases when, for whatever reason, people leave their home countries to live in another. The first phase is the 'honeymoon' period, when everything is exciting, new and beguiling. The second phase is 'resentment'. This is when newcomers lose patience with their new home and focus more on its negative aspects. During this period, expatriates start moaning about how bad mannered the Italians are and how they would kill for Thai food or some good sushi. Then, finally, comes the 'acceptance' stage. Some expats say they can go through all three stages in just one day.

The months turned into a year and, without knowing it, I was at the end of the honeymoon period, about to pass over into the resentment phase. Florentine life had become routine and lost its novelty. At the same time, my self-esteem was plummeting. Thankfully, I had enough work with Tutto Radio, 2UE back in Australia and USA Radio News to keep a finger in the radio journalism pie. The ABC's Radio National program, 'The Europeans', was also paying for interviews on the rapidly developing European Union. So, work wasn't the problem.

It was more a spiritual burden. It was as though the very nature of Italy, with its inflexible traditions and revered customs, was smothering me. Bound by duty, stymied by social expectations, it felt like the very fire that fuelled me as a person was being extinguished. I hadn't reckoned on finding Italy itself so stifling.

Paolo wanted me to convert to Italianism. He wanted me to become like the other women he knew and understood. He wanted me to replace his mother. He was happy with our relationship, but he couldn't understand why I refused to give in on the subject of housework. I knew that holding down a full-time job would be extremely tiring because there would be no sharing of the domestic duties at home. Of all the European countries, Italy has the lowest number of women in the workforce (only thirty-six per cent). It's no wonder, when you consider how much time it takes to tidy up the men's messes.

On the surface, our relationship was loving. Paolo was still the same deeply caring man. He wanted me to assimilate into Italian society. Whenever he wasn't involved in sport or work, he dedicated himself solely to me. We were also best friends, still enjoying aspects of sharing each other's cultures. We drove to Yugoslavia, Vienna, France and the Loire valley, adoring the travel that was so easy together. But underneath our love was a web of confusing demands and concessions. The road to a successful cross-cultural relationship is pot-holed with problems.

With the table set for two, the minestrone bubbling away on the stove and the steaks ready to go under the griller, Paolo arrived home one night to spring yet another surprise.

'The Gruppo FIST are on their way over for dinner. You'd better pull out a few more steaks and make some baked potatoes. Turn the minestrone off and put some water on to boil. They'll want some pasta.' Just like that. No help offered, just commands issued.

'*How* many people are coming?' My hands stole up to my hips and my feet moved apart into an aggressive stance as I turned to face him.

Brrring went the doorbell.

'Six. Here they are!'

'Listen, *mate*. This is not a friggin' restaurant. Why didn't you call to let me know they were coming?'

'It was a last-minute thing. You're always saying you're lonely. Well, here's some company.'

The troops spilled in through the door, noisily dragging chairs up to the table and calling '*Ciao*' as they sat down.

I had two choices. I could throw in the tea towel and tell them all to bugger off and find a restaurant. Or I could cook dinner.

I cooked dinner.

I allowed myself to be walked over for several reasons. Most Italian men have overwhelmingly strong characters. Their mothers have fostered in them a spirit of unquestionable self-righteousness. Paolo was also in his own home environment, which gave him boundless self-assurance at a time when my self-esteem was at its lowest ever ebb. Was Paolo just being a typical man, or a typical *Italian* man? Was this a universal problem or a cultural one? All I knew was that his work was more highly valued than mine. He brought the money home, and for that reason he couldn't be reprimanded.

Paolo sat down with his guests and had a great time while I cooked and served. His mouth was greasy from the steak. He wiped his fingers on the tablecloth, rubbed his bread down to the crust and looked more and more like Giovanni with every passing second. In my mind's eye I saw him in ten years' time . . . shouting, '*Qui! Qui! Tu devi stare qui!* Here! Here! You have to stay here!' pointing to the stove. Then there were our unborn children, little mini-mes with food dribbling down their chins, waving Mummy away as I tried to teach them not to speak with their mouths full.

To top it all off, RSVPs from the two hundred silver-embossed wedding invitations, telling all and sundry to come and celebrate our nuptials at the Consuma Church, were starting to come in. Ten, twenty, thirty people . . . with more RSVPs arriving every day. It seemed that everyone wanted to come to a wedding in the Tuscan mountains. They all needed accommodation, they all wanted help with their Italian. Mum's friends had begun to call, asking me to find them houses in Chianti. Did I know of a nice one with a pool? Could I find them a cook? I was overwhelmed with doubt about the marriage, but felt locked into an inescapable appointment at the altar.

The ground beneath me was beginning to shift. All the foundations that had felt rock-solid only a year ago now felt like sand. I was sinking.

The Contiki Villa, where the Australian, New Zealand and British Contiki tour groups stayed during their brief visits to Florence, felt like home. The villa staff were warm and friendly, and the bar was open from mid-afternoon. But it wasn't the booze that I needed, or wanted. It was the typical Australian humour, the larrikin behaviour, and the non-judgmental attitudes of the easy-going people who hung out there. Drawn to it on an almost daily basis, it was the only place where I felt I could really be myself. When at 6.30 I had to extract myself from the fun, the resentment at having to go home every night to cook dinner for Paolo built up in inside me like a pressure cooker.

One afternoon, the Aussie men were sitting around talking about how Italian men take lovers.

'Not bad, eh?' they joked. 'Reckon I wouldn't mind being a man here. They say it's almost standard behaviour and that the wives expect it. I must remember to have the right to have an affair included in my pre-nup contract. Ha, ha!'

'My fiancé doesn't think it's standard to have a lover.' I defended Paolo's loyalty, which I felt was beyond suspicion.

'Better check it out with him before you walk up the aisle, lovey!'

The conversation moved on, while our drinks tinkled and the evening sun hung ever lower in the pink sky. The villa's terrace overlooked the grassy hillocks beside Piazzale Michelangelo. The air was balmy, almost tropical with a scent of freshly cut grass. It all felt so much like home. I rang Paolo to say I wouldn't be back to cook dinner.

'*E io che faccio?* And what will I do?' he whined, stunned that he would come home to an empty house.

'Just take some meat out of the fridge. Make your own dinner.'

'But I can't do that. What are you doing? Who are you with?'

'I'm with a whole bunch of people – Australians, and I'm having fun.'

'You're up at the Contiki Villa! I'm coming up to get you right now.'

'Just leave me be, Paolo. I need the break away. I want the space.'

'No. I'll be there in fifteen minutes. Wait at the bottom of the driveway.' Click. He'd hung up.

Martha, a Canadian and the manager of the Contiki Villa, knew what was going on.

'You'd better go,' she said. 'Be honest with him. Talk to him, tell him of all your doubts. Ask him to confirm or deny your worries.' She was right. It was now or never.

Waiting under the trees for Paolo, I could hear echoing from the villa behind me an INXS song. It was from the new Michael Hutchence album that I hadn't yet heard. Like a snake being charmed out of its basket, I could feel the music pulling me back up the driveway. Someone shrieked and a man bellowed with laughter.

'Damn, damn, damn.' Feeling owned, no longer free, I kicked at the gravel driveway like a pubescent teenager huffily waiting for her dad to come and pick her up too early from a party.

When Paolo's *motorino* drew up, I grumpily heaved myself on behind him. His body was rigid.

'We're going home to talk,' he said through gritted teeth.

Up the stairs and into the apartment in indignant silence, we squared off to each other across the kitchen table.

'In six weeks we are getting married,' Paolo started. 'How is our marriage supposed to work if you want to party with Australians all the time?'

'Granted, I want to be with Aussies – but we have to look at *why*. It's because they don't expect things that I can't deliver.'

'Like what?'

'Like always being at home, because that's the role you expect your woman to play.'

'That will never change. You are the woman. You will have the children. You will always be needed at home.'

'OK. What about going back to Australia? Do you guarantee that I'll always be able to go home and visit? To take our children home to see their grandparents?'

'No, I can't guarantee that. We may not have the money for you to take our children back to Australia for visits. Anyway, *this* is your home now.'

'Taking our children to Australia is a *priority*. We'll have to do without other things, motorbikes, cars, expensive racing bikes, so that my kids can know my home.'

'No, you do not have my guarantee. Australia is no longer your home! Why can't you understand that, Lisa?'

The frustration made my chest constrict into sobs that, for now, were controllable.

'Right. Understood. While we're being so honest, can I ask you what you think about lovers?'

'Huh?'

'What would happen if I took on a lover?'

He laughed ruefully. 'The marriage would be over. When a wife takes a lover, there is no longer trust.'

'What would happen if *you* took on a lover?'

'That's different. Sometimes husbands do that. We would have to try and work it out.'

That night it became clear to me that my Italian lover of twelve years would never become my husband. It was the pivotal moment in our relationship, because my heart did a U-turn. Our marital expectations were too different for a partnership between us to ever work.

There was a wall in my head and it felt heavy. Each brick was another reason not to marry Paolo, and every day there were more bricks. The wall was so big now I could feel myself flailing, falling under its weight. The questions reeled, turned and came back again. Why won't he guarantee that

I can go home? Why is it different if he has a lover rather than me?

The sobs came, and he walked away from my tears. He could offer me no comfort, he was tired of trying. Our relationship hadn't been easy for Paolo. He was a good man, almost thirty-six years old, with normal Italian hopes and expectations. But our constant bickering was making him feel threatened and inadequate. He no longer felt sure of himself, or of me.

By mutual decision, we cancelled our wedding. The wedding dress, so lovingly designed and created by cousin Carla and Aunty Dina, was shunted into a cupboard like a disgraced family skeleton. Zio Franco's restaurant, the church, the priest, Paolo's family – all received the news with total incomprehension. Nothing so shocking as a cancelled wedding had ever happened in Consuma. To save face and heartache, we told the Consumi family and the Rossi aunties that perhaps the wedding would take place the following year. Whether they believed us or not is hard to say. Their only reactions were sighs of sadness and resignation. Gemma and Giovanni didn't assign blame. Their disappointment in the two of us was etched into their slow, deliberate words of shock and sympathy.

Finally I mailed out two hundred copies of a letter stating that the wedding would not take place. My family wasn't as shocked or appalled as Paolo's, because they'd known of my differences with Paolo. 'If you're not happy now, marriage is only going to make it worse,' they said, supporting and encouraging our decision.

We didn't break up, though. Still we hung on. We knew that, despite our differences, we still loved each other.

23

Summer, with its doomed nuptials, was behind us. In its wake were at least ten friends and family members who had paid for their tickets before the wedding was cancelled. They came to Florence anyway, bringing with them a badly needed sense of humour. Paolo and I did our best to be light-hearted and to entertain them, but it was difficult. We were grieving for something that was forever lost. Once the wedding guests left, we ate our meals together in remote silence, detached from each other's emotional turmoil. We knew that if our relationship wasn't moving towards marriage, staying together was pointless.

Over the following five dismal months, Shine and Paolo's cousin Claudia (Zia Maria's daughter) became my good friends. Both of them listened to my problems without comment. Claudia loved to trowel through flea markets in far-flung

Tuscan villages. She adored travelling to countries like Burma and Thailand – the more remote the place the better. She was curious and accepting of my foreign attitudes and patiently explained to me the ways of Italians.

The Leonardo Leather Works crowd and the gang across the road at Walter's Silver – Walter, Chris, Elizabetta, Jamie, Ottavia – were also warmly supportive when I most needed their friendship. They could see the loss in my eyes, so they included me in their circle at Francesco's bar. All of them a mix of nationalities – Canadian, Dutch, New Zealanders, British. All of us foreigners living with Italian men in Florence.

Soon another person began to form in my mind; a dream man. He embodied all of my male fantasies and was the image of a true-blue, ridgy-didge, dinky-di Aussie. My fair-dinkum dream fella was tall, with sandy brown hair and wonderful manners. He enjoyed good wine and food, and loved to cook. He valued my work, and would take paternity leave so that I could pursue career opportunities. He loved the beach, so he took our kids to Little Nippers because he'd been a lifesaver himself. He played cricket, and was the 'fire master' when we had backyard barbies. Of all his wonderful traits, the fact that he spoke and thought in Australian, so that we understood each other at a glance, was the most endearing.

Once Mr Ridgy-Didge (and the possibility of him truly existing somewhere in Sydney) had a firm foothold on my brick wall, any hope of rekindling my romance with Paolo was gone. For he, too, had been endowed with a wonderful dream woman. She had caramel skin, flashing black eyes, red lipstick and lots of gold jewellery. She loved cleaning and ironing, and had her brothers and sisters and childhood friends in Florence to keep her company while Paolo spent his weekends on the motorbike.

These fantasy people appeared because Paolo and I still cared deeply for each other. But we were tired of inflicting pain and so wanted peace for the other. By December, a few weeks before Christmas, there was little more than memories to hold on to and we knew it was time for me to return to Sydney. With the letting go came permission to like each other again, as people, as friends. With the friendship came relief, hope and great surges of energy at the prospect of getting on with our lives independent of each other.

Paolo and I spent our final weekend together up at Pratiglioni. He'd watched as I packed up my jackets and boots. Nodded in silence when I returned the diamond engagement ring. Playfully lunged at the gold Rolex when I told him it was staying on my wrist. He'd shrugged at the prospect of selling Shine. Laughed when I told him if he didn't stop dyeing his hair, he'd never find a girlfriend. Our moods swung from gaiety to melancholy. For the first time since we'd met, there was real conviction to our goodbye. Our circle of departures, arrivals and regrets was finally over.

Paolo would stay on in Consuma and have lunch with Zio Franco, while I drove back down to Florence alone. There would be no goodbye stops along the way. That would be more than I could bear. Just slip away.

Driving back down to Florence on that cloudy early morning, I felt the familiar pull of Australia, independence and freedom. Sometimes I wonder if I ever can, really, leave Italy. But I know that I must.

All that remained was the farewell to Gemma and Giovanni, and they had no idea that I was going.

The Consumis' new home was outside the city centre in a residential green belt near the Arno River. Happily retired from the Theatre Pergola, they spent their city time socialising with friends and ballroom dancing at their local *circolo* – the community council centres used by the elderly for daytime coffee sessions and night-time dances.

When I buzzed their doorbell, Gemma poked her head over the balcony to see who was there rather than pick up the intercom phone. She grinned widely and called down.

'*Un miracolo! E venuta Lisa a trovarci*,' she yelled. 'It's a miracle! Lisa has come to visit us.' Her comment was a dig at how rarely I popped in. Nothing would have pleased them more than a daughter-in-law prone to making unannounced visits.

She disappeared from view and the door of their building clicked open. With each step I took up the stairs to their first-floor apartment, my mind tried to rationalise my sense of guilt. My goodbye to Paolo had been punctuated with sadness and relief. During the drive down to Florence, my mood had swung between euphoria and confusion. Now, standing in Gemma and Giovanni's hallway, fidgeting with my jacket, I felt abject accountability.

A fresh tablecloth was being pluffed across the kitchen table as Gemma called out, 'Coffee or tea?' Giovanni gave a smoker's early-morning half-chuckle/half-cough when I requested an English Breakfast teabag instead of the customary Italian espresso.

He sat down across from me in the kitchen that they'd recently renovated in *stile montagna*, country mountain style, the most popular kitchen look in Italy. Rustic, dark wooden cabinets with ivory and brass knobs. Below them, long stretches of marble benchtops because there is no better surface than floured marble for kneading pasta dough.

'You left Giampaolo up there, eh? Do you have to work today?' asked Giovanni, reaching for his cigarettes.

'No, there's a million things to do, so I thought I'd come down early. He'll come down with Zio Franco later.'

Gemma fussed with the pot of water over the stove – Italians don't use kettles. My eyes moved from her back to Giovanni's face and I wondered if the wedding debacle with their only son had caused them shame. Small talk wouldn't come. General chit-chat felt superficial and I had no desire to feel shallower than I already felt.

'I've come to say goodbye,' I said.

Gemma turned to look at me. She knew from the gravity in my voice that the announcement was big. She came to the table and sat down next to her husband with her hands together on the table.

'Every time you've left us in the past, I've always asked if you planned to come back,' said Giovanni. His voice was paced, deliberate. There was no surprise to his reaction, as though he knew of my planned departure and had a speech at the ready. He put his cigarette in the ashtray, fanned both hands out on the tablecloth and looked down at his stretched fingers.

'I think this time it's final, Giovanni.'

'No,' he said. 'This time it *is* final.'

He reached across the table to take my hands in his while he shifted his gaze to my face.

'Lisa, you must promise me something now, and never, ever break the promise.' His words sounded so rehearsed.

'You must never return to Italy. You must leave my son forever. Do you understand? Do you promise me that?'

'Yes, Giovanni,' I said, nodding my head with heartfelt certainty. 'I promise you, I will never come back to Italy.'

24

One year later. A beach in Sydney's east.

A persistent seagull is trying to cajole me into sharing my dinner. It must be the same one from last night. His face looks familiar. Nielsen Park, with its quiet bushland and netted beach, has become my regular sunset picnic spot after work. The steps from the pavilion down on to the beach are perfect for leaning against to watch the activities on the harbour.

The sand here is coarser, yellower, than on the other harbour beaches. Cicadas rub their legs in a frenzied percussion that is as soporific as the curling, lapping waves. Birds swoop and squawk.

The beach is deserted and I am alone, as I always am. Paolo, Italy and the promise I made to Giovanni rarely come to mind. It's all so far away, so long ago. I have no regrets.

Three years later. Llandilo, Sydney's west.

It's not often you see a mature television reporter's brow creasing and bottom lip quivering as if she's about to burst into tears on the prime-time evening news. On this occasion, the journalist was doing a live cross to a residential street in Sydney's west, near Penrith, where a woman had died in her backyard. She had been digging fence posts when her borer struck electrical wiring. She had died on the spot, with her four young children, all aged under eight, playing nearby.

The camera took a close-up of the teary reporter recounting the facts, then the studio cut to footage of the backyard, complete with one of the woman's shoes and the kids' tricycles. The screen then went back to the reporter to sign off. The Channel Ten newsreader, Ron Wilson, followed with: 'Thanks, Lisa . . . now on to other news . . . '

'Maaaate,' came the chief of staff's voice into my two-way radio. 'You looked pretty bloody cut up. You're meant to look unaffected by the news you're reporting.'

'Ohh, my God!' I wailed. 'This is so *sad*. The woman's little children saw her die! We shouldn't even *be* here. This is a private, family tragedy. We should be leaving them in peace.'

'Listen, pal. Knock on their door and ask them for a photo of the woman, so that we can run it in *The Late News*. Then get back to the station,' the voice came back.

'You must be out of your mind! They're *crying* in there! I'm not doing it.'

'Death-knocks, mate. Part of the job. See you back here with the photo.' Static.

The cameraman, Scott Richardson, looked at me with an eyebrow cocked.

'Not doing it, Richo. We're outta here,' I said striding back to the Channel Ten news car. As we drove off up the street, one of the woman's neighbours stuck her head out of a window.

'FUCKIN' VULTURES!' she screamed at us. On this particular occasion, I agreed.

One year spent on the road for Channel Ten News had followed two years at 2GB Radio News Talk. After the fence-post lady, it was obvious that the buzz of reporting had waned for me. There was more baulk than barge to my journalistic approach, an attitude that wasn't going to secure me a reporter's position on *60 Minutes*. The morbid constancy of covering death produces a high burnout rate.

To solve the problem, Channel Ten's news director, John Campbell, suggested I come off air to produce.

'We need an associate producer for *The Late News*. Why don't you try writing for Sandra Sully?'

'Great. When can I start?'

'Next week. Your new hours will be 3 pm to 10.30 pm.'

After two years spent writing *The Late News*, it was again time to meet with John Campbell.

'So,' he said, his chair squeaking as he leaned back in his seat. 'I hear you enjoy working on *The Late News*?'

'Yeah, it's the right position for me.'

'Lisa, you're not getting any younger. You should think about increasing your responsibilities. What do you think about putting the news to air?'

I looked at him aghast. The top news producer's position involves sitting in the studio booth with a hundred screens and a microphone from your mouth into Sandra Sully's ear. If anything goes wrong, you have to decide what to do – move on to the next story – while simultaneously telling Sandra, the studio director and all the button pushers what to do and say next. The buck stops with you. I'd seen people take the position and go all grey and wrinkly from the stress overnight.

'No thanks, John. It's very kind of you to mention it – but really, I'm happy just writing.'

'Ahh, Lisa. I don't think you're quite understanding me. We *want* you to take the position.'

'But I don't *want* the position.'

'Then you should think seriously about where you want to go within the company.'

'Are you saying it's move up or out?' The word 'deadwood' (in the cut-throat, ambitious world of news, this isn't a good thing to be) kept ringing in my head.

'I'm saying it's move up, or think seriously about what Channel Ten can offer you.'

In other words, he was saying Channel Ten wanted me to move up. And if 'up' wasn't what I wanted, then may be it was 'out'.

So far, Mr Ridgy-Didge was proving to be elusive, but it wasn't for my want of trying. If there was a party on in Sydney or a freebie Channel Ten premiere, I was there. Not only that, I was the dressed-up eastern suburbs girl looking over everyone's shoulder to see if there were any single men arriving. To no avail. My bronzed Aussie either stayed in at night or didn't exist.

An old *Sydney Morning Herald* supplement on women's health provided a possible explanation. Apparently, only thirty-five per cent of all Sydney girls who had been born in the 1960s would marry. This remarkable statistic was attributed to a marginally lower male birthrate, some male 'brain drain' to other countries and a substantial increase in the number of gay men. All the lovely straight men had been snaffled up when they were young. Sydney's shortfall of eligible bachelors was more prevalent in the eastern suburbs, where I lived along with ninety per cent of the city's gay population.

Anyway, who was I kidding? A well-mannered lifesaver with a penchant for barbecues who would take paternity leave? He was a phantom, an illusion, just like my dream that Australian men had terrific attitudes to equal rights and opportunities for women. My married friends' complaints were evidence of the grip they were in when it came to shouldering the burden of cooking, cleaning and looking after baby. They were cornered just as much as Italian women were.

Fortunately, my other dreams had all been realised. I was financially independent with my own apartment and car. My brothers had both returned home and I was in close contact with them and an eccentric, indulgent auntie to my five little nephews. Life in Sydney, if a little empty on the romance side, was good.

On occasion, thoughts of Paolo would pop into my mind, but I would quickly squelch them. I absolutely refused to let my mind go back there. Thoughts of Paolo were a no-go zone.

What happens in the subconscious, though, is another matter. Once, when I was under the gas in the dentist's chair (they say it's akin to a truth serum), I had a vision of Paolo looming over me. He was explaining something in Italian with infinite patience. With his surgeon's hands he made round, soft circles in front of his face. In that gas-induced trance, I felt an inexplicable surge of comfort, which left me feeling unsettled for weeks afterwards. But there was no point in stopping to analyse it. If there was a battle going on between my heart and my head, I didn't want to know about it.

Then, one day, fate intervened. A journalist friend called to ask if I knew anything about a weirdly violent Florentine football game called Calcio Storico. Her boyfriend, the Italian photographer Daniele Mattioli, had already sold his fabulous Calcio photographs to the Ansett in-flight magazine, *Panorama*. But without a writer to explain the game, his photos couldn't be published. Meeting Daniele provided the career change that I needed when TV journalism had taken me as far as I wanted to go. Together, we went on to produce a dozen magazine stories on Tuscany.

It was time to take the leap of faith and quit Channel Ten for a full-time career as a freelance writer. Daniele had lined up five amazing stories for publication in some of Australia's most prestigious magazines and newspapers. There was only one problem. To write the stories, I had to go back to Italy.

There had been times over the past five years when I had been tempted to make a phone call to Gemma and Giovanni. How were they? How was Aunty Dina? Aunty Maria? Uncle Franco? Were there many porcini mushrooms in the woods this year? What *was* that recipe for *nudi*, because mine have the consistency and bounce of a super ball? My questions remained unasked, as it would have been ridiculous to keep in touch with Giovanni and Gemma but not Paolo.

In five years, there had been no contact with anyone in Italy, except for intermittent postcards from Claudia while on her travels. On the one hand, I thought, surely it would be possible to visit Italy without my presence being detected by the Consumi family. But I also felt that I owed them the respect of telling them that their errant almost-daughter-in-law was breaking her promise and on her way back.

'*Pronto.*' It was Gemma's voice. Presuming that their schedule had changed little, I had called at eight o'clock on a Sunday evening. I wasn't expecting to be so moved by the sound of Gemma's voice. It was great to know that she was at the other end of the line.

'Gemma, it's me, Lisa,' I said in the first Italian I'd uttered in five years.

'Lisa who?' she asked. My heart sank – she didn't even remember me.

'Lisa from Australia. Do you remember me?'

'*Oh, mamma mia! Oh mio Dio! Lisa? Dove sei? A Firenze?* Oh, my God! Where are you? In Florence?' Once she understood it was me, she sounded pleased. Her voice also sounded a bit hoarse.

'*Ciao!* I'm in Sydney. I know it's such a long time since we've spoken and I didn't want to disturb you. But how are you?'

'We're not so good. It's very sad over here right now. Giovanni passed away last month.' My heart skipped a beat. It didn't seem possible.

'Giovanni? Gemma, I'm so very sorry.'

'It was a long illness. Lung cancer. He died October 17.'

The hairs on the back of my neck stood up. Then the skin all over my body crawled as if someone had just walked over my grave.

'But that's my birthday! He died on my birthday?'

'*Si.* Peculiar, isn't it? Paolo mentioned it at the time.'

'How is Paolo?'

'He's not taking it very well. Giovanni's death has changed him.' Her voice became ragged. My tears started to flow.

'I can't tell you how sorry I am, Gemma. This call was to tell you that I must come to Florence for work. It seemed important that Giovanni knew I was breaking my promise to him.'

'Darling, come if you need to. Are you going to call Paolo?'

In truth, the thought of speaking to Paolo had been buzzing like an uncatchable blowfly in the back of my mind. But calling him would make too many firmly repressed emotions clatter to the surface. I didn't even ask Gemma if he was married or engaged.

'No. I hadn't planned to.'

'Maybe you should phone him. I think he would be pleased to hear from you.'

We talked further about Giovanni's death and how she was coping. Gemma didn't suggest that we get together. When I hung up, the loss of Giovanni and all that he represented made me feel so sad. The fact that he had died on my birthday seemed bizarre. In view of our pact, his timing couldn't have been more poignant.

Now there was no promise to break.

My girlfriends looked sceptical.

'You *have* to call him,' said Karen.

'She *can't* call him,' said Janet. 'She's spent the last five years getting over him. It's a can of worms. Let it go.'

'Who knows when she'll go back to Italy again? What's the harm in having a chat? I'd love to know if he's happily married. I bet he's still in love with Lisa.'

'It doesn't matter if he is. She can't go back to that relationship. You can never go back.'

'Whose talking about getting back with him?' said Karen. 'Maybe she has unresolved issues to work through.'

Love those girlfriends! You can sit back and let them sort out your life for you. My contribution to the discussion was a pained shrug.

'I honestly don't know. I think I agree with Janet. I don't want to see him. The thought fills me with a screaming terror.' So we left it at that. They concluded that if there was so much fear, then there must be some love left over for him. And that frightened everybody into a pensive silence.

Most of my family were dead against my calling him. My sister urged me not to, whereas Mum couldn't see any harm in it. My father recommended that I have a long hard think before I did anything rash, and my brothers looked at me like they were ready to schedule me into the nearest straightjacket.

'Jeez! You're a lunatic, a sucker for punishment. Go and write the stories and come back home. What do you want to contact Paolo again for?'

I couldn't let it go, because I couldn't work out what I felt for him. Now that thoughts of Paolo were allowed to resurface, the prospect of seeing him filled me with a shortcircuit of sparking emotions. But the feelings were an unfathomable, messy mass of wires that led nowhere. To call, or not to call, consumed my thoughts while I packed for the trip and during the flight to Rome.

Being back in Italy felt wonderful. I concentrated on appreciating the Italian culture once again, rather than focusing on painful memories. There was no healing process to be worked through, no unearthed pain. For the first time, I felt comfortable with the ways of the country and its people.

It was fun to join the Italians on their evening *passeggiata*, listen to their conversations and enjoy their humour.

Daniele and I covered three stories on artists, earthquakes and food in Umbria before heading on to Milan to interview the Australian supermodel manager, David Brown. My indecision about whether or not to contact Paolo continued. Soon it was time to leave Milan for Florence to do yet another interview.

As I lay on my bed in the overheated Milan hotel room, gazing at the pale-blue, fake-suede wallpaper opposite, I felt an inexplicable sensation of being pushed into picking up the phone to dial Paolo. Something beyond my understanding was telling me to do it. It didn't feel as though I *wanted* to, only that I *had* to. My inner voice told me that everything in my life had led to this one moment, that my life was about to change. I sat up and looked at the phone on the bedside table and felt sick with apprehension.

With a hammering heart, I clasped the phone tightly to my ear and dialled the numbers.

The sound of Paolo's recorded voice on his answering machine call made me freeze. The beep, a pause, and then my halting voice.

'Hi, Paolo, it's Lisa. I know we haven't spoken in a very long time, but Gemma told me that Giovanni has passed away. I wanted to let you know how sorry I am. I'm in Milan right now and will be coming to Florence. If you feel like calling, that's fine. If you don't, that's fine, too.'

I left him the hotel phone number and slumped back against the wall. The relief had made my body go weak. I had extended my sympathies. Now the ball was in his court. If he wanted to call, he could. For all I knew, his girlfriend was sitting on his couch listening to my message.

Brrring!

The ringing made me jump. It had to be him.

'Hello?'

'*Ciao, Lisa. Sono Paolo.*' My hand flew up to my throat.

'Hi. How are you? I hope I'm not intruding on your evening.'

'No, no. It was nice to hear your voice. Mamma told me you were coming to Firenze. I had hoped you would call.'

So my call was welcome. That gave me a rush of pleasure and made me smile. Once again, he spoke in Italian and I spoke in English.

'Are you OK? I'm so sorry about Giovanni.'

'I am very sad, but at least he is no longer in pain. He suffered terribly towards the end.' Paolo had that gravelly texture to his voice that men get when they are feeling emotional. But he didn't sound cold or resentful, as I'd feared.

'Is Gemma getting by?'

'She's managing. Spending a lot of time up at Consuma with her sisters.'

'What about you? Is there someone you can share this with?' The question came from the bottom of my heart. It wasn't about finding out if he was seeing someone. It was about making sure he had a close friend to share his grief with. I was suddenly aware of just how much I cared for this man.

'Lisa, there is no one in my life. There has been no one in my life since you left. There are a lot of things that I need to say to you, that's another reason why I'm glad you called.' Paolo's voice had taken on a tone of urgency, as if tightly held emotions were spilling from his chest.

'Uh-huh. All right,' I said tentatively, all wrapt attention focused down the phone line. What was coming was anyone's guess.

'Lisa, I'm sorry. For so long I've wanted to tell you that. When we were to marry, I never gave you the guarantees that you needed in order to be able to live here. *Of course* you could have visited Australia whenever you needed to. You had changed your whole life for me, and I changed nothing in return. I said those things because I was proud and stubborn and threatened and scared. Forgive me. I think I made big mistakes.'

I sat in a stunned silence.

'It's all right, Paolo,' I said softly. 'Truly. I don't think either one of us was to blame.'

'It's important you know everything.' His voice was tender.

'Really, it's all right,' I said. He went on, his voice growing warmer, a pillow-talk warm. It was as though he were whispering a lifetime of love in my ear.

'Since my father died, I've done a lot of thinking. I have grown up. I feel so different. You know, we never really talked properly about having children? That's the most important thing in the world for two people who love each other. Children.'

Hearing his emotional apology seemed to dissolve all the confusion surrounding my own emotions. Beyond any doubt, I knew then that I still loved him. I knew that I loved him more now than ever before, and that I had never stopped loving him.

'Paolo, I'm coming to Florence tomorrow and I'd like to see you. Would you like to have dinner together?'

'Very much.'

'I'll call you from the hotel in the early evening. And

Paolo, thank you for telling me all of this. It means a lot to me. I didn't know how much until I heard you say it.'

'*Ciao.*'

'*Ciao.*'

I flopped down on to the bed and felt an emotion so pure it was breathtaking. Talk about cloud nine. Wow!

Brrring! The phone! Again? Who could this be?

'Hello?'

'*Ciao*, it's me again. What if I jumped into the car and came up to Milan to get you right now? Would that be OK?'

I laughed excitedly. 'That would be fantastic! I'm on Via Monte, at Hotel Monte.'

'See you in three hours.'

Such exquisite anticipation. Those three hours were the longest in my life.

It was November – cold, misty and dark outside. I paced the hotel room, waited for Paolo and bit my fingernails down to their quicks. After three hours I moved my luggage downstairs, checked out and waited for him in the hotel lobby. When he walked in, his face and bearing revealed the changes he had undergone. His hair was thick and almost completely grey, not dyed, his blue and yellow eyes more captivating than ever.

When we hugged, the sensation of his body so close to mine was primal. I was shocked by my body's reaction to his smell. His familiar scent ignited a longing to touch him, hold him. The fact that he was so nervous he was trembling blew me away.

The drive down to Florence was unforgettable. Paolo

looked straight ahead at the highway and filled me in on the last five years, while I just listened. He recounted the many changes in his life with a surprising gravity and sensitivity. He wouldn't have been capable of those perceptions years ago. His features fell into new expressions, his eyes had a different depth. I looked at his profile and watched his hands on the wheel, all the while aching to touch him.

The death of a man's father can be a life-changing event. For Paolo, it meant a re-evaluation of everything he thought he understood. He was no longer the flippant, cocksure sportsman, but a deeper man with greater wisdom. His father's illness had consumed him. When Giovanni eventually passed away, Paolo was by his side.

In the lead-up to his father's death, many of Paolo's old distractions had fallen away. Sport no longer satisfied him. He had sold his trail bike, motorcycle and Shine. Karate had given way to weights. His gym routine was the only exercise he'd maintained.

The friends that he had held so close had also disappeared. The members of the Gruppo FIST had had a nasty falling out. They no longer took up his time and influenced his attitudes. Another change was in the way his mother looked after him. Gemma had nursed Giovanni for more than two years, leaving Paolo to do his own household chores. He said he now appreciated the mundanity and hard work that went into running a home.

Now in his early forties, Paolo confided that he had an odd feeling of having been left behind. His cousins and friends were married with children, and he was godfather to many of them. More and more, he wanted to have his own children.

When he pulled the car up in front of my hotel in Florence, we looked at each other and knew that it was too soon to say goodnight. We went back to the same old couch at Via Orsini to talk until the early hours of the morning.

Eighteen years after falling in love for the first time, we found ourselves doing it all over again. Only this time, there was something profoundly different about our love. Our past had given us a deep understanding of each other. By morning we knew that you *can* go back to an old relationship. When we fell into a peaceful sleep, we felt that there was nothing left to iron out, only the future to be lived.

I never moved out of Via Orsini. The same diamond solitaire engagement ring that I had handed back to Paolo with such certainty more than five years before, suddenly reappeared. It was to be mine after all.

Within two months, I was pregnant with our first child. The grandchild that Giovanni had so dearly desired was due to be born exactly eleven months after his death.

25

To confirm our lifetime partnership through pregnancy was a wise decision. The joy of being together was focused on the beginning of a new life, rather than on a ceremonial day – a much healthier scenario for two people still smarting from the stressful pressures of a looming wedding date.

By my fifth month of pregnancy we were ready to take our vows and married in a civil service in the Red Room of the Palazzo Vecchio, the town hall of Florence. Built in 1322, it is an imposing medieval structure next to the Uffizi Gallery, in the heart of ancient Florence. The floor of the Red Room is covered with thick red carpet, its walls with red silk, its windows with red velvet curtains and its ceilings with frescoes of cupids shooting arrows. The Municipality of Florence gives all newlyweds a sterling silver pot with a raised lily in its lid. The lily – or *giglio* – is the emblem of Florence. Inside the pot were love sonnets written by famous Florentine poets. None of my Australian family or friends was there to share in our happiness, only Gemma, Zia Maria and my witness, cousin Claudia. It was a very different wedding from the one we had planned originally, but it was the right balance for Paolo and me. Florence was my home now, and being married here, alone, was one of the steps I needed to take to help me come to terms with that.

It had been a long and tumultuous battle, this final giving up of my homeland. Letting my Australian family go in favour of having my own Italian one had been the challenge of my life. For many other girls, the decision to move to the other side of the world for a man is a snap. Not so for me . . . and I could never have done it without making some major changes to my own entrenched attitudes.

There are no more accusations of 'I gave up everything for you', but rather, 'I chose to be with you because I wanted to'. For our marriage to work, I cannot burden Paolo with responsibilities that are not his to bear. The decision to leave Australia permanently was mine, but the responsibility for helping me to make that decision in a supportive, caring way, was his. The biggest stumbling block to marrying Paolo all those years before had been his refusal to guarantee me the right to visit Sydney whenever I wanted. Whether or not I chose to take up the right, it was essential that I *knew* I had the choice. When love requires relocation to Italy, there has to be a clear runway out of Rome.

I also had to learn how to surrender my work. There was a baby on the way and I wasn't falling for the modern mythology being peddled by the glossy women's magazines: 'Girls! You can work, have quality time with your children *and* be a great wife! Let us show you how!' No way, too much guilt and hard work.

Another choice had to be made, and it was work that got the flick. I took the risk of being financially dependent upon Paolo, and if the gamble left me destitute with the kids after he absconded with his dental nurse, well then, so be it. My issue was *letting* a man take care of me, not fear of abandonment.

Sorting through the cultural differences with Paolo wasn't an overnight matter. It's an ongoing learning curve that requires patience and a lot of putting the shoe on the other foot. Paolo still takes his seat at the table and waits to be served. Always will. But one of his best attributes is that he doesn't mind being told what to do. So it's up to me not to make a scoresheet of his faults, because his habits are deeply entrenched. 'The pasta is in the pot, Paolo.' 'Ok,' he says, 'I'll get it myself, then.' 'Pick up the bread and milk on the way home, please, Paolo.' 'Ok. Do we need anything else?'

Paolo has been wonderful about putting my Aussie shoe on his Italian foot. He no longer expects me to convert to Italianism, but he understands now that there are no gender-based duties in most Australian families. He clears up, washes up and takes the washing off the line. It helps that these former domestic problems are an open window – they are well aired and, in typical Tuscan style, a fair target for a giggle and a tease. No grudges are allowed, ever.

Even though sport is still his obsession (speed-bicycle racing is the current passion), Paolo now cares for all his own sports gear. How my time is spent while he's out has had to be managed with the forethought and planning of an American election campaign, otherwise depression can still set in. It's remarkably easy to blame any loneliness I feel on him, but I can't expect him to give up what makes him happy; he'll only resent me for it in the long run.

The legacy of Giovanni and his mountain gruffness is also well and truly with us. It's there in the tone of Paolo's voice. Every day, I have to remind myself that Paolo's way of speaking is part of his cultural and family heritage. More and more though, Paolo is hearing it for himself. This morning he said, 'I'm sorry, I didn't mean to sound rude.' It was practically the most beautiful thing he has ever said to me.

A long-standing issue that hasn't changed, never will and could ultimately see us in the divorce court, is table manners. But it's a cultural thing that I just have to accept. The Italians approach their food with a hands-on relish that can make those of us with prim table manners appear repressed. At the end of the day, Paolo adores eating and is more knowledgeable about good food than anyone I know. Gotta love that.

There are three main ingredients in our mixed-culture marriage: love, a merciless sense of humour and the sharing of the same moral principles. If our values differed (including monogamy – no exceptions for husbands!), we'd be in deep trouble. We've also come to realise that our issues are similar to those in same-culture relationships. However, during arguments, we tend not to blame each other, but rather our cultural backgrounds. That way, neither of us is at fault! This could be considered cheating or denial, but who cares? It works for us.

A pregnant woman in Italy is fed all she can eat with exclamations of, 'You are eating for two'. Complimentary cakes arrive from benignly smiling bartenders in coffee shops, while unsolicited extra servings of everything drop on to your plate as if sent from heaven. In this Catholic country, where the mother-Madonna figure is often elevated to a position higher than Jesus, a pregnant woman is admired and revered.

I felt like a goddess lying on the couch at Pratiglioni while Gemma brought me tastettes from the kitchen. She was happy that I was back, but her smiles at my return paled into insignificance beside her sheer euphoria at my pregnancy. During the many times I was banished to Pratiglioni to incubate the baby in the fresh mountain air, Gemma plied me with her mountain spring water (less sodium) and nightly bowls of *farinata*, for my milk production. (Basically it's a white sauce. The magic is in the flour.) It was a shame, she said, that chestnuts were out of season, otherwise they too would have featured heavily on my mother-in-law's pregnancy dietary supplement list.

Whenever I ventured out for a walk, she would come hurtling up the path panting and calling my name. 'You can't be out of sight of the house,' she'd cry. 'What if your waters break? What if you fall?'

Her care was cloying but endearing, and not worth confronting her with. So I stayed within the prescribed precincts of the building, waving to our Nonna-to-be whenever she stuck her head out of a window to check on me (about every half-hour).

The Rossi aunties drooled over my stomach, and twittered as they lifted my T-shirt to inspect its shape and rub its bulge. Then the predictions started. The most common clue at the sex of an unborn child is the condition of the mother's skin. If it's a boy, his testosterone is in conflict with the mother's oestrogen. The signs are all in the luminosity.

'You're sallow, pinched – it's a boy!'

'You're rosy, smooth – it's a girl!' Or the less flattering, 'She's having a girl! Look! She's stealing her mother's beauty!'

If the baby is hanging low in the womb, it's a boy. High, a girl. If your shape is like an egg on its side, a boy. A basketball, and it's a girl.

Paolo was no less enamoured of our unborn child than were the Rossi sisters. According to the ultrasound, we were to have a little girl. He bawled great lumpy tears and grinned like a madman at the sight of our foetus on the TV screen. When it came to preparing the baby's nursery, the man who would rather stick needles into his eyes than go shopping spent Saturdays examining the benefits of cotton-lined woollen vests for newborns.

Still nervous about delivering in an Italian hospital, I pushed aside the raft of delivery horror stories and focused on finding the right obstetrician. The first one was crossed off the list after he took a social call on his mobile while giving me an internal examination. The second one was given the boot after hospitalising me at four months for a week with a drip in my arm over a non-existent threatened miscarriage. All this because every time I had a bowel movement, I spotted. To get out of the hospital I lied and said the bleeding had stopped. Upon being discharged I had an internal examination and a polyp, the cause of the bleeding, was found.

I found my third, and final, obstetrician through an American girlfriend who also recommended that I give the Italian public hospital system a miss and go private. After my week at the local maternity hospital, this sounded like just the trick. What upset me more than the trails of blood up and down the corridors, and the smears of it on the bathroom door handles and toilet seats, were the mothers miscarrying next to others in advanced labour. There was no sympathy shown for mothers who lost their babies in varying stages of advanced pregnancy.

Dr Lucosi was an experienced obstetrician who was well advanced in years and with no constantly ringing mobile phone. His only quirk was his aversion to black lace underwear on pregnant women. As my pregnancy progressed, we developed a good patient–doctor relationship, as long as I wore the modest white lingerie suited to a woman in my condition. Concerning the delivery of my baby, we differed on only one point. Epidurals. My fear of having a baby in Italy had a lot to do with the Italians' disdain for epidurals (no matter how long the labour). Everybody knows that labour hurts, it's just that in Italy the pain seems to be prized. Nurses, doctors and mothers explained, 'You must endure birthing pain because it is a suffering that all mothers, like our mothers before us, must suffer.' What *was* this, some kind of ancestral pass-down-the-pain kick? Grandma knew pain, therefore so must you?

Dr Lucosi explained that an epidural *could* be made available, but only if it was deemed necessary. Defining 'necessary' was one problem. Deciding on *who* could deem it as necessary was another.

The final fear I had to crash-tackle was my fear of giving birth in a foreign language. Words like 'dilate', 'labour', 'cervix' and 'breech' aren't part of your everyday Italian vocabulary. But it was nothing that my book *Tutto Sulla Tua Gravidanza – Everything About Your Pregnancy* – couldn't fix.

Fortunately, when Natalia June Consumi decided it was time to meet the world, she couldn't wait to join the party. Her delivery was quick and easy. Dr Lucosi and I never had a moment to haggle over the definitive nuances of a 'necessary epidural'. 'Save that for next time,' he 'ho ho-ed' during his bedside visit after the birth.

Throughout the birth, my husband had stood steadfastly by my side, supportive and tender. Mum had come to Florence and had held my hand as I was stretchered into the delivery room. She stared at Natalia all afternoon and marvelled that after five grandsons, she finally had her granddaughter. Later, my brothers and sister called, and my best friends in Australia sent an enormous bunch of flowers. After all my phobias and fears, childbirth in Italy hadn't been lonely or frightening. It had been beautiful.

We thought it remarkable that Natalia was born on Zio Franco's birthday. He was Giovanni's closest friend and brother; he was also Paolo's godfather. The coincidence made us laugh. 'What are the chances of *that*?' we said. And 'Got to hand it to Giovanni. He must be pulling a few strings up there to have his granddaughter born on his brother's birthday.'

Once I was home with Natalia, a whole new layer of Italian society was opened up to me. All of a sudden I was treated like a star. There was so much attention and praise. '*Brava, bravissima*,' people called, as though I were an opera diva who had just performed an incredible aria. I felt terrific because the other mothers, and especially the grandmothers, now shared their knowing looks of complicity with me. I had made it into the Mammas Club, no small feat when you consider they actually run the country.

The attention bestowed upon me, however, was nothing compared to the sheer adoration bestowed upon my baby. Simple errands now took hours because of the constant flow of admirers who stopped my pram for a peek inside. '*Ohhh, che bella*!' cooed elderly men. '*Ohhh, quanto tempo ha?*' clucked stylish young women. Young men had no fear of expressing their love and of interest in babies. *Everyone* wanted a glimpse of the precious little bundle and it filled me with pleasure. I was so far away from my own family's love that the endearing way in which these strangers worshipped my child greatly soothed my homesickness.

I appreciated the community's adoration of my child all the more because in Italy there are no council or community-run baby centres, drop-in support groups or free health clinics for new mums. The wonderful assistance and just plain old shoulder to cry on (or for your baby to cry on) that we take so much for granted in Australia simply doesn't exist in Italy. I survived by ordering all the baby-care books that I could find on the Internet. Natalia's weight, growth patterns and eating problems were all solved by reading books by Robin Barker, Miriam Stoppard and Penelope Leach.

While I didn't have Karitane to turn to, I *did* have Nonna Gemma – a reliably constant source of information and advice. She is no different from the great majority of Italian grandmothers – utterly at your disposal should you need them for any little thing concerning their grandchildren. What's more, she can cure your baby of any ailment, because Italian grandmothers spend their lifetimes gathering helpful home hints on every aspect of family life and Nonna is only too happy to pass them on, whether you want them or not. I found my mother-in-law's baby-care tips at best interesting, at worst, extremely intrusive. Rice or barley water were two of her favourites for a gas problem, though stewed fennel and bay-leaf water were also popular. A parsley stem gently inserted up Natalia's bottom was a sure remedy for her daily bouts of colic. Drops of warm grappa and milk placed in her ear would certainly do the trick for an earache. When she's older, bread dipped in wine and sugar is sure to calm her down. Nor does Nonna's advice diminish with Natalia's age. Natti must wear shoes at all times, or she'll pick up worms through the soles of her feet. Don't kiss her on her mouth, or you'll spread your germs. Don't uncover her stomach after dinner, or she'll catch a chill in her tummy. The sea air excites, so don't bother putting her to sleep. Maybe there is something to all this unconventional advice and traditional homeopathy – or nonneopathy, as we call it. Personally, I don't have the courage to administer or practise it. And there were many times when I curtly told Gemma to 'back off!' because her peering over my shoulder all the time sometimes made me doubt my own mothering skills. She soon learned, without too much offence taken, that her daughter-in-law was going to do everything *her* way.

Apart from her extensive pharmacopoeia, the Italian nonna also offers a very practical, helpful hand. No domestic duty was left unturned by our visiting nonna. She wanted to babysit and while doing so washed and ironed, and mopped all the floors. Not all nonnas are like mine, but the great majority are. When it was time for preschool enrolment, my council-run preschool furnished me with a government form to ascertain that there were no lazy nonnas shirking their familial duty to care for Natalia. It didn't seem fair to ask Nonna Gemma to look after Natalia full-time, so I listed her permanent residence as Pratiglioni – Arezzo – too far away for her to commute. I think Nonna Gemma was quietly relieved. Once it was established that our other Nonna lived in Australia, Natalia earned her place at preschool.

After trying to fathom this matriarchal selflessness,

I realised that Italian mammas show their love for their children and grandchildren by doing everything for them. Anglo-Saxon mothers demonstrate their love by teaching their children how to do everything for themselves.

When it comes to raising children, women tend to raise their kids the same way they themselves were raised. At night when I pulled Natalia's bedroom shutters closed at seven, only to see my neighbours laughing at me, I felt a little ashamed of my Aussie regimen. It's impossible to erase my childhood memories of a 6 pm dinnertime and 7 pm bedtime. However, doubts about my bedtime rituals last only until their two-year-old's exhaustion-induced tantrum echoes across our lawn at about eleven every night. The Italians let their children play until they drop. This includes a ridiculously late start to the Baby Disco dance party that is organised at every beach and ski resort in the country. My child never raged with the other toddlers because, in spite of that exciting sea air, when the mirror ball started to turn at 9.30 pm she was always fast asleep.

Though I dragged the chain at becoming an Italian mamma, I am amazed by how much I have conformed to Italian life, how much I now enjoy it. It has a lot to do with the baby, but I'm home every day happily cooking up pasta for lunch. I now love our special, mid-week, midday time together as a family. There's no more resistance at having to cook two meals a day, probably because Nonna Gemma has passed on her timesaving secrets and doing it isn't a big effort anymore. I also adore the siesta and the romance that an enforced one-hour nap induces.

My social behaviour has changed, too. I now speak loudly, talk over people and interrupt them. Put it down to cultural osmosis – it's a matter of survival. Another big change is in my driving skills. After years of driving in open-mouthed wonder at the antics of Italians on the roads, I've joined in and am among the worst of them. Yet again, it's about survival. If I never made an illegal U-turn, overtook on double lines or pushed in, I'd be sitting in the traffic right now, instead of writing this book.

My life is at the acceptance stage. The honeymoon and resentment phases have given way to an acquiescence to the Italian way of life. I still can't cut my bread the Tuscan way, though, and a breadboard is a central feature of my table.

Florence itself has helped me to reach this phase of my love affair with the city and with Paolo Consumi. Phone contact with Australia no longer costs three dollars a minute. (A twenty-minute phone call to mum used to cost sixty dollars.) Communication has been made less expensive with the advent of cheap phonecards, emails, the Internet and fax. Florence is also far more cosmopolitan than it used to be. The Chinese have infiltrated the city and opened Asian mini-marts on many of the historical street corners. They are open until late and throughout the siesta. They offer convenience and a change of tradition. I almost staggered into the noodle shelf in shock when Paolo recently pointed out the fresh tofu in one Asian mart fridge. Rice noodles, coconut milk, sweet potatoes, sweet chilli sauce, lemon grass and bok choy were available only in expatriates' dreams just ten years ago. Peanut butter, maple syrup, bottled tomato sauce and chocolate-chip cookies were sold exclusively through the expensive British Store; now they're on the supermarket shelves. Licensing laws for vendors have been extended to give bakers permission to sell milk, and there's been a revolution in the traditional shopping hours. Supermarkets are open all day; though when Italians want quality, and most do, they still shop at their local *ortolano* and *alimentari*. The result of the euro has been an astounding increase in prices, and this is having a more negative effect on the little food shops than the big supermarkets ever had.

Some Italophiles will see these changes to daily life as a corrosion of all that they love about Italy. But life is about change, the world is about migration and globalisation, and there is nothing we can do to protect or exclude medieval cities from experiencing an expansion of their fortified walls to include sushi, tacos, tofu and corner shops. Simply by virtue of having these products available, the often-narrow Italian mind and vocabulary has been enlarged to include more than just what is on their map. A new younger, better-educated generation is changing the old Italy, and it is only natural that this is so. The sad and unfortunate aspect to this is, what will happen when the last nonnas and nonnos, who keep so many traditions alive, are gone? Most young Italians aren't interested in having a vegie patch of their own. They don't want to slave over fresh homemade pasta for Sunday lunch. They have too many leisure-time distractions – TV, sport, computers and their games, CDs, DVDs and travel. Once the Nonna Gemma generation is gone, Italy will be very different.

The absence of Giovanni in our lives has created other changes. The Theatre Pergola has demolished its custodian's apartment so that the Consumis' old home is now a warren of changing and meeting rooms for actors and directors. No one goes up to Pratiglioni in the dead of winter anymore. There is no one to care for the road, which is now too steep and rough to handle with the extra hazard of snow. The heating needs to be on permanently to offer a comfortable night's sleep, and Gemma doesn't want to stay up there alone. She stays in the city and we go up to the house every summer to escape the suffocating heat of Florence. There are no more homegrown chooks or rabbits, but Giovanni's wonderful orchard of figs, plums, apples and pears grows well under Gemma's care.

Though Paolo has changed enormously since the death of his father, the elements of his character, the ones that I fell in love with so many years ago, are still the same.

He is constant, reliable and loyal, and has a strong desire to provide well for his family. Though he is not a *mammone* (mummy's boy), he has been brought up in the *mammismo* environment. As with most Italian men, this has made him caring towards women, marriage, his mother and his grandmother. He is not embarrassed to show love towards his mother or wife. Italian men have no qualms about expressing love and they know how to validate and respect women . . . because their mothers have taught them how.

At night, Paolo bathes Natalia, puts her into her pyjamas and tells her stories until she falls asleep. Her favourite story is the one about Nonno Armando careering down the hill near Pratiglioni as he tried to save the girl on the bike whose brakes had failed. Her great-grandfather is a hero in her eyes. She knows all about how Nonno Armando cut wood in Calabria to make money to bring home to Nonna Angiolina. Natalia listens wrapt as Paolo takes her back to when Pratiglioni was a working farm, to when Paolo himself was sent out into the woods all day with the sheep.

When it's my turn to tell the stories, Natalia hears all about wild brumbies, lost kangaroos and lonely koalas stuck up trees. She crosses between her parents' cultures, countries and languages with the ease of the innocent. Her first spoken language was Italian, though she has always understood English perfectly, too. For a child to be truly bilingual, both parents must speak to their children only in their mother tongues. From the moment she was born, I've only ever spoken to Natalia in English. For the first two years, she only ever spoke to me in Italian. It was difficult, as I desperately wanted her to call me 'Mummy' instead of 'Mamma'. Then one day, just as I was starting to give up hope of ever hearing my child speak the same language as me, Natti called me 'Mummy'. I whooped with joy. Then slowly, her every second word popped out in English. At this point, no one except Paolo and I understood her. Nonna now needed me to translate for Natalia. Her language had become a peculiar mix of English and Italian, depending on what word first sprang into her mind.

'*Dammi* toothpaste' – give me toothpaste.

'*Fa* bath' – have a bath.

'*Chi* coming?' – who is coming?

'*Questi* pants are *troppo smallie*' – these pants are too small.

Then Natalia herself told me that she was turning a lingual corner. In her stroller, she turned herself around to face me and said in Italian, 'Oh, you're speaking your funny way again, Mamma!' Rather than the words being a jumble that she understood but couldn't differentiate, she began to tell the difference between Italian and English.

Later, at three-and-a-half, the door in her mind that would let her wander fluidly between the two languages, opened. She could construct whole sentences in English and ask intelligent questions about words that ended with a feminine vowel.

'If Santa is a man, why does he have a girl's name?' Got me on that one.

Not only was her accent in English perfect, but also she could immediately tell who spoke which language and addressed people accordingly. Natalia would offer our English-speaking friends a cup of tea and our Italian friends a cup of coffee. Such is the perception of the cross-cultural, bilingual child.

Not all bilingual children are the same. Our friend's little boy thought all women spoke English and all men spoke Italian. Language to him was sex-based. Some children resent their second language and choose never to speak it. Others excel in their foreign tongue and struggle with the language of the country they were born in. Some continue to translate every thought that passes through their head, making them slower than their classmates until they are into their teens. Every bilingual child is different.

The change in Natalia's language skills happened when I became pregnant with our second child. A trip to Sydney was planned before the birth, as travelling to Australia with one toddler had been a nightmare. Making the twenty-four-hour journey from Rome to Sydney with two babies on my own was unimaginable.

Natalia had met her Australian family at three months when I'd gone back to Sydney to pack up my life there for the last time. She had gurgled in her cot while I gave away my furniture. Her toothless smile as I changed her nappy on the echoing floorboards while waiting for charities to come and collect the rest of my belongings had been my lifeline to happiness. Feeling more and more maudlin at the thought of leaving, her presence had buoyed my spirits during the sale of my home and car.

My family had been so brave at the airport when I'd said goodbye and held Natti's little arm up to wave. Their sadness at my permanent relocation to Italy had been difficult for them to conceal. The dynamics within my family had already begun to change. In the past, we had our set roles, which had been comfortable and well lived-in – the protector, the peace-maker, the communicator, the rebel. But with my leaving, my family's energy was changing.

I held back the tears and delayed taking my leave of the people who had sustained me all my life. With Natalia clutched to my shoulder, I held each of them closely and squeezed their hands. In my heart and mind, I knew I had to let them go, but physically I clung on. I wanted my brothers to know my baby, my sister to share in her first steps, for them all to be with me on Natalia's first birthday. I thought of my Australian friend in Florence, Catie Cellai, who had married her Italian boyfriend twenty-five years earlier and had told me that the dreaded goodbyes to your ageing parents and your rapidly growing nephews don't get any easier. She'd said that as the years go by, the goodbyes get harder.

Mum could no longer talk for the tears in her throat. The harder she tried to show courage and strength, the more frail and sad she looked. Finally, Dad led me towards the doorway into Customs control. His voice wavered and cracked as he said, 'Off you go now. You have a bonny baby.' At those words, I lost all composure. Hot tears coursed down my crumpled face. Turning away, I held Natalia as close to my cheeks as I could and left my home in Australia behind.

The Italians have a story about destiny. It's called *La Morte* – Death. It's about a soldier who is celebrating the end of the war. He has survived the fighting, and is celebrating together with his comrades and much wine around a big campfire. Suddenly, he sees *La Morte* – the Grim Reaper – beside the fire. From under the shrouds of his dark hood, *La Morte* sees the soldier too, but his face shows surprise at seeing the soldier. The young man is so frightened he mounts his horse and gallops for two days, until he is exhausted and can go no further. He stops at a village, but again he sees *La Morte* who says to him, 'When I saw you by the campfire, I was surprised, because I knew your fate was to die, here in this village, in two days' time. I wondered how you would be able to travel all this way here in time to meet your destiny.' The soldier then had an accident on his horse and died.

I think of that story sometimes when I'm out in the garden or putting on the kettle. It makes me realise just how patient and planned destiny is. You cannot outrun your destiny, for it will find you. You cannot fight fate, for it bides its time and waits patiently for the right moment in which to reveal itself to you. Italy had always been my fate, and Paolo had always been my destiny. I know that in my heart.

I am finally, truly settled in Italy. It's a beautiful place to live and I never tire of the mystical medieval wonderland that is my Florence. I no longer moon with longing for Paolo with a sentimental rush of emotion when I hear Italian songs. There is no more lying awake at night wondering about his life and loves. The sight of all things Italian on television or in magazines doesn't give me pangs. There is no more suppressed emotion for a man who lives so very far away. For he is always close. I will always miss Australia and my family. That is part of my life. But there is no more indecision. Paolo and I are together, and I am content living in my adopted home.

My son was due to be born on 23 January. We had decided to call him Leo because, like Natalia, it is an easy name in English and Italian both. But if he was born on 12 January,

Paolo had made me promise to call him Giovanni because that was Giovanni's birthday. I had agreed, thinking that the chances of my son being born eleven days early, on his grandfather's birthday, were remote.

My waters broke and I delivered my son on 12 January. Paolo looked at me, so happy and proud with his newborn son in his arms. 'You promised. We'll have to call him Giovanni. I mean, it's just so incredible that he came today, of all days.'

Dear reader, you may think this story is make-believe, but it's not. Giovanni had his hand in the birth of his long-awaited, dearly loved grandson after all. And he let us know it by bringing him to us on his birthday.

But I refused to call my son Giovanni. That name is far too old-fashioned and Italian for an Australian mother like me. I called him Leo Giovanni instead.

Another broken promise.